Persistent poverty

PERSISTENT POVERTY

Underdevelopment in plantation economies
of the Third World

GEORGE L. BECKFORD
University of the West Indies

New York
OXFORD UNIVERSITY PRESS   1972
London   Toronto

Preface

This book presents an interpretation and analysis of the phenomenon of persistent underdevelopment in the plantation economies
of the world. It is concerned with the welfare of people living in
plantation societies—why we are poor and what we can do about
it. It seems clear that a virtual revolution is required in order to
bring about significant improvements in the welfare of all Third
World peoples. This book is offered as a small contribution to
that revolution.

Before that revolution can come about we need fundamental
perspectives on the causes of underdevelopment. Why have Third
World countries remained underdeveloped for so long? Contrary
to popular belief, most of these countries have a long history of
exposure to so-called "modern" influences. But they seem to be
caught in an underdevelopment trap. Our study of plantation
economy and society suggests that underdevelopment derives
from the institutional environment—the nature of economic, social, and political organization. This should not, of course, be
surprising, for it is through institutions that human activity is
organized. Nor is the idea new—Latin American economists have
emphasized this for some time. In every society the institutional
environment is a legacy of historical forces. So that the analysis
must be historical in orientation. What this means is that we are
really engaged in a study of political economy—a study in which

all aspects of human activity are synthesized in a holistic analysis.

The general approach is exploratory. More questions are raised than perhaps are answered. This may be so because the intention really is to provide a broad canvas on which details can later be inserted. The objective is to open up avenues for further inquiry and to provide a kind of framework for new perspectives of Third World problems. Our analysis of plantation economy and society seems to provide useful insights into two general problem areas: underdevelopment in the major plantation areas of Asia and of America (mainly the Caribbean, U.S. South, and Northeast Brazil), and dispossession among black people in the New World. The latter will be considered more specifically in a separate volume.

The present study is offered to other Third World social scientists as a contribution to the challenge to pursue more rigorously our own independent analyses of the problems facing our societies. Too often we view our problems through the eyes of metropolitan man; and our analyses of these problems depend too inordinately on analytical constructs developed for, and appropriate to, North Atlantic society but which may be inappropriate for the Third World. Even our pattern of research and style of presentation suffer on this account. No apology is necessary for directing the book to a Third World readership. It is true that others may find it helpful, but it is obvious that Third World problems can be solved only by Third World peoples. We alone have the basic understanding of our problems and the necessary commitment to overcome them.

The book is intended to present a genuinely Third World perspective to a wide readership of both professionals and non-professionals. The professional reader is likely to be irritated by a certain degree of repetition. But I am of the view that repetition is necessary for the lay reader to grasp the essential points of the argument—especially in view of the fact that time-honored myths about plantations are being challenged. In general, the philosophical orientation, the style of presentation, and the obvious omission of detail represent a kind of break with traditional academic work. Again, it might appear to the professional reader that I have taken many "liberties" which scholars normally do not like to

take. But in fact the question must be raised as to whether many
of these are liberties in any real sense. For example, the question
of whether one is absolutely right or wrong is really a phony issue.
I do not mind being charged with over-generalization and under-
documentation. This is an "ideas" book. What we need most are
studies pregnant with ideas, not studies full of sterile detail. Ideas
are what help people to understand problems and to pursue further inquiry. Yet another consideration is that traditional social
science scholarship operates under a veil of "objectivity." How
human beings can engage in anything which is objective is really
beyond my comprehension. Worst of all is the study of human
activity. As Myrdal has suggested, real objectivity in social research is achieved by explicitly stating the value premises on
which a study is based.

The valuations throughout the present book are clearly those
of a Third World writer. Many of these valuations are made quite
explicit from time to time. In this connection, I wish to make it
clear from now that when I refer to improvement of the welfare
of Third World peoples, I do not mean just material welfare, as
measured by higher incomes, but social welfare in general. An
important and often-neglected aspect of social welfare is, in my
view, *genuine independence*—that is, the full freedom of a people to control the environment in which they live and to manipulate that environment in any way they desire.

I am, of course, concerned with material advancement as well.
But this *material advancement can be satisfactory only if it pre-
serves the quality of life that people regard as important.* Although
people in underdeveloped countries may aspire to the levels of
material comfort that people in the advanced countries have
achieved they do not necessarily want the same quality of life
that obtains in those societies. The appropriate kind of material
advancement will, therefore, vary from one society to another. But
I feel certain that *all* people wish to be independent. To have to
be dependent on others is dehumanizing. This value premise
may be stated more strongly by saying that, in my judgment, people would rather be poor but free than to be slaves living in material comfort.

All countries of the Third World are, in varying degrees, dependent on the more advanced countries of the North Atlantic. Neo-colonial economic relations between the two sets of countries ensure this dependency and contribute as well to low levels of material advancement in the Third World. This book deals with *the agricultural dimension* of this general phenomenon. Other dimensions have been, and are being, explored by other scholars (including many of my colleagues at the U.W.I.). Many studies dealing with mineral exports, foreign investment, and multinational corporations are complementary to the present agriculture-oriented one. Our study, like some of these others, indicates that the dependence of Third World countries is detrimental to their economic, social, and political advancement.

My whole view of plantation economy and society has been profoundly influenced by Lloyd Best. We have been discussing continuously the problems considered in this study for many years. Several of the ideas relating to possibilities for change are perhaps as much his as they are mine. Norman Girvan, Owen Jefferson, Al Francis, Clive Thomas, and Havelock Brewster also have influenced my thinking considerably. Our discussions over the years in the Economics Department and in the New World Group at Mona provided the infrastructure for this book. More indirectly, the work of Celso Furtado, William Demas, and the whole school of Latin American and Caribbean structuralists has left an indelible imprint on my intellectual development. And, as is obvious from the references, I owe much to the plantation studies of Edgar Thompson, Sydney Mintz, and Charles Wagley.

Several individuals and institutions contributed directly to the study. The University of the West Indies granted a sabbatical year which, supplemented by a Ford Foundation grant, enabled me to devote full time to the work at Stanford University. There Professor W. O. Jones, Director of the Food Research Institute, provided me with all the necessary facilities for research and writing. Some of my colleagues at Stanford read the entire first draft. Of these, Kenneth Leslie, W. O. Jones, and Gerald Meier gave me the most detailed and critical comments. Bruce Johnston and William McKenzie also gave helpful suggestions. Individual chapters benefited from the comments of the following individuals: Professors Hayami and Ruttan, Chapter 2; Professor R. T. Smith,

Chapter 3; Professor D. G. Hall, Chapter 4; Dr. N. P. Girvan, Chapter 5; Mr. Havelock Brewster, Chapters 6 and 7; Mr. and Mrs. Joseph Harris, Chapters 8 and 9. Peggy Sothoron and Eva Larsen typed the first draft and Minnie Jurow edited and typed the final draft of the manuscript. Officials of a number of plantation enterprises were kind enough to supply me with information relating to individual companies. Among these, the most co-operative were Tate and Lyle, United Fruit, Standard Fruit and Shipping, Booker McConnell, and Unilever.

To all those who have assisted me in one way or another, I express my sincere gratitude. I can only hope that they will regard the final product as being worthy of the assistance they gave. None of the persons and institutions mentioned are to be held responsible for my errors or for whatever misinterpretation of fact there might be in the presentation.

Mona, Jamaica   G.L.B.
August 1971

Contents

Tables

Illustrations

Introduction

Latin America and the Caribbean, Africa, and Asia comprise what is now popularly described as the Third World. Although vast in area and rich in resources, the Third World does not now provide adequate levels of living for its people. Very low levels of income, malnutrition, disease, poor housing, sanitation and medical services, and little or no education are the lot of the majority of people. The task of improving the welfare of Third World peoples is the most important and formidable one confronting mankind today.

The countries of the North Atlantic—stretching from the United States and Canada on the one side to the Soviet Union on the other—have managed, on the whole, to achieve high levels of material advancement. It is becoming increasingly clear that the fortunes of North Atlantic peoples are closely related to the misfortunes of Third World peoples, in many fundamental ways. For a long time the Third World has relied heavily on trade ties with the more advanced countries but, for various reasons, trade expansion has not proved to be a sufficiently effective stimulus to economic development in the Third World. More important is the fact that the North Atlantic has come to own a considerable share of the resources of the Third World. Plantations and mines are important sources of income generation and potential "engines of growth" in many Third World countries. But these are, in most instances, owned by metropolitan corporations.

The present study is concerned with plantations. However, our concern goes somewhat beyond economics, as narrowly conceived. In general, this book presents an analysis of the way in which plantations have influenced many different aspects of human activity in those countries where the plantation is the dominant economic and social institution. And it attributes the persistence of underdevelopment in these countries to the plantation influence. The particular kinds of economic relations between these countries and the North Atlantic that are associated with the plantation system are not unique to those countries which we describe as plantation economies. Parallels can be drawn for mostly all Third World countries which tend inordinately to rely on metropolitan countries in different ways—in mineral exploitation, in banking and financial intermediation, in trade and the processing of raw materials, in technological innovation, and even in policy formulation. Insofar as Third World countries exhibit characteristics of colonial economies, parts of the present analysis have direct relevance to the entire group.

External relations alone do not account for persistent underdevelopment. Accordingly, the internal pattern of economic, social, and political organization is analyzed in an attempt to uncover those factors which constrain development in plantation economy and society. It is argued that the institutional environment of this particular type of economy and society has several unique characteristics which are directly associated with the plantation influence and which contribute importantly to continuous underdevelopment. In this respect, the analysis is of less relevance to countries where the plantation influence is absent or weak. But the general approach used here may provide a useful framework for undertaking specific analyses of underdevelopment in other countries where the institutional environment is different from the one studied here. Whether or not this is so depends on how successful our approach is in creating a better understanding of the development problem in the plantation case. We leave that to the reader's judgment.

The concern with means of promoting development in Third

World economy and society has increased considerably in recent
years. Economists and other social scientists have undertaken
many studies, official as well as independent. For the most part,
these studies have relied heavily on lessons and generalizations
drawn from the experiences of the more advanced countries. Insufficient recognition has been given to the fact that the institutional environment of underdeveloped countries differs in fundamental respects from that of the more advanced—not only at
present, but in the past as well. In addition, far too much attention has been directed to the promotion of development in these
countries without prior understanding of the nature and causes
of underdevelopment. Practitioners of medicine realize that diag-
nosis must precede prescription in order to increase the probability
of making correct prescriptions. That social scientists generally
have not followed the same course in their development prescriptions is largely attributable to an unstated assumption that development and underdevelopment derive from the same causes
everywhere. So that if we know how Europe developed, for example, we can say what is required for underdeveloped countries
today. Such an assumption is dangerously misleading.

One must approach the problem with a recognition of the need
to understand the phenomenon of underdevelopment. This is a
necessary prelude to devising appropriate policies and strategies
for promoting development. Furthermore, it is necessary to probe
beyond the observation that underdevelopment derives from short-
ages of capital and skills and from the use of backward techniques.
In order to find out why these conditions exist (and persist) one
must explore the social and economic environment. Institutional
environment varies from place to place, so to avoid studying
every country individually—though this is necessary at some
stage—one must devise ways of grouping countries together according to apparent similarities in social organization. Rural institutions have an important influence on the social order of most
Third World countries. It therefore seems to be a useful exercise
to classify countries according to the nature of dominant rural
institutions. This is why the plantation economy and society is
here identified in a particular class or type.

There are several other ways in which the present study differs

from most "development studies"—conceptually as well as ana-
lytically. It is important therefore to outline the general perspectives that inform the analysis.

1. Development and underdevelopment

Much of the current development concern is with raising the average levels of income in underdeveloped countries. Economic development is said to occur whenever there is an increase in real
per capita income which is sustained over a long period of time.
This kind of concern generally ignores two important considerations: first, in most underdeveloped countries the distribution of
income among the population is very unequal; and often, an increase in per capita income may not change, and may even
worsen, these inequalities. The second consideration is that all
Third World countries are, in one way or another, colonies of the
North Atlantic—that is to say, the underdeveloped economies
are controlled, in important ways, by the North Atlantic.

Meaningful development for Third World countries must therefore serve to correct these two basic deficiences. In other words,
in addition to a sustained increase in per capita incomes, what is
required as well are more equitable patterns of income distribution and the emergence of genuinely independent societies. This
independence must reach the point where the people of individual
Third World countries at least have full control over their resources and the whole environment in which they live. This is a
basic precondition for the achievement of full human dignity
which is of crucial and ultimate importance to all people.

An increase in average real incomes simply means that the
output of goods and services in a particular country is increasing
at a faster rate than its population is. The incidence of widespread
poverty in the Third World today has led many people to advocate
restrictions on population growth in order to promote economic
advancement and/or to ward off some imagined prospect of
world famine. This study is concerned with the more positive
side of the equation—how to increase the rate of growth of output and how to secure a more equitable distribution of the output
produced. The level of national output is determined simply by

the quantity and quality of various inputs—or what are sometimes called factors of production—and by the techniques of
production. Increased output can be secured by increasing the
quantity of inputs, by improving the quality of these inputs, by
introducing superior techniques which raise the productivity of
existing inputs, or by any combination of these. Much emphasis
is usually given to the importance of technological change and
capital accumulation (including human capital).

The process of economic development itself involves much
more than increasing the rates of technological change and of
capital accumulation. It is a dynamic process that involves major
adjustments in the structure of economy and society. Changes in
the mix of goods and services produced will be required as incomes increase; some industries will decline while others rise;
the occupational composition of the labor force will change in
the process; towns and cities grow at the expense of the country-
side; people have to learn new skills as old ways of doing things
are discarded; changes in the distribution of population lead to
adjustments in the distribution of political power; and so on.

The whole process is complex. Here it is necessary to note only
that certain preconditions must exist before development can take
place. Among these, the most important, it would seem, are a
highly motivated population willing and able to make the sacrifices involved, and appropriate institutional arrangements that
provide the necessary incentives and reward for effort. These are
matters which are of central concern to us in the present study.

Underdevelopment is not normally considered to be a dynamic
process in the same way as development is accepted as being. Instead the view is usually taken that an economy is in a state of
static underdevelopment and remains so until some stimulus initiates the development process. The view taken in this study is
that underdevelopment is itself a dynamic process—that there
are systematic forces which operate in the direction of keeping
underdeveloped countries continuously underdeveloped, so much
so that powerful development stimuli (such as trade) do not ini-
tiate a process of sustained development. The analytical framework of this study is based on the hypothesis that the dynamics
of underdevelopment of the plantation economy and society in-

here in the institutional environment. To this extent, development can hardly be expected to occur without a change in the institutional environment.

Social, cultural, political, psychological, and other non-economic variables influence the economic behavior of individuals and groups in every society; and these factors are important in determining the pattern of development or underdevelopment. For example, we know that social organization and structure are important determinants of social mobility. And we know that the distribution of political power and the nature of political organization determine the extent to which different individuals and groups are able to participate in decisions affecting the whole society. The fact is that patterns of economic, social, and political organization vary considerably from place to place though many countries have features which are common to others.

Patterns of agricultural organization are important in the study of development and underdevelopment for at least two reasons. First, most societies evolve from an initial position in which agriculture is the main activity. In consequence, we find that rural institutions subsequently influence the nature of the social environment of the society as a whole. Second, in most countries of the Third World today agriculture accounts for a large percentage of all economic activity and the bulk of the population in these countries live in rural areas. So that whatever affects the welfare of the rural population is of great significance. The agricultural scene is important in yet another dimension: the voluminous literature on the role of agriculture in economic development has emphasized that increases in agricultural productivity and expansion of agricultural output are essential to economic development. And in this connection, we must recognize that the potential for agricultural development per se depends, in large measure, on the nature of agricultural organization and the structure of rural society.

In surveying the situation in the Third World today, we can identify certain types of agricultural systems which reflect different economic, social, and political situations. The plantation system, the peasant system, the tribal system, the feudal system, and the state-controlled system all represent different institutional environments. And within each system, there are certain characteristics which serve to enhance the development potential and others which promote underdevelopment. The success with which development programs can be executed depends, in large measure, on the degree to which underdevelopment biases within each system can be overcome. The present study indicates that the plantation system creates considerable underdevelopment biases. Whether the same situation applies to the other systems can be determined only by specific inquiries of the kind carried out here.

2. Toward new perspectives: the plantation case

Plantation agriculture has been one of the chief means by which numerous countries of the world have been brought into the tributaries of the modern world economy. "Tributaries" because although many of these countries have been participating in modern world commerce for some four hundred years, they still cannot be said to be part of the mainstream of the world economy. None of the plantation economies of the world is today among the select group of advanced or developed countries. It is perhaps true that per capita income levels are on average higher for plantation economies than for other underdeveloped countries. But that is no consolation for countries where modern development began (with the establishment of plantations) almost at the same time as it did in the present-day advanced countries. Again, it is true that the plantation was an instrument of modernization in the sense that it served to "open up" previously undeveloped countries and regions. It brought roads, ports, water supplies, communications, health facilities, and so on. But the fact still remains that the plantation economies of the world have been left outside of the current of development and change that has swept many other countries along since the Industrial Revolution.

The question which we must seek to answer is Why? Why have the plantation economies been left behind? Why is it that after four hundred years of direct participation in the modern world economy the plantation economies of the world still find

themselves underdeveloped countries with the bulk of their inhabitants living (rather, existing) in the most wretched conditions
of poverty? Perhaps there are factors inherent in the plantation
system which serve to impede transformation from a state of
underdevelopment. Let that be our working hypothesis, because
we really do not know. If the hypothesis is correct then we must
seek to find out what these factors are, how they operate to limit
the process of transformation, and what can be done to remove
these constraints. In rather general terms, that is the purpose of
the present exercise.

The plantation was introduced into certain countries of the
Third World by the metropolitan nations of the North Atlantic
for the benefit of those nations. The peoples of these Third World
countries have inherited the plantation system and all the legacies which come with it. Although many of these countries have
achieved constitutional independence, the plantation system (with
all its inherent economic characteristics, internal social hierar-
chies and central authority, and dependence on the outside world)
still dominates the lives of their people in fundamental ways.
The problem now facing these countries is essentially that of
harnessing the plantation for the benefit of the welfare of their
peoples. Initially, to do this will require a thorough understanding of the plantation in all its dimensions. Hence the imperative
of a study in political economy. It would be arrogant, to say the
least, to imply that a thorough understanding could be accom-
plished by this study alone—especially in view of the fact that
the bulk of the existing literature on which such a study must
draw is the product of metropolitan scholarship and therefore
is cast in a different mold. The present study is offered as a kind
of introduction in this area of inquiry in the hope that it will
stimulate other scholars to contribute to the task outlined.

Economists concerned with problems of development are becoming increasingly aware of the limitations of a single-disci-
pline approach. Economics alone cannot explain the development process, and the need for political economy is reasserting
itself. Nowhere perhaps is the need as pressing as in the study
of plantations, for the plantation is an institution of wide-ranging
dimensions. This study tries to broaden the disciplinary focus

by drawing on history, sociology, anthropology, and geography. The end product has the broader focus, and it is hoped that a satisfactory disciplinary integration has been achieved.

The basic concern of the study is development—how to improve the welfare of the millions of people living in the plantation economies of the world today. The point of departure is the observation that the plantation was indeed the means by which previously *un*developed areas of the world were brought into the modern world economy; that it was a modernizing institution in the sense that it created social overhead capital and transformed "primitive" economies into money economies. But the further observation is made that plantation economies today remain *under*developed. Thus it seems that although plantations are effective in transforming a state of undevelopment they are less effective in combatting a state of underdevelopment. In pursuing the question of whether or not the plantation system contributes to persistent underdevelopment, we are led naturally into an analysis which is strongly historical in orientation. Consequently, more attention is given to the experiences of the oldest plantation societies in the world—those in Brazil, the Caribbean and the United States South—than to the newer plantation areas of South Asia and Africa.

Inclusion of the United States South requires some explanation since we have designated the Third World as our constituency of interest. As in the Caribbean and Brazil, black people were brought to the United States in the service of the plantation. The plantation South of the United States has been an important influence on the lives of black people in that country, even though a large percentage of them have migrated from that region to other parts of the country. The analysis in this study suggests that dispossession among black people in the United States stems from causes which are similar in many respects to the causes of poverty in the Third World. Consequently, it is important to include the United States South in the analysis, and to consider black people in that country as part of the general class of Third World people. Another consideration is that a comparison of the development performance of the South with that of the rest of the United States will help to identify plantation influences with respect to development and underdevelopment, since it is the plantation that really differentiates the South.

Chapter 1 provides information on the general nature of the plantation system. Detailed description of the economic organization of plantations as units of production are in an appendix to the book for those who are not familiar with plantation agriculture. The description there also differentiates between different types of plantations. In addition Chapter 1 identifies those countries which are plantation economies and considers the impact of plantations on peasant activity in these countries. Descriptive material related to the selection of countries is placed in an appendix and can be consulted for reasons why individual countries are classified as plantation economies.

Chapter 2 provides an outline of the political economy of change in plantation economy and society. The discussion there relies heavily on the experience of social, economic, and political change in the Caribbean, beginning with European colonization of the New World up to the present time. It tries to identify the main factors which have contributed to social change, broadly conceived; and it describes the basic contours of the society and economy today in a way that reveals the historical legacy.

Chapter 3 examines the social and political dimensions of plantation society and develops a model of social dynamics appropriate to this kind of society. It is demonstrated that plantation society has certain unique characteristics associated with the plantation influence. Specific patterns of social and political organization create an environment which makes underdevelopment endemic. Rigid patterns of social stratification associated with race and color inhibit social mobility and severely restrict the participation of large groups of people in economic and political affairs. Plural societies pregnant with race conflict exhibit instability which is inimical to development. And the concentration of economic, social, and political power within the society prevents the emergence of a highly motivated population.

Chapter 4 considers changing patterns in the development of plantations. In particular, it is concerned with how changing circumstances influenced the use of labor and land, and how plantations affected the livelihood of people in various places over time. In addition, it identifies changes which have taken place with respect to the ownership and management of plantations. The two most important findings in the chapter are that monopoly of land by plantations has increased over time, and that there has been an increase in the concentration of capital as a result of the declining importance of individual proprietary planters and a corresponding rise in the importance of metropolitan corporate enterprise.

Chapter 5 provides an analysis of the growth of corporate plantation enterprise. Certain dynamic factors are identified and matched against historical evidence. These enterprises are also described as they are now and inferences are drawn concerning the influence of these firms on the development potential of the plantation economies.

Chapter 6 considers the question of resource mis-allocation in plantation economy. The analysis there indicates that plantations create major misuses of resources and that their presence accounts for the prevalence of gross underconsumption existing along with resource underutilization and poverty.

Chapter 7 brings together the major conclusions of earlier chapters to explain how the plantation influence contributes to persistent underdevelopment. There it is demonstrated that the economic, social, and political environment creates formidable underdevelopment biases which cannot be overcome without breaking up the plantation system. Chapter 8 considers how this can be done. It provides a general outline of possibilities for transformation and change. Chapter 9 briefly restates the fundamental problems and raises certain issues related to the transition process. Inferences are drawn there concerning the relevance of our findings for the numerous Third World countries which do not come directly within the purview of the present study.

Persistent poverty

1

Plantations in third world economy

The plantation economies of the world are found chiefly in tropical America and tropical Asia. (There is only a sprinkling of them among the countries of tropical Africa.) In these areas the plantation has been the dominant economic, social, and political institution in the past, continues to be in the present, and from all indications will continue to be in the future. It was an instrument of political colonization; it brought capital, enterprise, and management to create economic structures which have remained basically the same; it brought together different races of people from various parts of the world to labor in its service and thus determined the population and social structures now existing in these places. As Edgar Thompson has said, ". . . Elements of the present problems of many interracial societies, such as those of the American South and South America, were set up in an older plantation order." [1] The plantation introduced new crops to many countries and the cultivation of many of these still represents the chief means of livelihood (however tenuous) of high percentages of the populations of these countries. In short, it has fashioned the whole environment which the people of these countries have inherited.

1. Edgar T. Thompson, *The Plantation—A Bibliography* (Washington, D. C., 1957), p. iv.

PLANTATIONS AND DECOLONIZATION

The era of political colonization is said to be at an end. Since World War II, numerous colonial countries have achieved independent *constitutional* status. Winds of change were said to have swept through the Third World. On closer examination one sees that though the winds may have swept, they have not swept clean. The plantation system was an integral part of the political colonization of tropical America and tropical Asia. It was set up for the benefit of the metropolitan colonizers and therefore it is not surprising that it was also an integral part of the process of de-colonization. Plantations were a major target in the independence struggle of many colonial peoples. As a result of their hegemony of scarce land in some places and the depressingly low level of wages and living conditions everywhere, the pressures which they created on the peoples of plantation economies gave rise to peasant movements and labor unions. These were the basic organizations which served initially to mobilize the colonized peoples and ultimately provided the basis for the organization of parties and revolutionary movements that whipped up the winds of change.

It is ironic that although plantations were one of the main sources of conditions that generated the winds of change, they have managed to withstand the tempest. Or was it a tempest? Most of the postwar literature on plantation agriculture speculated that the days of the foreign-owned plantation would soon be ended as the plantation colonies secured their independence. Given the background outlined above it was what independence was supposed to have been about. However, the plantation withstood the test everywhere it was threatened after independence. In Ceylon, the political party with a program for nationalization of the foreign plantations soon found itself occupying the opposition benches in the national assembly with the government offering guarantees of non-nationalization to the foreign plantation owners. In Indonesia, the Sukarno government managed to take over the Dutch-owned plantations but eventually Sukarno was ousted and the Dutch owners invited back. In Guatemala, the same pattern existed. And elsewhere—in the Caribbean, for example—independent governments have introduced all kinds of incentive legislation to encourage foreign plantation (and other) investment. And so the plantation remains entrenched in all of these countries.[2]

Either the plantation was too solid an institutional structure for the force of the winds of change or the winds were in fact only a breeze. It might of course be both. And so it seems. As the next few chapters indicate, the plantation has become deeply rooted in the environment of many underdeveloped countries, and to shake it may well threaten the entire economic and social order. On the other hand, the so-called winds of change have brought constitutional independence to many countries but have left them with a legacy of economic, social, psychological, and indeed even political dependency.[3] Again, as the discussion in the rest of the book will show, this continued state of general dependency can also be traced to the plantation influence.

1. The plantation system and plantation economy

The plantation has many dimensions. It is a system of agricultural production and a social institution as well. The term "plantation" has fallen into such widespread use that it will be useful for us to look briefly at the meaning attached to it in the present study. There will be occasions when reference is made to plantation production, that is, as a type of agricultural organization; on other occasions, reference will be made to the plantation system; and on still others, reference will be made to plantation *economies*.

In considering the economic aspects of the plantation as an ag-

2. Although Cuba is not one of the newly independent countries it should be noted here that this is the only country which has successfully taken over the foreign plantations. But even here the structure of the plantations has remained intact. The change has been from foreign-owned private plantations to government plantations maintaining their specialization in sugar production.
3. The distinction between "constitutional" and "political" independence is one that is important to recognize. The former refers to the trappings of independence—constitutions, flags, anthems, a seat in the United Nations, and so on. Real political independence derives from the ability and power to control and manipulate the environment for the benefit of the people of the independent state. It derives in large measure from the degree of control of the economic resources of the country.

ricultural producing unit (that is, plantation production), our definition here follows that of Jones:

A plantation is an economic unit producing agricultural commodities (field crops or horticultural products, but not livestock) for sale and employing a relatively large number of unskilled laborers whose activities are closely supervised. Plantations usually employ a year-round labor crew of some size, and they usually specialize in the production of only one or two marketable products. *They differ from other kinds of farms in the way in which the factors of production, primarily management and labor, are combined.*[4]

It bears emphasis that the special factor combination that distinguishes plantation production from other kinds of farming is the bringing together of as many unskilled laborers as is economically profitable with each of the few highly skilled supervisor-managers who direct production. As Jones succintly puts it, "the plantation substitutes supervision—supervisory and administrative skills—for skilled, adaptive labor, combining the supervision with labor whose principal skill is to follow orders."[5] We would wish therefore to exclude from our constituency of observation certain large-scale, highly capitalized farms where field operations have become so mechanized that only a small number of skilled machine operators comprise the labor force. Examples of these are fruit and vegetable "plantations" of California in the United States.[6]

On plantations, production of the crop (or crops) is undertaken solely for sale. In most of the underdeveloped countries the sale is in an overseas market so that export production is the objective. However, we do not wish to restrict our definition to these plantations since production for the home market is important in some cases. (The Southern plantation in the United States is a case in

4. W. O. Jones, "Plantations," in David L. Sills (ed.), *International Encyclopedia of the Social Sciences,* Vol. 12 (1968), p. 154. Emphasis added.
5. *Ibid.,* p. 156. Edgar Thompson somewhere in one of his several contributions has appropriately described plantation agriculture as "military agriculture."
6. For other examples of these enterprises found mainly in the advanced countries, see H. F. Gregor, "The Changing Plantation," *Economic Geography,* June 1965.

point.) However, even in these cases the markets for the plantation output are normally located outside the regions of plantation production so that in terms of the regional (as distinct from the national) economy, production for export is still the objective. Wolf and Mintz have argued that export-oriented production is an important characteristic of plantations and that this is one factor which distinguishes them from certain other large-scale, centrally directed farming units like the hacienda.[7] However, in the present exercise we do not wish necessarily to maintain the distinction emphasized by Wolf and Mintz. But it will be used as one of the characteristics by which we differentiate different types of plantation agriculture. In the plantation regions of Brazil and the United States, production is partly for the home market and partly for export. Elsewhere in the world, it is predominantly for export (defined in the usual way).

It may be useful to classify types of plantation agriculture on the basis of ownership of the producing unit. Various types of ownership patterns exist; among these we can identify private individuals, families, limited liability companies, partnerships, cooperative societies, and state ownership of one kind or another. The three main types in world agriculture are the limited liability companies, private family and individual plantations, and government plantations. Historically, there has been a dramatic shift in the relative importance of these three types. Private family and individual plantations have systematically been transformed into limited liability companies and today they are the dominant types in world plantation production.[8] Government plantations exist in many places but they constitute the dominant type in very few countries. Cuba is the most outstanding of these. In the underdeveloped countries, the plantation companies are predominantly foreign-owned with shareholders, directors, and centers of decision making located in a metropolitan country—usually the one which initially exercised political control over the plantation colony.

7. E. R. Wolf and S. W. Mintz, "Haciendas and Plantations in Middle America and the Antilles," *Social and Economic Studies,* September 1957.
8. Sir Bernard O. Binns, *Plantations and Other Centrally Operated Estates* (FAO Agricultural Studies No. 28, Rome, June 1955), p. 33.

There is a relatively high degree of vertical integration in the plantation company. The company owns facilities for processing its own plantation output and for supplying many of the inputs in its plantation production. This has been the result of certain historical forces which are described in Chapter 5. And the effects of this vertical integration of production and services are significant for the patterns of resource use and the development prospects of plantation economies, as the analysis in Chapters 6 and 7 indicates.

When we use the term *plantation system* we refer to the totality of institutional arrangements surrounding the production and marketing of plantation crops. To understand the systemic dimensions of the plantation it is necessary to review briefly its historical development. The colonization activities of the metropolitan countries took three general forms, the establishment either of colonies of "settlement," of "conquest," or of "exploitation." In the first case, people migrated (individually, as families, and as groups) from the metropole and settled in the colony. In the second case, metropolitan interest was simply in establishing sufficient administrative and military organization to facilitate the transfer of wealth (chiefly precious metals) from the colony to the metropole. In the third case, metropolitan interest was in production for trade. North America, Australia, and New Zealand were representative of colonies of settlement; mainland Spanish America of colonies of conquest; and the Caribbean Islands and those of Southeast Asia of colonies of exploitation. The plantation was the institution best suited to metropolitan needs in colonies of exploitation.

The plantation is one type of settlement institution. According to Thompson, "It is one of that class of institutions that pattern the relationship of people to the land and largely determine how people shall live on the land and with one another." [9] As a settlement institution the plantation was the means of bringing together enterprise, capital, and labor from various parts of the world into

9. Edgar T. Thompson, "The Plantation Cycle and Problems of Typology," in Vera Rubin (ed.), *Caribbean Studies—A Symposium* (University of the West Indies, 1957; reissued University of Washington Press, Seattle, Washington, 1960), p. 30.

a new location where land was available to be combined with these for the production of a particular staple. In the nature of the case a system of authority and control was vested in the institution. As Lloyd Best puts it:

Where land is free to be used for subsistence production, the recruitment of labour exclusively for export production imposes a need for "total economic institutions" so as to encompass the entire existence of the work force. The plantation which admits virtually no distinction between organization and society, and chattel slavery which deprives workers of all civil rights including the right to property, together furnish an ideal framework.[10]

R. T. Smith in the original application of the Goffman concept of "total institution" to plantation society describes it as a "bureaucratically organised system in which whole blocks of people are treated as units and are marched through a set of regimentation under the surveillance of the small supervisory staff." [11]

From the very outset then the plantation began as a unit of authority with control over all aspects of the lives of people within its territory. Because it had to rely on immigrant labor of different ethnic and cultural origins it also provided the locus and rules of accommodation between these different groups. "The resulting power structure . . . gives the plantation all or many of the characteristics of a small state with a classification of people into different statuses together with a formal definition of the relationship between them." [12] Thus caste became an important aspect of the slave plantation society and it still persists in some plantation areas such as the United States South.[13] And wherever plantations exist at present we find the phenomenon of plural societies of a

10. Lloyd Best, "Outlines of a Model of Pure Plantation Economy," *Social and Economic Studies,* September 1968, p. 287.
11. R. T. Smith, "Social Stratification, Cultural Pluralism and Integration in West Indian Societies," in S. Lewis and T. G. Mathews (eds.), *Caribbean Integration* (Rio Piedras, Puerto Rico, 1967), p. 230. Smith attributes the general concept to Erving Goffman, *Asylums* (New York, 1961).
12. Edgar T. Thompson, "The Plantation Cycle . . . , *op. cit.,* p. 31.
13. As far as the United States is concerned, although the caste system originated in the plantation South it has subsequently become an integral feature of the entire U.S. social order.

type in which the only common elements of social values and aspirations can be traced directly to the influence of the plantation.[14] Chapter 3 will provide further elaboration on this and other aspects of the social and political organization of plantations.

To view the plantation as a system we need to identify, at least for the purpose of exposition, two of its systemic dimensions. First, the plantation as a social system in the territory in which it is located (the internal dimension) and, second, the plantation as an economic system both in the territory of its location and in the wider world community (the external dimension). The two are of course interrelated but are separated here to make it easier to discuss them. By "system" we simply mean a set of relations governing the component parts that make up the whole. In any such network of relations there is a coming together of the component parts at some point and for some common purpose. It is this organization that makes the set of relations a system. The institution which provides the organization governs and gives character to the whole—the system.[15]

From what has been said in the last few paragraphs, the contours of the internal dimension of the plantation system should be sufficiently clear although there are other aspects, such as the usual monopoly by the plantation of the means of livelihood for population groups within its territory, which will emerge in due course. For the time being we will draw directly from Thompson to summarize the all-pervasive character of the internal dimension of the plantation system.

The plantation is an institution in just as real a sense as the Catholic Church. It arises to deal with certain seemingly eternal problems of an ordered society. . . . It is made up of people but, like the

14. The concept of plural societies originally formulated by Furnivall in his examination of Dutch Indonesia has more recently been revived by M. G. Smith in his studies of social structure in the West Indies. See J. S. Furnivall, *Colonial Policy and Practice* (Cambridge, 1944), and M. G. Smith, *The Plural Society in the British West Indies* (Berkeley and Los Angeles, 1965).
15. See Edgar T. Thompson, "The Plantation as a Social System," in Pan American Union, *Plantation Systems of the New World* (Social Science Monographs, VII, Washington, D. C., 1959), p. 26.

church, it is an impersonal and implacable automatism having a set of norms which control all the people who constitute it, planter and laborer alike, who "belong" to the estate, as though the estate were something existing apart from its people: the plantation demands and dictates. The individual members acquire particular beliefs and ways of participating which become part of the very fibre of their lives. Further, they acquire from the plantation that firm element of assured behavior which all institutions give to their members and which contribute toward social order and stability.[16]

The external dimension derives from two characteristics of plantation production—its export orientation and foreign ownership in most of the cases in which we are here interested. Mention was made earlier of the fact that plantations were, and are, the product of metropolitan capital and enterprise. This and its orientation to overseas markets ties it to the wider world economic community in very precise ways. Plantations are only one part of a much wider economic system consisting of a set of relations which meet at a metropolitan and industrial center far removed from the plantations. The locus of discretion and control usually resides at this center on which the plantations are dependent.[17] Control may take several forms: property ownership, political connections of one kind or another which influence prices and tariffs, financial control through the branch banking system, or the specificity of raw-material export to metropolitan refining capacity, shipping, and so on. The degree of metropolitan control of plantations will of course vary according to the type of plantation. Thus we would expect metropolitan control to be greatest for the foreign corporate plantations and least for the state plantations, at least at the level of the plantation producing unit. However, regardless of the type of ownership the external relations are always of consequence and need to be recognized.

In the course of our discussion the term *plantation system* will be applied in some instances to what we have described as its internal dimension and on other occasions to the external dimension just described. However, the specific context in which the term is

16. *Ibid.,* p. 27.
17. I. C. Greaves, "Plantations in World Economy," in Pan American Union, *Plantation Systems of the New World,* p. 15.

used will make it clear to the reader what is meant at the particular point.

Plantation economy is the term we apply to those countries of the world where the internal and external dimensions of the plantation system dominate the country's economic, social, and political structure and its relations with the rest of the world. We have argued above that the plantation is all-embracing in its effect on the lives of those within its territory and community. It follows that wherever several plantations have come to engross most of the arable farm land in a particular country which is predominantly agricultural, that country can be described as a plantation economy or society and its social and economic structure and external relations will be similar to those described for the plantation system.

In some cases the community of plantations in a particular country will consist of units owned by different individuals, families, and companies. This is so in most of the tropical island economies—all of the Caribbean excluding Cuba; Mauritius and Réunion in the Indian Ocean; Ceylon, Malaya, Indonesia, and the Philippines in Southeast Asia; and Hawaii, Fiji, and certain other islands in the Pacific. In other cases the community of plantations may be substantially owned by a single company as is the case in Guyana, British Honduras, and Liberia. In either case the plantation system pervades all aspects of life in these countries and their development problem must be viewed in this light.

Elsewhere in the world the plantation is of lesser significance except for its dominating influence in certain regions of larger economies. The chief of these regions are the United States South, the Northeast of Brazil, and the Caribbean lowlands of Central America. In the first two, most of the producing units are owned by nationals whereas in the last case they are for the most part foreign-owned. These plantation regions of wider national economic communities display characteristic features of the plantation system and have followed a development path different from the paths of the rest of the national economies of which they are a part. It will be useful therefore to include them in our field of observation although we must recognize that we are dealing with sub-systems in this particular class of plantation economy. These sub-systems are of particular interest in the study of plantations because they provide a unique opportunity to isolate the effects of plantations on the development pattern. Since they are part of a larger system which, in the United States's case at least, is not dominated by the plantation, a comparison of the development experience of the sub-system with that of the rest of the larger system will help to isolate the plantation influences.[18]

We may note in passing that the dominating influence of plantations in our class of economies is not measured simply by the number of such units in relation to other farming units in the particular country. In most cases the number of peasant farms in these places exceed by a wide margin the number of plantations. However in terms of quantity and quality of land (and other agricultural resources) the peasants come nowhere near the plantations. And indeed in most cases the peasants themselves are dependent in one way or another on the plantations. The peasant sectors of these economies are really sub-sectors within the general framework of the plantations. And the development of the peasantry is interwoven with that of the plantation.

2. Plantation economies of the world

Plantation agriculture exists in numerous countries of the world. However, its influence on national economies varies quite widely from a degree where it is insignificant to one where it pervades all aspects of national life. The present study is concerned primarily with its wide-ranging influence.

Our criteria for identifying the plantation economies of the world is based on the following considerations: plantation share of national economic aggregates, such as total output, capital, land area in cultivation, income, and employment; plantation contribution to government revenues, and the country's foreign exchange earnings; evidence of effects of the plantation on social and politi-

18. An interesting initial attempt at this was made by Douglass North in "Agriculture and Regional Economic Growth," *Journal of Farm Economics,* December 1959, and in his book, *The Economic Growth of the United States, 1790–1860* (Englewood Cliffs, New Jersey, 1961).

cal structure and organization; and evidence of what, for want of a better term, we describe as a general plantation psychology—in other words, the extent to which the national community reflects the over-all plantation characteristics already described. Sufficient data (quantitative and qualitative) are not available on all these aspects to permit what one could claim to be an exhaustive survey of all the Third World countries that are likely candidates. However, we have managed to assemble sufficient information on the greater number of these. This information is presented in Appendix I. The following is a summary listing of the plantation economies and their population base (in thousands): [19]

A. The plantation economies of the world

I. The Caribbean and Latin America

1. Cuba	5,830	10. Dominica	60
2. Jamaica	1,610	11. St. Lucia	87
3. Haiti	3,098	12. St. Vincent	80
4. Dominican		13. Grenada	89
Republic	3,048	14. Barbados	233
5. Puerto Rico	2,350	15. Trinidad	828
6. Antigua	55	16. Guyana	561
7. St. Kitts	57	17. (Brazil)	(70,968)
8. Guadeloupe	284	18. British	
9. Martinique	291	Honduras	91

II. Africa

19. Liberia	1,017	22. (Cameroon)	(5,017)
20. Portuguese		23. (Congo-	
Guinea	522	Kinshasa)	(12,769)
21. Rio Muni	184	24. (Angola)	(5,400)
		25. (Mozambique)	(7,200)

19. The data on population are recent estimates (mainly in the early 1960's) and are derived principally from United Nations, *Demographic Yearbook, 1967* (New York, 1968), Table 2. Figures are all rounded upward. Data on Hawaii and the U.S. South are from U.S. Department of Commerce, *Statistical Abstract of the United States, 1969.* For the U.S. South the figure shown is the total for the "South Atlantic" region, excluding Delaware, Maryland, and Washington, D. C.; all of the "East South Central" region; and Arkansas and Louisiana in what is described as "West South Central."

III. Indian Ocean

26. Mauritius	682	28. Comoro	
27. Réunion	349	Islands	184

IV. Asia

29. Ceylon	10,591	31. Indonesia	96,319
30. Malaya	6,279	32. Philippines	27,088

V. Pacific

33. Fiji	477

B. Plantation sub-economics

1. Brazil Northeast	25,000	3. U.S. South	38,907
2. Carribbean Lowlands of Honduras, Guatemala, Costa Rica and Panama		4. Hawaii	633

The table shows that the greatest concentration of plantation economies is to be found in the Caribbean but the greatest concentration of population is in Ceylon and Southeast Asia. It also indicates that the countries and regions concerned vary substantially in respect of size of population and in area as well, although area is not shown. The countries listed are those with which this study is primarily concerned. The common plantation influence gives the set of countries a certain homogeneity: each is fundamentally similar to the other, in terms of not only economic structure and economic problems but also social structure, political organization, and other aspects of human life.

The plantation influence is more pervasive in some countries than it is in others. In most of the countries we have identified, the influence can be traced to virtually all aspects of human life because plantations are fully integrated in the economic and social order. For these, "plantation economy" is an appropriate description. In certain cases, however, the plantation sector is more or less cut off from the rest of the economy and society—as in Liberia. Such cases may be better described as "enclave plantation economy." There are even different kinds of enclave plantation economy. In Kenya, Rhodesia, and South Africa, European plantations exist, but these are kept so separate from the African sectors of those countries that it seems best to ignore them in the present study. For the most part, we are concerned with the more prevalent cases where the plantation influence affects the entire social order.

A brief word now about what we have described as plantation sub-economies. The two most important are those of the United States South and the Northeast of Brazil. Although by definition these sub-economies are part of larger national economies, it appears that their economic relationship with the rest of their national community is very much akin to that between plantation economies and their metropolitan counterparts. Writing about the United States South, for example, Johnson *et al.* indicate that "Even under slavery the chief capital supporting cotton cultivation was not available in the South, a situation which kept the whole area in secondary slavery to the capital of the North." [20] And Rupert Vance in *Human Geography of the South* has advanced the thesis that the U.S. South is a "colonial economy" because (1) finance capital from the North was responsible for the development of the South; and (2) southern manufactures (for example, textiles) were exported to be finished and marketed in the North. And the result was that accumulation of capital and utilization of technology was retarded in the South. As James Allen summarized the position, ". . . The chief point of resemblance between southern economy and a present-day colonial economy . . . is the plantation system with its slave survivals" and "the most important social expression of the existence of the plantation is the oppression of the Negroes." [21]

The pattern described above is similar to that which obtains in the Northeast of Brazil in the sense that it was the surpluses generated in that earlier established plantation region which provided much of the stimulus for industrialization of the Center-South (the São Paulo-Rio de Janeiro axis) in much the same way that the

20. C. S. Johnson, E. R. Embree, and W. W. Alexander, *The Collapse of Cotton Tenancy* (Chapel Hill, North Carolina, 1935), p. 25.
21. James Allen, *The Negro Question in the United States* (New York, 1936), p. 131.

West Indies provided stimulus for the industrialization of Britain
(and to a lesser extent, France). And like the plantation economies
of the world, the plantation sub-economies of the United States
and Brazil have lagged behind their internal "metropolitan" centers in the process of industrialization and structural transformation. The Brazilian Northeast, for example, is an area of great relative poverty. Per capita income levels are only one-half of the
national average and only one-third of that of the industrialized
Center-South. The Northeast "is the oldest, the poorest, and until
recent years the most populous of Brazil's major regions." It has
18 per cent of the land area of Brazil and 32 per cent of the country's population but it produces only 16 per cent of the national
income. (Its population of 25 million is greater than that of any
other South American country except Brazil itself and its land
area is surpassed only by Argentina and the rest of Brazil.) [22]

The other significant plantation sub-economies are the Caribbean lowlands of the Central American countries. There the pattern is somewhat different from the two just considered. Whereas
the sub-economies of the Brazilian Northeast and the U.S. South
are integrated in important ways to the national economies because of the internalization of "metropolitan" connections, those
of the Central American lowlands are not. The metropolitan center which provides the capital, management, technology, and a
market for these banana plantation sub-economies is located outside their borders—in the United States. The sub-economies in
this case are therefore enclaves within those national economies
and have very limited connection with the larger national community apart from revenue payments to the national government. For
all practical purposes, these are really not sub-economies at all but
plantation economies in their own right. However, legal convention regarding nation states forces us to consider them as plantation sub-economies.

PLANTATION AMERICA

Finally we wish to note that the spatial continuity of plantation
economies in the New World has led the social anthropologists to

22. Stefan Robock, *Brazil's Developing Northeast* (Washington, D. C.,
1963), pp. 2, 21, and 45.

recognize a community of nation states, territories, and regions of two nations as representing a culture sphere. Charles Wagley has labeled this culture sphere plantation America. According to Wagley: Briefly, this culture sphere extends spatially from about midway up the coast of Brazil into the Guianas, along the Caribbean coast, throughout the Caribbean itself, and into the United States [South].[23] In Wagley's scheme, the rest of the New World consists of two other culture spheres: Euro-America and Indo-America—both labels reflecting the character of the dominant races. For consistency Wagley could have described plantation America as Afro-America or black America because black people are the majority of the population in this culture sphere. This is of course not surprising because the black presence in the New World derives from the plantation. We should therefore approach the study of black dispossession in the New World through the medium of plantation economy.

In his article, Wagley elaborates on some of the common features of plantation America and describes a series of cultural characteristics common to the region. Among the common features are "monocrop cultivation under the plantation system, rigid class lines, multi-racial societies, weak community cohesion, small peasant proprietors involved in subsistence and cash-crop production, and a matrifocal type family form." While the common cultural characteristics are reflected in similarities of the peasant crops, production techniques, and marketing arrangements; the cuisine; the music and dance; the folklore; religious cults; and a series of traditions, values, attitudes, and beliefs.[24] As implied by the label used by Wagley, all these similarities can be traced back to the common experience which black people in the New World have undergone as a result of the pervasive influence of the plantation on their lives.

3. Peasants in the political economy of plantations

In most of the countries in which plantations are important they coexist with peasant producers who normally are engaged in farm-

23. Charles Wagley, "Plantation America: A Culture Sphere," in Vera Rubin (ed.), *Caribbean Studies—A Symposium*, p. 5.
24. *Ibid.*, pp. 9–11.

ing cash crops (sometimes the same crop as the plantation) in addition to providing for their own subsistence. These peasant farmers are affected by the plantations in at least two important ways: competition for land and other resources and the provision of wage work on the plantations to supplement their incomes from the main pre-occupation of farming on their own account. What evidence there is suggests that normally peasant farmers are reluctant to undertake wage work on plantations. This is clearly the case in the West Indies (and other ex-slave plantation areas) where the legacy of slavery has resulted in a high premium being placed on an existence independent of the plantation. It also appears to be the case in plantation Asia as well. For example, Boeke writing on Indonesia asserts that

A man who takes service on a plantation does so because he finds it impossible to make a living as an independent cultivator. Contrariwise —and the Outer Provinces furnish proof positive of this assertion— anyone who can manage to earn a living as an independent cultivator refuses to hire himself out as a wage laborer on a plantation.[25]

And Blake writing at a later date notes that the existence of labor shortage for plantation agriculture alongside substantial unemployment and underemployment in both rural and urban areas is attributable to the fact that Sumatran peasants prefer own-account farming even if it involves squatting on prepared plantation land. According to Blake the Sumatran regards plantation work as "inferior if not degrading." [26] It would seem then that as concerns the welfare of peasants the more important consideration is the effect of plantations on the availability of land and other resources for peasant production.

Competition for resources is particularly intense in certain countries where land is in relatively short supply and the intensity has substantially increased in recent decades with the accelerated rate of population expansion. Very often this has resulted in increasing social tension and political conflict, as the following examples indicate.

25. J. H. Boeke, *The Structure of the Netherlands Indian Economy* (New York, 1942), p. 135.
26. D. J. Blake, "Labour Shortage and Unemployment in Northeast Sumatra," *Malayan Economic Review*, October 1962.

In Ceylon the peasant-plantation conflict appears to be most severe in the Kandyan uplands where, according to Farmer, the expansion of peasant villages has been severely restricted by the presence of European tea plantations and is a constant source of political conflict and tension. This is supported by Forrest who cites the *Report of the Kandyan Peasant Commission* and other sources to substantiate the claim that the expansion of plantations coupled with increasing population have placed a "sharp limit on village expansion" and on peasants' access to land.[27] For the Philippines, Luna describes the plight of peasants in Basilan Island; he indicates that in spite of assistance from the government's homesteading provisions, peasants have great difficulty in securing quality land because plantations have already alienated the best land in the northern and southern portions.[28]

In Fiji the tension between peasants and a monopoly plantation company erupted in the 1960's in the so-called cane dispute over the terms for sale and purchase of sugarcane. According to Watters the underlying factors in this conflict situation are:

. . . The latent feelings of insecurity and fear of the Indian smallholder—feelings that arise from the context of the whole Fiji problem, with its Indian land hunger, mounting population pressure, cultural cleavage and racial antagonism, unrelenting traditionalism of the powerful Fijian community, and the precarious foundations of the economy as a whole. But above all, animosity towards the company represents both the incipient nationalism and marked sectionalism of [the] people.[29]

27. *Report of the Kandyan Peasant Commission* (Colombo, 1951); B. H. Farmer, "Peasant and Plantation in Ceylon," *Pacific Viewpoint,* March 1963; and D. M. Forrest, *A Hundred Years of Ceylon Tea* (London, 1967).
28. T. W. Luna, Jr., "Some Aspects of Agricultural Development and Settlement in Basilan Island, Southern Philippines," *Pacific Viewpoint,* March 1963.
29. R. F. Watters, "Sugar Production and Culture Change in Fiji," *Pacific Viewpoint,* March 1963, p. 49. Reference to "the company" is to the foreign-owned Colonial Sugar Refining Company which has a monopoly on the milling of sugarcane in Fiji. The term "Indian" is applied to those indentured laborers and their descendants who now make their home in Fiji while the term "Fijian" in the above relates to the indigenous population.

For Indonesia, Karl Pelzer notes that since World War II there has been increasing pressure on the land in Sumatra and the squatting of peasants on plantation land has become an important source of conflict between the two groups. He indicates that although population density is low there is a "scarcity of land which is easily accessible, well-drained and protected against destructive floods or the encroachment of tidal salt water." And Fryer also says that there is a strong conflict between estate and peasants for land and water in Java. All this has been further documented by Jacoby.[30]

In Mauritius, Brookfield describes the situation as follows: ". . . The renascence of the plantation economy is leading to a progressive reduction in the proportion of small growers' land and the circumstances of the [sugar] industry are sharpening the differential between the big and the small man." [31] And the peasant land hunger is said to be acute in neighboring Réunion and in the Comoro Islands because of the alienation of the best lands by plantations. According to Harrison Church et al., some fifty plantations with over a thousand acres each monopolize the coastal plains of Réunion and peasants are forced to eke out an existence in the eroded and "useless" highlands. And in the Comoro Islands peasant holdings are said to be small, highly fragmented and dispersed as a result of "Islamic inheritance law, the destruction of indigenous society and *competition for land by plantation holders*" who maintain large estates that are, for the most part, hardly developed.[32]

Finally, the West Indies provides outstanding examples of the peasant-plantation conflict. Since the plantation has a longer history here than in the other countries mentioned above it will be useful to consider the West Indian case at somewhat greater length

30. Karl J. Pelzer, "The Agrarian Conflict in East Sumatra," *Pacific Affairs*, June 1957; D. W. Fryer, "Recovery of the Sugar Industry in Indonesia," *Economic Geography*, April 1957; and E. H. Jacoby, *Agrarian Unrest in Southeast Asia* (New York, 1961).
31. H. C. Brookfield, "Problems of Monoculture and Diversification in a Sugar Island: Mauritius," *Economic Geography*, January 1959, pp. 32–33.
32. R. J. Harrison Church et al., *Africa and the Islands* (New York, 1965).

so as to make clear the full dimensions of the problem. In the West Indies the problem is greater in the sugar islands of St. Kitts, Antigua, Barbados, and Jamaica. In the first three the plantations had alienated the best lands long before the emancipation of the slaves in the nineteenth century so that a peasantry hardly emerged at all. Augelli writing on Antigua, for example, notes that apart from a modest land settlement scheme, "the predominant systems of land tenure and tenancy are only slightly modified forms from the pre-emancipation days" and the resulting pattern is one of a large landless peasantry living in constant economic distress.[33] In most of what follows we take the somewhat less extreme case of Jamaica to analyze the nature of peasant-plantation resource competition and to consider the effects of this on the welfare of the peasants.

The West Indian peasantry is the outgrowth of the slave plantation system. The abolition of slavery in the nineteenth century was followed by a movement of the ex-slaves away from the plantations in an effort to establish an independent existence as far removed as possible from the brutalities of the slave plantation. In the process they "started small farms 'on the peripheries of plantation areas,' wherever they could find land—on abandoned plantations and in the mountainous interiors of the various territories." [34] As Mintz has described it, this process "represented a reaction to the plantation economy, a negative reflex to enslavement, mass production, monocrop dependence, and metropolitan control. Though these peasants often continued to work part-time on plantations for wages, to eke out their cash needs, their orientation was in fact antagonistic to the plantation rationale." [35] The success with which the ex-slaves managed to establish small farms depended in large measure on the availability of land. Since the plantation had already engrossed most of the best lands, little or none was available in some territories while in others what was available was either inaccessible or of very poor

33. J. P. Augelli, "Patterns and Problems of Land Tenure in the Lesser Antilles: Antigua, B.W.I.," *Economic Geography,* October 1953.
34. W. K. Marshall, "Notes on Peasant Development in the West Indies," *Social and Economic Studies,* September 1968, pp. 252–53.
35. S. W. Mintz, Foreword to R. Guerra y Sanchez, *Sugar and Society in the Caribbean* (New Haven, 1964), p. xx.

quality. Barbados, St. Kitts, and Antigua fall in the first category while Jamaica, the Windwards, Trinidad, and Guyana fall in the second. In Jamaica and the Windwards the mountainous interior had not been touched by the sugar industry and in Trinidad and Guyana small population bases and not yet fully established sugar industries left available supplies of land. With Emancipation, the plantations lost direct control over the labor services of slaves, and the high independence aspirations of the ex-slaves raised the reserve price for wage work on plantations and led to a depletion of plantation labor supplies.

From the very outset peasant production in the West Indies had to compete directly with previously established plantation production for very scarce resources, in particular land and labor. As our analysis of the Jamaican experience below shows, the stranglehold of the plantations has remained to this very day and has served to limit the accessibility of resources to the peasants. Consequently, the present-day situation still reflects a struggle by the peasantry to break through an institutional setting that is biased toward its stagnation. In the one hundred and thirty-odd years since Emancipation, the Jamaican peasantry has not managed to secure very much of the country's agricultural land and other resources. And what little they have achieved can hardly be maintained in the face of continuing stiff competition from the plantations. In spite of attempts by government to provide assistance to the peasants in recent decades, incremental agricultural resources tend to flow toward the plantation sector and the peasantry increasingly has been forced to seek possibilities for advancement through migration and/or wage work on the plantations. Thus the situation has reverted to very much the same pattern that existed just after Emancipation.

The present distribution of *land* in farms in Jamaica shows a very unequal pattern—farms of under five acres in size (constituting the land of the bulk of the peasantry) represent 71 per cent of all farms in the country but together they occupy only 12 per cent of total farm acreage. On the other hand, plantations are less than 1 per cent of all farms yet these occupy 56 per cent of total farm acreage. When account is taken of differences in the quality of the land, the pattern is even more grossly unequal. Norton and Cum-

per, in a recent exercise, found a distinct correlation between the
Census-revealed occupancy pattern of plantations with the geolog-
ical boundary of the alluvial deposits and of peasant farms with
the lower and less precipitous hills, slopes, and accessible river
valleys.[36] This situation exists in spite of relatively intensive attempts by government to assist the settlement of peasants. The impact of government land settlement schemes (which began around
the turn of the century and were intensified after World War II)
has been limited in part because land which became available for
settlement was what plantations no longer required for their own
use or what was mountainous forested Crown lands. Usually it
was the least viable plantations which sold out to government and
their limited viability was not entirely unrelated to the quality of
land. Redwood has calculated that of all the land settlements acquired by government between 1929 and 1949 only 4 per cent
were of the most fertile soil type.[37] In addition the politics of settlement dictated that each property acquired be divided between
as many people (votes) as possible. Thus we find that at least half
of these holdings are less than four acres. Given the poor quality
of the land farmers can hardly make a living on these small holdings and are forced to seek outside work. It has been estimated
that "13 per cent of the settlers under these schemes supplement
their income by seasonal work and as many as 24 per cent in regular part-time work." [38]

The position of the peasants with respect to land has varied
over time in accordance with changes in the fortunes of the main
plantation crop—sugar—and with changes in the demographic
picture. In the early decades after Emancipation when more land
was available, the movement of the peasant population was dis-
tinctly from the plantation lowlands to the mountainous backlands.
It appears that this trend has been reversed more recently. In a

36. A. V. Norton and G. E. Cumper, " 'Peasant,' 'Plantation,' and
    'Urban' Communities in Rural Jamaica: A Test of the Validity of
    the Classification," Social and Economic Studies, December 1966.
37. Paul Redwood, A Statistical Survey of Land Settlements in Jamaica,
    1929–1949 (Ministry of Agriculture, Jamaica, mimeographed report,
    n.d.).
38. H. R. Brewster and C. Y. Thomas, The Dynamics of West Indian
    Economic Integration (Mona, Jamaica, 1967), p. 117.

1954 study of one of the major plantation parishes, Cumper discovered "a considerable local migration from the peasant areas
. . . into the cane lands" which he attributed to two factors: the rationalization of the sugar industry and its rising fortunes since 1938, and the inability of the infertile mountain areas to absorb an expanding peasant population.[39] In a more recent survey of land and population in the sugar belt of Jamaica, Alan Eyre noted:

There are . . . populous centres which are entirely rural. These are associated with zones of small-scale subsistence farming on the periphery of the cane zone. The important fact about these centres is that while their "subsistence" area has decreased or remained static, the population has in many cases more than doubled. . . . Some of these peripheral centres have so increased in population that there is not the slightest possibility that without massive depopulation they can ever again be considered basically villages of subsistence farmers. . . .

It is quite clear that the nature of these erstwhile "subsistence" districts has changed rapidly as they become increasingly hemmed in by expanding capitalised large-scale monoculture.[40]

Thus it appears that opportunities for peasant production have become increasingly restricted with the expansion of plantations on the one hand and population growth on the other. The development of the peasantry will remain constrained so long as plantations remain entrenched on the best available lands.

Peasant development is further constrained by the influence of plantations on resources other than land. In the case of labor, shortage of land restricts the use of peasant family labor in own-account production. And with expanding population on a limited land base the tendency has been toward increasingly smaller farm sizes in the peasant sector. Peasant farms are therefore increasingly incapable of fully utilizing the available peasant labor supply and of providing sufficient income to sustain the families. In the labor market as a whole, plantations have a distinct advantage as

39. G. E. Cumper, "A Modern Jamaican Sugar Estate," *Social and Economic Studies,* September 1954, p. 121.
40. Alan Eyre, *Land and Population in the Sugar Belt of Jamaica* (University of the West Indies, Department of Geography, n.d. [ca. 1966], mimeo.), p. 8.

well. The reasons for this are (1) the more advanced techniques of plantations result in a higher labor productivity making possible the payment of higher wage rates; (2) employer-employee relations are more impersonal on plantations than on small farms; and (3) the plantation provides steadier employment than the individual small farm does. As a result of these considerations, peasants have great difficulty attracting hired labor unless they follow patterns set by the plantations. The closer peasants are located to plantations the greater the influence. In a 1956 survey, M. G. Smith found that

small settlers located in or near to an important property or estate area, tend to adopt the estate patterns of task, piece or job work; and that labourers faced with the competing alternatives of rural small-farm, estate, and urban or semi-urban employments, shift away from the former towards the better paid or more regular employment.[41]

He went on to indicate that even where small settlers are capable of paying wage rates equal to or greater than plantations near to them, labor is likely to be more available to plantations on account of the greater amount of work offered. For instance, "some properties were paying 2/3 a hundred to pick and husk coconuts while adjoining small settlers were paying 2/6 to 3/-; but in fact a man could make as much as or more per day's work on the property at this task than on any of the small settlers' holdings." [42]

Turning to capital and credit, again we find the dominating influence of the plantation. The metropolitan-based branch banking system was developed to service plantation production and the associated export-import trade. At most times therefore plantations have been able to secure sufficient credit for whatever capital expansion they contemplated. In addition the foreign-owned enterprises could always draw on the resources of metropolitan parent companies. On the other hand peasant producers have very limited access to outside financial capital and have to rely almost exclusively on their own limited savings and personal loans from friends and/or relatives. Even when, in more recent times, gov-

41. M. G. Smith, *A Report on Labour Supply in Rural Jamaica* (The Government Printer, Kingston, 1956), p. 3.
42. *Ibid.,* p. 18.

ernments have attempted to provide credit assistance, either this was insufficient or it made demands on the peasants that were too difficult for them to meet. As concerns the commercial banking system, Thomas has noted: "Agricultural production for the home market and small-scale industry centred on the same market find it most difficult to match the existing demands and standards of the commercial banks." [43] The result of this is that plantations (in particular, sugar) get a much greater share of financial capital resources than may be warranted. As a recent study concluded, "Despite the greater contribution made by agriculture other than sugar cane to the GDP, commercial banks have accommodated sugar agriculture to a greater extent than all other agricultural products." [44]

The plantation system also has largely determined the existing fund of knowledge and related technology in agriculture. Both the plantations and government have invested significantly in research related to export crop production whereas little effort has been directed to peasant crops. Edwards has revealed that the "volume of research effort directed . . . to the problems of sugar cane and bananas, was substantially greater than the average for all other products." [45] Whereas plantations have the resources to invest in agricultural research, individual peasants do not and therefore have to rely on the output of government research. But because of the importance of export crops in the economies and the "plantation psychology" of government officials very little government research expenditure has been channeled into crops grown chiefly by the peasants.

In addition to its influence on peasant resource availability, the plantation system also affects certain policy and institutional arrangements which serve further to impede development of the peasantry. In the area of marketing and prices, for example, we

43. C. Y. Thomas, *Monetary and Financial Arrangements in a Dependent Monetary Economy* (Mona, Jamaica, 1965), p. 68. Thomas's study relates to the Guyanese experience but the nature and structure of the banking system in Guyana is identical to that in Jamaica.
44. B. C. H. Gayle, *The Financing of Sugar by Commercial Banks in Jamaica* (University of the West Indies, Department of Economics, 1968, Mimeographed report), p. 8.
45. D. T. Edwards, "An Economic View of Agricultural Research in Jamaica," *Social and Economic Studies,* September 1961, p. 333.

find that because of the plantation legacy the infrastructure for processing and distribution of export crops is highly developed whereas that for domestic output is not. Again most of the export crops have guaranteed metropolitan markets while peasant production for the domestic market is forced to compete with cheap food imports from other countries where farmers are subsidized. Furthermore, a great deal of foreign economic relations are fostered by government activity which brings benefits to export producers. It is hardly surprising therefore that even the peasants participate significantly in export crop production and in so doing are brought into further dependence on plantation activity. Peasant production of sugarcane, for example, depends on processing facilities provided by plantations.

The general picture of peasant-plantation conflict and the dominating influence of plantations on peasant welfare described above for Jamaica is more or less representative of the pattern in the West Indies as a whole, with only minor variations.[46] The conclusion that emerges is that peasant development in the West Indies is constrained by the institutional legacy of the plantation system. And so long as the agricultural resources of the region remain scarce as they have been in the past, peasants are unlikely to secure a sufficient base for the expansion of production and advancement of their levels of living.

The West Indian case seems to be similar to the pattern existing in other plantation areas. The book by Clifford Geertz on Indonesia shows that the plantations there have a debilitating effect on the Indonesian peasants in a multi-dimensional way. The influence of plantations on peasant culture and society is considered in socio-ecological terms and the conclusion is reached that peasant

---

46. W. K. Marshall, *op. cit.*, in his study of peasant development in the West Indies provides information on some of these variations. In analyzing the growth of the peasantry from Emancipation to the present, he has identified three broad phases in the process—the "period of establishment" from 1838 to 1900, the "period of consolidation" from 1900 to 1930, and the contemporary "period of saturation" during which the land accessibility has become increasingly restricted to the peasants. He concludes his analysis with a plea for "reconsideration of the role of the plantation" in the community.

welfare in Java has suffered from the impact of plantations.[47] And Erich Jacoby looking at the land problem in Indonesia puts the problem this way:

The peasants' claim for land against the rights of the plantation in East Sumatra places the agrarian problem in its proper focus. . . . Under the present economic, social and political conditions the suitability of the plantation as a tenure type can rightly be questioned since it is an obstacle to the realization of peasants' claim for land. . . . it is unquestionably fateful to deny land to a peasant population who identified the struggle for national independence with the fight for land. To maintain plantations in spite of the land crisis might involve the danger of sacrificing the possibility of a democratic development for a few hundred million dollars of foreign exchange per year.[48]

Jacoby also summarizes the plantation experience in several countries by saying that plantations "have always resulted in the social demotion of the indigenous cultivator to a landless worker who lives in complete social and economic dependence on the plantation" and that plantations normally exercise excessive and adverse influence on land distribution and use—everywhere they occupy the best lands and push peasants on to marginal hillsides in the process and the consequence is almost always fragmentation and low living standards for the peasants.[49]

47. Clifford Geertz, *Agricultural Involution—The Process of Ecological Change in Indonesia* (Berkeley, 1963).
48. Erich H. Jacoby, *Agrarian Unrest in Southeast Asia* (New York, 1961), pp. 72–73.
49. ———, "Types of Tenure and Economic Development," *Malayan Economic Review*, April 1959.

2

The political economy of change
in plantation economy and society:
an outline

1. Colonial expansion and the plantation frontier

As indicated in the preceding chapter, the plantation is one of a type of "settlement institution." The questions for consideration here are what are the elements which distinguish it from other such institutions, what factors give rise to its establishment, and what are the important features which create an institutional legacy which forms the structural foundations for subsequent development in the plantation frontier.

The plantation was an instrument of colonization. Colonization is the process of bringing territory and people under new and more stringent forms of control. After the period of the great discoveries, the nations of Europe embarked on an extensive campaign of colonial expansion. This resulted in the extension of their "territory" over vast areas far removed from the metropolitan centers. These new areas were regarded as components of the resource base of the colonizing countries and so became "frontiers" for their further economic development. With the competition for frontiers and colonies, the problem of political control over these new areas became paramount. This control took different forms and varied from place to place according to circumstances. So too did the form of colonization.

All colonies were regarded as a source of wealth for the colonizing power. In some cases the wealth was provided by access to precious metals, in others by the supply of agricultural produce, in others by access to trade. The pattern of colonization depended essentially on three general sets of conditions: the basis for the transfer of wealth, the resources of the new territory, and the resources and state of development of the colonizing power. If the basis for the transfer of wealth was the acquisition of precious metals in a territory with a well-settled and organized population, military and administrative organization was all that was required. The same applied to colonies which were strategically located along trading routes and which therefore were a source of wealth through access to trade. However, where wealth was to be provided by the supply of agricultural produce much more was usually required of the colonizing country. In addition to military and administrative organization, an institutional framework for the bringing together of land, labor, capital, management, and technology had to be provided. The plantation provided such a framework. It is one of a class of such institutions which include the family farm, agricultural missions, the manor, the ranch, and so on.[1]

According to Thompson, the family farm is perhaps the simplest settlement institution. In this case, the farm "is a 'human unit of land,' that is, it is a piece of land which the farmer and his family have domesticated and made a member of the family as a working partner."[2] The ranch, on the other hand, is a kind of "migratory farm." Man-land relationships are tied to livestock which have to be followed and husbanded. On the ranch a man works on the land but does not work the land itself. Because it is concerned with a commodity which can transport itself to the market, the ranch "is usually located further inland than is possible for commercial agriculture without cheap transportation."[3] The

1. Edgar T. Thompson, "The Plantation as a Social System," in Pan American Union, *Plantation Systems of the New World* (Social Science Monographs, VII, Washington, D. C. 1959), pp. 27–30. The discussion of these types of settlement insititutions that follows draws from this source.
2. *Ibid.*, p. 27.
3. Edgar T. Thompson, "The Plantation as a Social Institution," Chapter 1 of "The Plantation" (dissertation, University of Chicago, 1935), p. 6.

large agricultural mission is somewhat similar to the plantation in many respects, even in the sense that it often produces commodities for sale in the market; "but the agricultural mission is fundamentally an institution maintained specifically for the assimilation and education of the native." [4] Thompson makes the distinction rather nicely when he states that whereas the mission governs its membership for the glory of God, the plantation does so "for the material advancement of His planters."

In some of the early writings on plantations, there was much confusion arising from the fact that the plantation was regarded as a feudal institution. Some of this confusion persists even today. The reason for this is that the plantation has several features similar to the manor. Both are large landed estates based on agricultural production in which large numbers of people are governed on the principle of authority, with lord or planter exercising judicial and state functions. Consequently it was assumed that the manorial system of preindustrial Europe had been transferred to the colonies in the form of plantations. The essential difference between the manor and the plantation is that in the former, initial production was directed toward self-sufficiency. The manor arose in isolated inland areas and production for trade outside these areas came later with the development of towns. The *raison d'être* of the plantation was production for overseas trade and it naturally arose in coastal regions. Its present-day concentration in the island regions of the world is not unrelated to this historical fact. This difference is also reflected in several other ways, one of which is the cropping pattern. The manor is characterized by diversification while the plantation is based on crop specialization to the extent that even food requirements of the population are imported.

The closest modern parallel of the traditional manor is perhaps the Latin American hacienda. Although the hacendado's production is normally for sale there are two significant differences in relation to the traditional plantation: sale is normally to markets within the same country and the hacienda as a unit is more self-sufficient than the plantation. Self-sufficiency arises from the pro-

4. *Ibid.*, p. 6.

duction of the hacienda workers on plots of land which the hacendado provides for the workers' own cultivation and subsistence requirements. By attaching workers to plots, the hacendado ensures that sufficient labor is always available for his own production needs. The plantation is similar to the hacienda in several other respects. Both require large numbers of unskilled workers and this contributes in large measure to the extended land area they normally cover. For in order to secure labor for its almost exclusive service, the institution must somehow ensure that no (or few) other means of livelihood exist for the population. Modern plantations are normally more heavily capitalized than are haciendas and, because of their corporate structure, are more profit-oriented and their impersonal employer-employee relations contrast sharply with the personal face-to-face relations on the hacienda.[5]

The main point to be established here is that the plantation is a highly capitalistic enterprise. And this above all else distinguishes it from other agricultural settlement institutions. Whereas the family, religion, social status, and other considerations enter into the calculus of decision making in other settlement situations, the guiding consideration of the plantation is production for profit. This determines how the factors of production are combined. And its orientation toward export trade helps to determine what it produces.

Mintz and Wolf have provided a simple framework for considering the conditions which give rise to the establishment and subsequent continued existence of the plantation.[6] Preconditions for the establishment of the plantation as a settlement institution include: (1) capital sufficient to allow the plantation organization to secure needed factors of production; (2) land in sufficient quantity and of quality adequate for present and future production; (3) labor in sufficient quantity to minimize production costs and so

5. For further discussion of the differences between haciendas and plantations, see E. R. Wolf and S. W. Mintz, "Haciendas and Plantations in Middle America and the Antilles," *Social and Economic Studies,* September 1957.
6. Although the basic reference is to the foregoing citation, the discussion here draws more directly from S. W. Mintz, "The Plantation as a Socio-cultural Type," in Pan American Union, *Plantation Systems of the New World,* pp. 45–47.

maximize profit; (4) technology of a sufficiently high level for "modern" production; and (5) sanctions of a political-legal sort to maintain a disciplined labor force and to regulate distribution of the surplus. In addition, the system needs (6) a sizable industrial market for its staple and (7) a system of class stratification that differentiates those with capital from those with only labor services to sell. Once established, the survival of the plantation is ensured if capital is in continuous supply, land monopolized, the labor force in oversupply and its control standardized, and technological change adopted as quickly as necessary and feasible; and if, in addition, the market remains stable and ensured.

During the seventeenth and eighteenth centuries the industrializing countries of Europe provided the necessary capital, markets, and technology to exploit the "new" lands of the Western Hemisphere—particularly the coastal tropical lowlands where the original inhabitants practiced shifting cultivation on land which was relatively sparsely inhabited. The problem from the very beginning was how to secure adequate labor supplies and for this purpose the system of slavery was introduced. Because of its extensive land requirements the plantation normally can be established only in "open resource" situations in which all of the land is not already in permanent settlement. But herein lies the problem, for the population resident in a situation of open resources is in a position to secure an independent existence on the land and is not then normally available for plantation work. Thus compulsion becomes an essential mechanism of control. This is exercised at first on the indigenous population and then, when this source becomes inadequate, on the new labor recruits which the plantation brings from elsewhere. Subsequently, by engrossing as much land as it possibly can, the plantation soon transforms the open resource situations it finds on invasion to a "closed resource" situation which guarantees a labor supply even in the absence of legal compulsion.[7]

In general, the execution of a scheme of colonization depended on several other factors. Among these, geography and climate

7. See H. J. Nieboer, *Slavery as an Industrial System* (The Hague, 1900), especially pp. 420–21, for the distinction between open and closed resource situations in relation to the plantation and slavery.

played a part. In some places, for example, mountains and forests presented effective barriers to penetration and conquest; as a result, rights of trade and control had to be secured through treaties with local chiefs. Also, the suitability of the climate for European settlement was of some consequence; the difference between New England with its temperate climate and the West Indies with its humid, tropical environment is a case in point. Another factor influencing the pattern of colonization was the numbers and state of organization of the indigenous population. In the highland regions of America and in parts of Asia the Europeans found societies which were highly organized politically. There the customary organization was used to form units of government through which the metropolitan power exercised control.[8] The scheme also depended ultimately on the resources of the colonizing power. In some cases, rapid industrialization and growing populations provided the basis for overseas investment and migration while other countries with lower levels of industrialization and no surplus populations were less able to mobilize resources for colonial development. Compare Britain and Spain in this connection.

The nature of the plantation and of the conditions which gave rise to its establishment left a very distinctive imprint on the plantation colonies. This was also true of other settlement institutions. Students of colonization long ago detected certain of the peculiarities of plantation colonies as compared, for example, with what have been described as "farm colonies." Farm colonies are the same as those we described earlier as colonies of settlement. In those instances, massive migration from the metropolitan country was the basis of settlement. There the unit of migration was normally a group such as the family or a religious sect. This migration was permanent. The groups had left their homeland either to avoid oppression of one kind or another, or to secure a better livelihood in the new environment. They, therefore, carried with them patterns of social organization and definite ideas about the kind of society they wished to create. The basic unit of social organization was the family. On the other hand, migration to the plantation colonies normally consisted of individuals (males) who viewed plan-

8. See I. C. Greaves, *Modern Production Among Backward Peoples* (London, 1935), especially pp. 32–33.

tation production as a means of accumulating wealth over a relatively short period; then they planned to return to the home country to enjoy the good life on the accumulated wealth. The family of the planter either came much later or never at all, so that his point of reference was always the home country and not the colony. His sojourn in the plantation colony was regarded as a temporary affair. With his family far away, he had to establish a temporary "family."

These differences in the pattern of colonization left a legacy of social organization and patterns of production which have been summarized by Keller as follows. The farm colony bears a closer resemblance to the "mother country" in terms of the composition of population, institutional structure, and so forth. Its development is based on self-sufficiency in food production which leads to an independent economy and polity in which there is equality and widespread popular participation. On the other hand, the plantation colony develops as a racially mixed society specializing in production for export. It remains dependent on the mother country, economically and politically as well.[9] Internally, political authority and control are centralized in the hands of the planters whose dependence on the home country is in turn reflected in the total dependence of the plantation colony as a whole. The economic and political dependence of the colony reinforces the personal dependence of the planter on the mother country and this creates a society with a deep-seated psychological dependence on the outside world in general and on the mother country in particular. This psychological dependence is a phenomenon that has persisted, and it continues to be, as will be evident in due course, one of the chief obstacles to change and transformation in the plantation economies.[10]

9. A. G. Keller, *Societal Evolution: A Study of the Evolutionary Basis of the Science of Society* (rev. ed., New York, 1931); Chapter IX. See also his discussion in *Colonization: A Study of the Founding of New Societies* (Boston, 1908), Chapter I. Keller naïvely attributes the conditions giving rise to the establishment of the two types of colonies to climate alone. However, his conclusions regarding the differences in the institutional legacy are worthy of note.

10. See, in particular, the discussion in Chapter 8.

2. The plantation in political and social change

By its very nature the plantation is an institution of international dimensions. As we have seen, its establishment necessitated bringing together enterprise, capital, and labor from different parts of the world into new locations. Internally it developed as a total institution and externally it continued to depend in fundamental ways on the outside world. It is therefore not surprising to find that it has been at the center of political and social change of one kind or another. In the nature of things it had to adjust to forces emanating from the external environment and the people within its territory in turn had to make adjustments to these changes in the plantation. Stimulus from outside, response, and reaction have characterized the whole history of the development of plantations. As Greaves has summarized it, because of its character "the plantation has been associated with most political and international developments of modern times: mercantilism and free trade; slavery and independence; capitalism and imperialism." [11] To understand the structural dynamics of the plantation we need to review briefly its historical and continuing role in these broad areas of political and social change in the world community in general and in the plantation economies in particular.

As already indicated, the plantation was a mercantilist creation of the metropolitan countries of Europe. Its wholesale transplantation of forced labor under a system of slavery served to create entirely new societies. In the Caribbean, for example, the sparseness and low levels of social organization of the indigenous population led to their rapid and complete decimation at the hands of the invading Europeans. As a source of labor supply for the plantations, slavery and then indenture resulted in the legacy of societies which consist totally of transplanted peoples. The plantation therefore influenced the racial and sex composition of the population, the social structure, and every other aspect of social organization. It

11. Ida C. Greaves, "Plantations in World Economy," in Pan American Union, *Plantation Systems of the New World,* p. 14.

also created, therefore, the seeds of social dynamics. These we will now briefly consider.[12]

The creation of a new social order from elements drawn from different societies and cultures could be achieved only if there was sufficient authority and control to bring these diverse elements into line, for a common purpose. The plantation provided the basis for this. Through systems of legal compulsion the planter was able to exercise authority. And this was reinforced by a class structure which completely restricted mobility from sub-ordinate to super-ordinate status. Race was the basis of this caste system. The early plantation societies of the New World were made up of three groups: the white European planters and slaveowners at the top of the social and political hierarchy; the free white intermediate group; and the large body of black slaves at the bottom.[13] The slave class was in a real sense similar in status to cattle and was on the whole an undifferentiated mass. The planters drew their slave supplies from African people of different cultures and social background so that their original culture was eroded in the process of assimilation on the plantation. Communication, for example, was a problem, and the solution lay finally in a modification of the planter's language on the plantation. Communication is important, for in the plantation setting it is the means by which orders from the top can be communicated to those below who must implement them. Each plantation was a self-contained unit or territory with ultimate control and jurisdiction (even to the point of deciding the life or death of a slave) vested in the planter. Plantation society was simply the agglomeration of these units in any one country.

The brutality and inhumanity of slavery forced the slaves into a total rejection of the plantation. This led to numerous revolts and escape. Those that revolted laid the foundations for subsequent political and social change. Those that escaped established remote Maroon colonies engaged in subsistence activity. As the planters found it more and more difficult to maintain law and order, they

12. Detailed discussion of the patterns of social and political organization is presented in Chapter 3.
13. This general classification ignores the free colored group which varied in size from place to place but was of decidedly minor importance in the total social order.

had to rely increasingly on metropolitan military and political intervention. Thus, for example, we find that a few years after the abolition of slavery the ex-slave populations naturally sought to secure an existence independent of the plantation. This led to the creation of a peasantry in places where land of one kind or another was still available for settlement. It also led to a new wave of immigration of plantation labor which introduced new racial and cultural groups into the plantation societies,[14] with corresponding effects on the social structure and social dynamics.

After the abolition of slavery the social structure of the New World plantation colonies was somewhat adjusted. The system of caste remained (and still persists in some places). But opportunities for a limited mobility of the ex-slaves became possible through independent peasant cultivation and, more important, through education. Relatively small numbers of the black population were able to acquire clerical skills through the educational system. But because the educational system was itself a metropolitan creation, the black people who passed through it further assimilated the metropolitan culture and became essentially black Europeans. Their importance in the dynamics of change, however, rests on the fact that they were able to articulate the circumstances and needs of the more dispossessed mass of the black society which helped them to create the organizational infrastructure for political and social change. Thus we find "educated" black men playing important roles in the creation of political parties and trade unions which served eventually to transfer constitutional power from the European Crown back to the colonies—this time to the population as a whole.

The low levels of wages and the wretched living conditions of those who continued to secure a livelihood from plantation labor led to numerous uprisings and social unrest. We find therefore that worker organization and metropolitan intervention (under Crown Colony government) led to the introduction of social legislation of one kind or another. This varied from legislation governing condi-

14. This occurred mainly in the relatively open resource parts of the Caribbean where indentured labor from India was important from the mid-nineteenth century until 1917.

tions of indenture to conditions of work. As the International Labour Organization has stated:

Much of the social legislation in a number of countries is related, in one way or another, to the development of plantations (and mining). Although the evolution of this legislation had been slow at the early stages (19th century), it was relatively rapid during the present century, in particular since the first world war concurrent with the development of the commercial economy of these countries.[15]

There are at least two general aspects of the politics of all plantation colonies which need to be noted at this point. They are, first, the direction given by public authorities in order to achieve the objectives of plantation development; and, second, regulation of the conditions of life and work of the population involved in plantation production. However, we need also to note that in all instances the second was subsidiary to the first—that is to say, the regulation of conditions of life and work was carried only to a point which would serve to minimize the degree of social unrest and thereby keep the plantation structure intact. This is obvious since the basic conditions for success of plantation development is the low wages that it pays its labor. Legislation cannot therefore at one and the same time seek to maximize the profitability of plantation production and the welfare of plantation labor.

The present social and political organization in plantation economies throughout the Third World fundamentally reflect that which existed in the colonial period. Social structures with rigid patterns of stratification based on race, color, and other ascriptive characteristics; cultural pluralism; and highly centralized government and political organization are today typical of all the countries involved. The social dynamics of the period since World

15. International Labor Organization (ILO), Committee on Work on Plantations (2nd Session, Havana, 1953), *General Report* (Geneva, 1953), p. 75. R. T. Smith has recently reminded us that "plantations were among the first industrial organizations in which the workers were separated from the means of production and subjected to something like factory discipline," in "Social Stratification, Cultural Pluralism and Integration in West Indian Societies," in S. Lewis and T. G. Mathews (eds.), *Caribbean Integration* (Rio Piedras, Puerto Rico, 1967), p. 231.

War I led ultimately to the creation of new nation states out of the former plantation colonies, mostly since World War II. The governments of these new nations predominantly consist of (and are often headed by) the corps of European educated black men who helped in the mobilization for better living conditions for plantation labor that led to independence. However, these national governments have all failed to achieve the objectives of the campaign. The reasons for this general failure derive in part from the strengthening of the economic power of plantations during the present century and, in part, from the incapacity of the national leaders, the leaders' incapacity being directly related to the psychological legacy of the plantation on the minds of the colonized peoples. The first consideration is taken up and analyzed in Chapter 5; the second is now briefly considered.

The model adopted here is one developed by R. T. Smith in his analysis of the evolutionary basis of social stratification and cultural pluralism in the West Indies. According to Smith, the sequel to plantation society after the abolition of slavery was creole society. But his description of creole society indicates that it differed only in degree (not in structure) from plantation society. For example: "The basic facts about creole society are that it was rooted in the political and economic dominance of the metropolitan power, it was colour stratified and was *integrated around the conception of the moral and cultural superiority of things English.*" [16] And "the value standards pertaining to the whole society were 'English' or 'white people's.' " Since the plantations were English-owned and since they provided the integrating mechanism during the slave period, it follows that creole society is fundamentally the same as plantation society. However, the important clue concerning the social and psychological legacy of the plantation comes from the following:

The very forces that were used to integrate creole society—religion, education, the law, medicine, journalism, the civil service—resulted in the creation of a creole élite which, by the end of the nineteenth century, was referring to itself as "the intelligentsia." This group owed its position within the society to achievement in the sense that it filled

16. *Ibid.*, p. 234. Emphasis added.

valued occupational roles and commanded and manipulated "English" culture, but it is evident that its members came to believe themselves to be *qualitatively* different from the other non-Europeans by virtue of their "refinement." [17]

The pattern is essentially the same as that of the slave-plantation period when the only significant basis of differentiation among the slaves had been that between those engaged in field labor and those engaged in housework or a skilled craft. The "intelligentsia" of creole society are the equivalent of the "house slave" of the earlier plantation society. Although Smith makes the case that West Indian societies have now passed from the stage of creole society to "modern society" he admits that the structure of these societies is still that of colonial creole society.

Two basic incapacities of the national political leadership follow from this analysis. First, the leaders treat the plantations as being beyond their control since these are the immediate embodiment of the "superior" culture. Second, they naturally underrate the capacity of the "unrefined non-European" element of the population. This partly explains why in every instance, except Indonesia and Cuba, the national governments of the plantation economies have sought to encourage, instead of threaten, the continued existence of the plantation. Even in the one case of Indonesia, the threat to the foreign plantations was reversed a few years after their take-over by the national government in 1957–59. In Ceylon, legislation introduced in 1958 forbad the fragmentation, by sale, of estates over a hundred acres and in 1961 the government of that country promised not to nationalize the foreign-owned plantations for at least ten years. In the Caribbean area, national governments have created the conditions for the entry of new plantation undertakings (United Fruit bananas in Surinam and Tate and Lyle sugar in Belize, for example) and have provided legislation to consolidate the position of old undertakings (capital-investment incentive legislation for sugar in Jamaica, for example). And in the younger plantation countries of Africa we find Liberia, after some forty years of domination by a rubber planta-

17. *Ibid.*, p. 237.

tion company, introducing a formal "open door policy" for new plantation investment.[18]

In spite of what is normally regarded as dramatic political and social change in the plantation economies (and more generally in the Third World) during the last forty years (especially the last twenty-five years or so), the plantation remains in a firmly entrenched position. This leads us to reject the only existing theory of social change of the plantation. In this theory an analysis of the natural history of this system leads to the conclusion that there are forces within it leading to its disintegration. Edgar Thompson's theory of the plantation cycle can be summarized as follows: the plantation gets established in a situation of open resources; this is followed by immigration resulting in a mixture of races and the emergence of new classes in the social structure. Over time, population growth leads to a shortage of land to create a closed resource situation which leads ultimately to the development of a peasant system of social organization with the establishment of co-operatives, rural credit, and so forth. An important rider to this theory is that the cycle may be lengthened or shortened by either (a) a change in market relations; (b) discovery and cultivation of a new and more profitable staple; or (c) a fresh invasion of foreign capital and superior technical methods of production.[19]

A generous interpretation of Thompson's theory would lead to

18. In all these countries, the plantation has set the pattern for a general open door to foreign investment of all kinds, not just for plantation activity, and they are currently in process of developing manufacturing, mining, and service activities which are of the same general nature as the plantation. Lloyd Best has described this process elsewhere as a "ratooning" of the plantation system. An analysis of the effects of this process of "industrialization by invitation" now sweeping the Third World is to be found in Lloyd Best and Kari Levitt, *Studies in Caribbean Economy*, Vol. I; *Models of Plantation Economy* (forthcoming).

19. The theory was first elaborated in Edgar T. Thompson, *The Plantation*, especially pp. 26–41; and in subsequent articles (see Bibliography). The "open" and "closed" dichotomy used by Thompson is borrowed from Nieboer, *op. cit.,* and is used in relation to the particular "state of the arts"; in other words, a closed-resource situation for one set of people may be open to another set with superior production techniques.

the conclusion that the consolidation of the plantation system in all areas of the world over the past few decades has been really a lengthening of the cycle as a result of the factors listed above, c in particular.[20] But then it is difficult to explain why the plantation has failed to disintegrate in places where the phase of closed resources has long since passed—Barbados and St. Kitts, for example. It would seem instead that even where a peasantry emerges in the cycle, its existence depends in large measure on the plantation and there are in fact no social forces leading to the disintegration of the system. The analysis in the present study supports this theory and concludes with the general hypothesis that the social forces inherent in the plantation system serve to perpetuate its existence and indeed to increase continuously its hegemony over the economies those social forces dominate. The disintegration of the system cannot result from evolutionary processes—a hypothesis to be confirmed or rejected when we arrive at a general social theory of the plantation.

3. Plantations and economic development

Imperialism, mercantilism, and slavery ensured that all the benefits of plantation production up to Emancipation accrued to the metropolis. In economic terms the plantation colony was simply an overseas extension of the metropolis. Nineteenth-century British economists were quite correct in describing the West Indies as a place "where England finds it convenient to carry on the produc-

---

20. This would be a generous interpretation because Thompson himself views the appearance of peasant farms in the West Indies and the U. S. South as evidence of the end of the plantation system in these areas. On the other hand, one might argue that it is necessary for the plantation to engulf the economy so much that it then sets up the social conditions for its own destruction. In this case the present phase of deepened entrenchment coinciding with newly won independence is a prelude to the subsequent disintegration. Haiti and Cuba, which are among the few plantation colonies that have been independent for some time, have indeed experienced a disintegration of the system in some way. But what about Brazil and the United States South?

tion of sugar, coffee, and a few other tropical commodities." [21]
The income generated from plantation production served to promote industrialization and development in the metropolis.[22] The
plantation colony was not an economy in any meaningful sense. It
consisted of a number of units, each of which was generally a
self-sufficient economic entity. The plantation unit was organized
to produce an export staple and almost all its resources were deployed to that end. Insofar as production of the staple did not utilize all the resources all of the time, some were used to produce
goods and services required to maintain the unit. The balance of
inputs for staple production and consumption requirements were
met by imports. Merchants and bankers in the metropolis played
an important role. The merchants provisioned the plantation with
supplies of consumption and capital goods and handled the sale of
staple output in the metropolis; and the bankers provided the necessary credit to lubricate these transactions.

The character of the slave plantation was such that it created
only subsistence income for the residents of the plantation colony
and it could not generate spread effects for economic development
in the colony because of the almost total absence of linkages outside of the unit itself. Lloyd Best has described the situation ex-
ceptionally well in his "Outlines of a Model of Pure Plantation
Economy." [23] What follows draws from that exposition. The slave
plantation economy has three important structural characteristics
which determine the pattern of development. First is that it is
structurally a part of an "overseas economy" consisting of a metropole which is the locus of initiative and decision, of product
elaboration and disposal, and of the provisioning of capital, technical and managerial skill, and other services. This means that the

21. This quotation from John Stuart Mill is cited by Greaves in "Planta-
    tions in World Economy," Pan American Union, *Plantation Systems
    in the New World*, p. 16.
22. See Eric Williams, *Capitalism and Slavery* (London, 1964) for an in-
    dication of this relationship between the West Indian plantation col-
    onies and Britain during the seventeenth and eighteenth centuries.
23. Lloyd Best, "Outlines of a Model of Pure Plantation Economy,"
    Social and Economic Studies, September 1968; see in particular pp.
    287–92 and 301–11.

plantation colony is simply a locus of production of the export staple. The second characteristic is that the slave plantation economy is really a "segmental economy" consisting of a number of firms, each of which is a self-sufficient unit almost completely independent of the rest of the economy. The individual units are held together by "little more than a system of law and order." (Each plantation even supplies its own civil government.) The earlier description of the plantation as a total institution applies as well to the economic structure. The third characteristic is what Best describes as "incalculability." As a result of the first two characteristics, "the commodity flow from stage to stage does not involve any considerable money flows. Accounting takes the form of imputing prices. There is thus a large measure of price indeterminacy." [24]

A number of consequences follow from these characteristics. First, an analysis of adjustments and resultant development in the plantation colony is meaningful only within the context of analysis of the whole overseas economy of which it is a part. Second, because linkages are confined to activity on each plantation unit and its corresponding metropolitan connection, there are no significant spread effects from staple production within the plantation colony. And since the product elaboration takes place in the metropolis the lion's share of the value added accrues there. Third, the nature of the transactions involved in production and sale of the staple is such that money flows in the plantation colony are kept to a minimum. So far as the colony is concerned then, very little money income is available to its residents from plantation production and the plantation does not provide the impetus for development. As Best indicates:

The economy can be complexified and diversified only to the extent first, that Maroons gain legitimacy and together with settlers gain land, create intermediate and final demand linkages between and among themselves and with the urban trades; and secondly, to the extent that the embryonic domestic monetary and banking system . . . is able to create money to lubricate these exchanges. [25]

24. *Ibid.*, p. 308.
25. *Ibid.*, p. 307. The reader should refer to the accounting framework presented by Best for a dramatic pictorial exposition of the structure of the slave plantation economy.

The dynamic for economic development is therefore not within the plantation sector but outside of it. Economic progress in the plantation colony can come only from the efforts of those outside the direct orbit of the slave plantation.

We need now to consider the pattern of economic development in the plantation colonies in the period after Emancipation to identify the dynamic forces and, of course, to bring our focus back to consideration of the present-day structure and dynamics of the plantation economies. Again the West Indian case is used to illustrate the pattern so. as to maintain the link here with our discussion of social and political change in the preceding section. In the period since Emancipation, two general economic trends need to be noted. The first is the establishment and growth of a peasantry and the second is the evolution of the multinational plantation enterprise. After the experience of the brutality of plantation, the ex-slaves sought every opportunity to secure an existence for themselves as independent of the plantation as possible. Where land of whatever quality was available they established subsistence plots which eventually were able to produce marketable surpluses. A considerable degree of diversification of the economies was the immediate result. In addition to production of foodstuffs for sale in the domestic market, the ex-slaves also introduced new export crops, such as bananas. Because the plantations had engrossed all of the best land, this peasant activity was restricted to the poorer hillside lands which nevertheless yielded enough for peasant subsistence as well as surpluses for sale. The money economy expanded, an infrastructure of footpaths (rudimentary roads) developed in the mountainous interiors, an internal system of marketing emerged, a rudimentary domestic banking and credit system gradually took form, and linkages between the different production and service sectors were established.

The plantation sector continued to concentrate on production of the export staple, mainly sugar. Fluctuations in prices, competition from other sugar-producing countries, and technological changes made it increasingly difficult for individual planters to survive. And the corporate plantation enterprise emerged to consolidate the plantation sector. These enterprises consistently evolved into multinational firms operating in several plantation countries and in the metropolis where decision making and product elaboration are centered. In addition, these firms have grown into vertically integrated enterprises supplying much of the inputs of goods and services required in plantation production and carrying out the processing and marketing of the plantation output as well. These phenomena are of direct relevance to the present development problems of plantation economies.

The emergence of the vertically integrated corporate plantation enterprise has really served to preserve the character of the slave plantation system. The three characteristics of that earlier institutional environment—appendage in overseas economy, total economic institution, and incalculability—have been preserved and strengthened in the period since Emancipation. On the other hand, the growth of the peasantry was equivalent to an expansion of the Maroon sector of the slave plantation economy. It is this expansion which has been the chief source of economic development of the West Indian economies since Emancipation. However, the plantation still dominates the economic life of the region. It owns and controls the use of the best land, has access to credit and technology, owns all the factory capacity for the rudimentary processing of plantation crops in the islands, provides services for the marketing of the export staples (shipping, insurance, overseas distribution, and so forth), and influences government policy in fundamental ways. In addition, the legacy of life on the plantation is reflected in the economic behavior of the peasants. For example, the taste for imported foodstuffs (like saltfish and flour) is well established and this pattern of consumption influences the effect of consumption spending on the economies. And finally the peasants still rely to a large extent on wage work on the plantations to supplement their own production, a substantial part of which consists of export crops which involve dependence on the plantation in one way or another (for example, processing or marketing).

What we have, therefore, are what the economists call "two sector" economies in which the dynamic sector for growth (the peasant sector) is bottled up by the other sector (the plantation sector), which contributes more to growth elsewhere. The development problem is therefore essentially one of breaking the constraints bottling up the dynamic peasant sector. The extent to which peas-

THE POLITICAL ECONOMY OF CHANGE   49

ant production is constrained by plantations varies from place to place according to circumstances. But it does seem, from information provided in the last chapter, to be of general occurrence in most of the plantation economies. Our conclusion here regarding the nature of the economic development problem in plantation economies (based on the historical experience of the West Indies) is so significantly different from that depicted by the existing literature on economic development that it is necessary briefly to review some of those contributions in the light of the present study.

The two-sector models of the development literature depict a situation in which there is a "modern" sector, in which inheres the dynamic for development, and a "traditional" sector, which is stagnant. And the development problem is seen as one of transferring resources from the traditional to the modern sector. In the underdeveloped countries to which these models refer the modern sector is usually comprised of either plantations or mines. The implicit assumption of these models is that because the so-called "modern sector" utilizes production techniques that are similar to those found in the more advanced countries of the world, it offers development possibilities akin to the development patterns of those countries. And the problem is really one of transferring all resources—in particular, labor—to this sector. It is further assumed that the expansion of the modern sector is facilitated by unlimited supplies of labor from the traditional sector.[26] Any seri-

26. The original statement of this position is to be found in W. A. Lewis, "Economic Development with Unlimited Supplies of Labour," *The Manchester School of Economic and Social Studies,* May 1954. Lewis subsequently extended the discussion in "Unlimited Labour: Further Notes," *The Manchester School* . . . , January 1958. And the model has been refined, extended, and garnished by numerous writers among whom Ranis and Fei perhaps deserve particular mention so far as the garnish is concerned. See Gustav Ranis and J. C. H. Fei, "A Theory of Economic Development," *American Economic Review,* September 1961, and *Development of the Labor Surplus Economy: Theory and Policy* (Homewood, Illinois, 1964). The Lewis two-sector model is the foundation for much of the existing economic formulations of the development problem. In all these formulations "modern" and "traditional" are defined in terms of production techniques. The modern sector utilizes relatively capital intensive techniques which contrasts with relatively labor intensive techniques of the traditional sector. Thus we have a high-income,

ous analysis of the history of plantations will reveal that the main problem of plantation agriculture from the outset to the present day has been and is one of securing adequate labor supplies (see Chapter 4). In all the plantation economies today a shortage of labor for plantation work co-exists with massive unemployment and underemployment. This suggests that those who make up this pool of unemployed labor services have a higher reserve price for plantation work than can be met by existing plantation wages. Far from facing a situation of unlimited labor supplies, the plantation sector is actually constrained by extremely limited labor supplies.

However, our contention with the two-sector models in vogue does not end there. We need seriously to question the assumption that the plantation (modern) sector provides the dynamic for development and that, therefore, the development problem resolves itself simply into bringing more resources into that sector. Again history is instructive here. If the West Indian case is a good example of the general case, and it seems to be as the rest of this study will indicate, then the development problem would seem to be the reverse of what is suggested by the two-sector models. The reason for this is that, as we have already suggested, the plantation sector dynamizes development elsewhere than in the plantation economies. This is a proposition that is developed and substantiated in much of what follows (see, in particular, Chapter 7). The two-sector models that place the plantation sector at the center stage of development in the countries with which we are concerned are therefore misleading.

The legacy of the two-sector models of economic development has also served to inform current thinking on the problems of *agricultural* development. In this more restricted field of inquiry everything tends to be cast in terms of the same classification of modern and traditional. Modern agriculture is said to be in a state of continuous disequilibrium in which rates of return on investment are sufficiently high to consistently generate improved technology and encourage the use of new inputs. Traditional agricul-

---

high-productivity sector on the one hand and a low-income, low-productivity sector on the other hand. The development problem is essentially one of expanding the high-productivity sector at the expense of the low-productivity one.

ture is said to be in a low-level equilibrium trap in which returns to investment are so low that farmers cannot be induced to adopt new inputs and new techniques. And the problem facing underdeveloped (or traditional) agriculture is simply one of breaking out of this equilibrium trap.[27] So far as the plantation economies of the world are concerned this formulation is grossly inadequate. The plantation sector of these economies fits the characteristics of modern agriculture but that does not guarantee a developed agriculture so far as the countries involved are concerned. Furthermore, it would appear that one of the chief obstacles to increased investment in the peasant sectors of plantation economies is that the rates of return on new investment and improved techniques are low because of the poor quality of land which is available to peasants as a result of the monopoly of good land by the plantations. And, in addition, the banking system and other financial intermediaries are too geared to servicing plantation needs to provide sufficient credit for peasant production. Insofar as peasant production in this setting fits the characterization of traditional agriculture the agricultural development problem must be seen in strictly structural terms, not in the marginalist tradition of the Schultz model and its derivatives.

In general, only a small portion of the existing literature on economic development adequately portrays the development problem in the plantation economies of the world. A few contributions have dealt with certain aspects relevant to the plantation but there are none that embody sufficiently the structural characteristics of plantation economies to really fill the bill. Identification of the problems of the general class of "export-propelled economies" and formulations of models of "open economies" and "dependent economies" have been on the whole quite useful.[28] But the more

27. The original formulation of this position was advanced by T. W. Schultz in his *Transforming Traditional Agriculture* (New Haven, Connecticut, 1964). Like the Lewis model of economic development this contribution has stimulated much extension and refinement and is the foundation of most current theorizing on agricultural development.

28. Among these, the contributions of Levin, Watkins, and Seers deserve special mention. See J. V. Levin, *The Export Economies* (Cambridge, Massachusetts, 1960); Melville Watkins, "A Staple Theory of

significant contributions have come from a very small number of scholars who have treated the plantation case as a special type in the general category of export economies. Baldwin, North, and Myint are the chief people involved here.[29] These writers have indicated that in addition to the general problem of export dependence, special problems of development derive from the special character of the production function, the unequal distribution of income, the limited development of linkages, and the low skill content of labor, all of which characterize plantation agriculture.

However, we need to expand on this limited base: to consider why the characteristics just mentioned inhere in the plantation structure; to introduce into the picture other economic aspects of plantations (the influence of the multinational enterprises, for example); and to integrate all that with sociological, psychological, and political considerations. That is precisely what this book is about.

Economic Growth," *Canadian Journal of Economics and Political Science,* May 1963; and Dudley Seers, "The Mechanism of an Open Petroleum Economy," *Social and Economic Studies,* June 1964. For an interesting and recent application of the export model to a plantation economy, see Donald Snodgrass, *Ceylon: An Export Economy in Transition* (Homewood, Illinois, 1966). The limitations of the general export model for analysis of development in plantation economies are revealed by Snodgrass's study which naïvely equates constitutional independence with a change in the traditional institutional order.

29. The references we have in mind are R. E. Baldwin, "Patterns of Development in Newly Settled Regions," *The Manchester School . . . ,* May 1956, and more recently "Export Technology and Development from Subsistence Level," *The Economic Journal,* March 1963; D. C. North, "Agriculture and Regional Economic Growth," *Journal of Farm Economics,* December 1959, and his book, *The Economic Growth of the United States, 1790–1860* (Englewood Cliffs, New Jersey, 1961); and Hla Myint, "Mines and Plantations," Chapter 4 of his book *The Economics of the Developing Countries* (London, 1964, and New York, 1965).

3
Social and political dimensions of plantation society

In Appendix II is described, in some detail, the nature of the economic organization of different types of plantations as can be found in various parts of the world. It is clear from those descriptions that all types of plantations have certain things in common: they cover relatively large areas, numerous unskilled workers are involved, decision making is highly centralized, the pattern of management organization is authoritarian, and workers and decision makers are separated by social and cultural differences. The particular pattern of economic organization associated with any one type is a variant of a general pattern which ensures effective communication from the decision makers at the top to those below who must implement the decisions. Authority and control are inherent in the plantation system.

Geographical isolation of the plantation unit reduces the extent to which those who live and work in it can have intercourse with other people outside its boundaries. In the least extreme cases this outside intercourse is mostly a weekend business whereas in the more extreme cases it may be virtually non-existent. On account of this isolation, people living and working on a plantation make up a distinct community which derives its full flavor from the system itself. Thus, in addition to being a system of production, the plantation is a community.

Since the community owes its being to the unit of production, it follows that its social structure and the pattern of interpersonal relations will be a reflection of the type of economic organization that governs production. The authority structure that characterizes the pattern of economic organization extends to social relationships. So we find that the plantation community is one with an inherently rigid system of social stratification—normally with white European-stock owners or managers at the top, culturally mixed skilled personnel in the middle, and culturally different unskilled laborers at the bottom. There is virtually no mobility in either direction within this system of stratification, and every aspect of life on the plantation reflects the social structure. Housing is perhaps the most obvious to any visitor; on a tour of any plantation the differences in quality of housing provided for owner or general manager, staff, and workers are quite dramatic. Recreational facilities, social group activities—everything is in tune with the pattern of stratification deriving from occupational status on the plantation.

Plantation work does not alone determine the social structure. For those living on the plantation, the institution is not just a place of work; it is their whole life. It is more normal than not that the plantation runs a store for selling supplies to workers and provides the only link between them and the outside world. In a sense the institution affords them the very means of survival, so that regardless of cultural or ethnic differences, the plantation is a binding force that welds people on it together. It is unifying. Everyone owes his existence to it. To rebel against it is to threaten one's own survival, for alternative opportunities are normally hard to find.

So far as concerns the plantation owner, the *primum mobile* is to extract as much labor services as possible out of the labor force available. This naturally leads to a pattern of exploitive authoritarian management organization which was at a peak on the slave plantation. Since the abolition of slavery, however, the pattern has become less exploitive and more benevolent. And the modernization of plantations in more recent times has given rise, in a few instances, to less benevolent and more consultative patterns of management. Benevolence and paternalism have been a necessary part of the strategy of plantation owners to keep the plantation community welded together. And this became so ingrained in many of the older plantation areas that modern corporate enterprises which have taken over planter units inherited a legacy of paternalism which is difficult to dislodge. Foster and Creyke noted this as one of the problems confronting Bookers after they acquired the Jamaican plantation described in Appendix II. And Hutchinson notes the same phenomenon in his study of a similar situation in Brazil as follows:

> The present social system tends to follow the old, traditional, family-oriented, slaveholding complex. The pattern of face-to-face interpersonal relations, developed during centuries of sugar-cane monoculture based on slavery, persists in modified form. . . . there is still the highly personal, intimate relationship based upon mutual rights and obligations and a sense of the obligations of nobility. Even the *usina* system perpetuates this paternalism to a high degree.[1]

It is easy to change the characters in the system but hard to change the system itself.

The plantation is a total economic institution. It binds every one in its embrace to the one task of executing the will of its owner or owners. And because it is omnipotent and omnipresent in the lives of those living within its confines, it is also a total social institution. Social relations within the plantation community are determined by the economic organization that governs production. Now imagine an economy composed of only plantation producing units. In such a case, the social structure and distribution of political power in the country as a whole would merely be a larger reproduction of that existing on the individual plantation. No country is purely an aggregation of plantations, in fact. But, as the discussion in this chapter indicates, the plantation economies and sub-economies of the world reveal social and political characteristics almost identical to those found within the individual plantation community. Thus we can appropriately define plantation society as a particular class of society with distinguishing characteristics of social structure and political organization, and laws of motion governing social change. The rest of this chapter develops this point.

1. H. W. Hutchinson, *Village and Plantation Life in Northeastern Brazil* (Seattle, Washington, 1957), p. 8.

1. Demographic characteristics of the plantation economies

The present-day composition of population in all the plantation economies of the world is a direct result of the movement of labor which the plantation system effected in the past. All the black people in the New World were brought here by the plantation. So also were all the East Indians now living in this hemisphere and in other plantation economies of the Indian and Pacific oceans and Southeast Asia (including Ceylon). Cultural plurality is a characteristic feature of all plantation societies because the plantation brought together people of different races and cultural backgrounds to carry out the task of production. Everywhere in the plantation world today we find national population groups that consist of people and sub-groups different in race. We are not here concerned with the fact that differences in racial composition of population exist in countries where plantations are not dominant. The argument is simply that the dominance of plantations in any particular situation is *alone* a necessary and sufficient condition for the existence of a mixed population base.

Before the arrival of the plantation, the plantation areas of the New World had been peopled by the red Indians. The plantation brought white Europeans at first, then brought black people from Africa as slaves, then brought the East Indian people as indentured laborers. The indigenous Indians never managed to survive the European conquest. And today black people, East Indians, and white people make up the populations in the New World plantation economies—roughly in the same proportion as existed on an individual plantation. Throughout the West Indies, for example, white people are a very small percentage while black people make up the bulk of the population because numerous workers were associated with individual plantations which normally have one or a few white families as owners or managers. Similarly, the relative importance of Negroes and East Indians in a particular country and the distribution of these two races throughout the region are linked directly with the plantation. For example, plantations in the smaller West Indian islands did not need to rely on indentured labor after Emancipation because the ex-slaves there had little choice but to continue working on the plantation as all the land had already been alienated. But in Jamaica, Trinidad, and Guyana, indenture was necessary and East Indians were brought in. East Indians are a relatively small percentage of population in Jamaica as compared to the proportion in Trinidad and Guyana, and this reflects the fact that resource situation was far less open in Jamaica after the abolition of slavery. The sugar industries of Trinidad and Guyana developed rather late and, for the most part, after slavery had been abolished. Consequently, the plantation need for indentured East Indian labor was greater there. These workers were brought in during the period 1836–1917; at present East Indians are more than 50 per cent of the population in Guyana and roughly 40 per cent in Trinidad.

Elsewhere indentured migration of East Indians also rapidly transformed the composition of populations. In Mauritius, this migration began in 1835; ten years later Indians made up a third of the island's population and by 1861 had reached two-thirds, remaining about the same up to the present time. In Fiji, indentured migration of East Indians lasted from 1879 to 1916; at present Indians outnumber the indigenous Fijians, being about one-half of the total population. The same pattern obtains for Ceylon, Malaya, and to a lesser extent Indonesia. The Ceylon plantations drew large numbers of contract indentured workers from the south of India—mainly Tamils. Today these Indians are over 10 per cent of Ceylon's population and they are roughly 70 per cent of the labor force working on plantations. Malaya also recruited plantation labor from the same part of India beginning in the late nineteenth century. Between 1911 and 1920, these laborers were brought in at the rate of 90,000 a year. Although the indenture system was ended in 1910, the *kangany* or gang system of recruitment from India continued until the Government of India termi-- nated it in 1938. Today the Indians are over 10 per cent of the population in Malaya, and most of them work on rubber and tea plantations.[2]

In the plantation sub-economies, population composition can

2. William Morgan, *Economic Survey of the Tea Plantation Industry* (International Federation of Plantation, Agricultural and Allied Workers, Geneva, 1963), pp. 28 and 46–47.

also be directly linked with the plantation influence. The predominantly black population of the Caribbean lowlands of the Central American republics came from the Caribbean islands in the service of the plantation. And the substantial percentages of black people in the populations of the United States and Brazil are a legacy of the slave plantation. In these two countries, the percentage of black people in the plantation sub-economies is much less than would normally have been because of internal migration to other parts of the country. Today, black people make up more than 10 per cent of the total population of the United States. If all these people were still concentrated in the plantation South they would represent well over half of that region's total population. In Brazil, black people are about a third of the total population which is equivalent to more than half the population of the plantation Northeast.[3] It should be pointed out, however, that these two areas differ somewhat from the other old plantation areas of the New World. In the United States South numerous "poor whites" had been involved in the plantation system (or were within its pale), whereas in Northeast Brazil, the indigenous Indians remained a relatively important group since they were able to minimize contact with Europeans in the vast territory available. Consequently, black people do not constitute as large a portion of the population of these two areas as in the West Indies.

In general, then, we can conclude that the basic population characteristics of all the plantation economies of the world reflect the plantation influence very significantly. Different races that comprise the plantation work force in different countries represent significant shares of national or regional population. The presence of Negroes and East Indians in the New World, and East Indians in most other plantation areas, is a direct legacy of the plantation. So also is most of the European presence. In addition to these two groups, we should also expect to find a sizable percentage classified by the censuses as "mixed." These people represent the out-

---

3. There are about 22 million black people in the United States as a whole, whereas the figure, given in Chapter 1, for the plantation South is about 39 million. In Brazil, race is officially an elusive concept. The estimate of one-third is based on what the census defines as "black" and "pardo," which includes black people of mixed ancestry.

come of a natural union between the white plantation owners and managers and non-white women from the plantation work force. The actual percentage distribution between these three basic ethnic groups will of course vary from place to place; but these variations can be explained in terms of the relevant history of the plantation system in particular places.

It is clear that the plantation can take credit for the original adjustment of population composition in the countries under study, for it actually transplanted people. What is not so clear is whether over time differential rates of population growth can be associated with groups directly within the plantation orbit and those without (that is, growth rate of plantation population vs. total non-plantation population in a country); and between the different racial groups within the plantation community. We can offer a few hypotheses in this connection. First, it is to be noted that plantations resorted to the importation of labor partly because of a shortage in the host environment but also partly because people far from home and their families are easier to control than indigenous people in their own home environment. And after it became increasingly difficult to secure imported labor, plantations had to rely on the labor services of the children of people imported earlier.[4] Plantation owners, therefore, have a vested interest in encouraging plantation workers to have many children and may employ incentives to this end. Woofter's studies of plantations in the United States South suggest that something of the sort was operative there. He points out that plantation owners would assign acreage to tenant workers "on the basis of the family labor available" and concludes that "the plantation system by placing a premium on large families perpetuates a high rate of natural population increase in the South, and that this high rate of increase by producing a surplus labor supply in turn tends to perpetuate the plantation system."[5] From these considerations it does not seem

4. Edgar Thompson makes this point in his "The Plantation: The Physical Basis of Traditional Race Relations," in Edgar Thompson (ed.), *Race Relations and the Race Problem* (Durham, North Carolina, 1939).
5. T. J. Woofter, *Landlord and Tenant on the Cotton Plantation* (U.S. Works Progress Administration, Research Monograph V, Washington, D. C., 1936), p. 7.

too unreasonable to speculate that, generally, population growth is likely to be more rapid among groups engaged in plantation work than among others in plantation society. And barring migration, we should expect to find the plantation worker group increasing in relative importance over time.[6]

The population mix that derives from the influence of the plantation system directly influences the character of society in many ways. For one thing, the different races bring with them different cultures and cultural plurality is the result. In every plantation society in the world we find two or more racial and cultural groups living side by side but having a minimum of cultural intercourse. Black people throughout the New World plantation belt have a cultural identity distinct from that of the white plantation owner and manager groups. In Trinidad and Guyana the East Indian and Negro groups live together with different cultural traditions. The same is true of the "Fijians" and the Indians, the Sinhalese and the Tamils in Ceylon, the Indians and the white-planter class in Mauritius, and the Malays, Chinese, Indians, and white people in Malaya. However, in spite of these basic differences in cultural traditions among the groups, they manage somehow to live together. And, as will be argued subsequently, this welding influence can be attributed to the plantation system. In every instance, however, the weld is continuously under pressure because of the underlying inherent social and cultural differences.

2. Social organization and structure in plantation society

The plantation influence can be traced almost directly in every important aspect of social life in the plantation societies of the world. As with plantation community, plantation society derives an ordering of social status of different groups and individuals within a country which is directly correlated with occupational status and rank in the authority structure of the plantation itself. Of course, correlation alone does not establish causality. To establish this we need to explore the historical legacy somewhat to determine what forces have molded the pattern of social organization

6. This seems to be the case with East Indians in Guyana, Trinidad, and Fiji.

which we find today in these societies. The New World experience perhaps provides the clearest illustration of plantation influence on social structure. Since this area has the longest history of continuous plantation influence, the experience there should provide useful insights into the general phenomenon.

The slave plantations of the New World brought together a few white people from Europe as owners, and large numbers of black people from Africa as forced laborers. The black people came from different parts of the west coast of Africa and were generally an odd mixture of people from different tribal and cultural backgrounds who, most often, did not speak the same language; the slave groups were mixed in terms of sex but men usually outnumbered the women, as more of them were required for the arduous task of sugar- and cotton-plantation work. On the other hand, the white Europeans who came were chiefly plantation owners, managers, and skilled laborers; and these were mostly males who viewed their association with the plantation as a temporary affair. The two groups were thrown together with one single purpose— production of the plantation crop. This meant, therefore, that the structure of authority established for this exercise would influence the entire social order on the plantation. We have already established that the slave plantation had the character of a total economic and social institution. Raymond Smith describes such institutions in the following way:

. . . "Total institutions" are organised groups with well-defined boundaries and with a marked internal hierarchical structure approaching an internal caste system. Examples would be asylum inmates and staff, prisoners and warders, officers and men on board a ship at sea, slaves and masters. . . .

It is characteristic of total institutions that people enter them as already socially formed human beings with a culture and a set of attitudes which need to be reformed so that the inmate can be "handled" as a lunatic, a monk, a prisoner, a slave or whatever it might be. Mechanisms are brought into play designed to effect a clean break with the past and a destruction of the inmate's old self so that a new set of attitudes—a new "identity"—can be imposed.[7]

7. R. T. Smith, "Social Stratification, Cultural Pluralism and Integration in West Indian Societies," in S. Lewis and T. G. Mathews (eds.), *Caribbean Integration* (Rio Piedras, Puerto Rico, 1967), p. 230.

The slaves were put through a process known as "seasoning" to adjust them for work on the plantation. And since then, right up to the present, the black experience in the New World has been a continuous process of acculturation and socialization to the norms of the plantation system.

The social structure of the slave plantation took shape from the social organization necessary for production. White European planters and administrators stood at the top and were separated by a system of caste which placed the black slaves firmly at the bottom. An intermediate group of skilled white people also existed. And among the black people there emerged a group of racial and cultural half-castes resulting from the exploits of white males with black females. This group was generally more privileged than the pure blacks and frequently made up the staff of house servants whose tasks were less arduous than those of other blacks.[8] Slave plantation society as a whole was simply made up of individual plantation communities. As Smith suggested, "one may say that this was a segmentary society with the plantations constituting a simple linear series of segments having little or no organic inter-relation."[9] The society as a whole was therefore rigidly stratified by race and color directly correlated with occupational status on the plantation and without any kind of social mobility whatever.

On each plantation, the white owner or administrator was lord and master and his mansion was the center of social life for all within the community. All decisions affecting the lives of the black people emanated from there. No church, state, or other social institution had direct access to the slaves. Church facilities were provided on the plantation by the master who also exercised juridicial and state functions. The political order was despotic with commands issued by the master to the slaves through an

8. The structure described here is a simplification of what obtained in fact. But the abstraction is fairly representative of the situation in most cases. For a detailed exposition on the social structure of the slave plantation, see H. Orlando Patterson, *The Sociology of Slavery* (London, 1967). For modifications of the general pattern described here, see, for example, W. E. Moore and R. M. Williams, "Stratification in the Ante-Bellum South," *American Sociological Review*, June 1942.

9. R. T. Smith, *op. cit.*, p. 229.

overseer. Slaves were herded together as an undifferentiated mass in compounds that had a kind of village character. Because the slaves were drawn from different cultures, they had to develop a language on the plantation in order to communicate with each other. And a common language was also necessary to facilitate the chain of command from master to slave. In the circumstances what emerged was a language which was a simplification and modification of the tongue of the masters. These are the so-called creole languages of the plantation societies today. This pattern of acculturation was to have a lasting effect on the lives of black people. For, as Thompson pointed out,

. . . Language is bound up with the system of social control. With its acquisition there tends to develop at the same time an acceptance of the situation. The meanings of the terms of the language develop in the general atmosphere of authority and against the background of cooperative activity involved in agricultural production. As this takes place, authority and obedience are determined more by moral and less by material factors.[10]

In the process, black people were increasingly emasculated culturally and socialized toward the culture of the planter class. However, they did succeed in retaining some of their original culture, and this was blended with the other to create what is now a clearly distinct sub-culture in plantation society today. Slave plantation society, therefore, had certain distinctive features: a caste system based on race, rigidly stratified social structure based on occupational status on the plantation and divided along race and color lines, and cultural plurality with integrative elements deriving from the common destiny to production of the crop for everyone in the plantation community. This last feature of the system is one which has largely escaped the notice of most plantation scholars. Yet it is one that is of great importance in explaining certain aspects of plantation societies today. The different groups on the slave plantation interacted with each other in one main area of activity—production of the crop—and from day to day, season by season, year in and year out, this was the chief bond between

10. Edgar Thompson (ed.), *Race Relations and the Race Problem*, p. 211.

them. Because production of the crop was the only reason why these groups were brought together, it is not surprising that this dominated their lives. For the white masters who owned the slaves and governed the plantations, the pattern of tolerable social organization was one that would maximize profits on production. Rigid control of the labor supply was critical and this involved control over the movement of slaves in space and status.

Although slavery has been formally abolished for about four generations or so, the basic structure of plantation society in the New World is very much what it was during slavery. The reasons for this are not very hard to find. The white-planter class monopolized the means of production on the land and were therefore in a position to maintain their dominant position. In addition, their ranks were reinforced with the arrival of non-agricultural enterprises owned and managed by their kith and kin in more recent times, so the means of production were further concentrated among that group. On the other hand, there was little that black people could do to improve their lot. Scarcity of land limited independent peasant production which meant continued dependence on the plantation. Barring emigration, the only significant scope for social mobility open to them was education. During slavery educational opportunities had been restricted. Slaves were trained only in skills useful to the plantation—artisan skills which could make the slave a more productive and contented servant. Illiteracy was almost universal among them because their masters believed that skills of reading and writing would not increase their productive value, and might even put ideas of insurrection in their heads. After Emancipation, educational opportunities for the slaves opened up somewhat. But the assimilation of what was being offered served further to acculturate black people to the culture of the dominant white class. And this served simply to expand the ranks of the intermediate social group rather than to effect any significant change in the general social structure.

Among the ranks of black people educational opportunities opened up more for the half-castes than for the rest. What limited social mobility they could achieve as a result depended in large measure on the extent to which they could succeed in divorcing the culture of black people and assimilate that of the whites. This set the stage for a dynamic process by which black people sought social mobility by aspiring continuously to a European way of life. Education, residence, manners of speech and dress, religious beliefs and practice, social values and attitudes, and general life style all served to distinguish the blacks who had "made it" from those who had not. The white sub-culture of plantation society was thereby reinforced by the joining of the club by some of the blacks. But even so the caste line still prevents their total acceptance by the dominant white class.[11] The sub-culture of the rest of the black people has remained basically that which they developed on the slave plantation. Consequently, plantation societies today maintain the traditional features of stratification by color and race, as well as a certain degree of social integration. All black people in these societies regard the white European culture as superior and, in a dynamic sense, they all aspire to it. Those still fully immersed in the plantation sub-culture aspire to getting their children away from it, even if they see no possibility of getting "out" themselves.

We find therefore that the plantation societies of the New World have the rather unique characteristic of exhibiting both cultural pluralism and social integration. This curious blend derives from the fact that cultural pluralism is operative in a static sense while the motivations and aspirations of people exhibit a kind of social integration. In terms of analyzing the dynamics of social change the social-integration concept is appropriate. But in describing the social structure at any point in time cultural pluralism seems more relevant. Our general conclusion that the basic structure of plantation society in the New World today remains much the same as that of the slave era finds support in numerous studies by sociologists, social anthropologists, and historians.[12] And of course those who live in these societies know it well.

11. As will be argued below, the caste line still exists in all New World plantation societies. The distinction between the caste system now operative in the West Indies and Brazil as compared with that in the United States is simply one that reflects differences in the definition of race.
12. In this connection, see the following: for the West Indies, R. T. Smith, *op. cit.*, and his *British Guiana* (London, 1962); Lloyd Braithwaite, "Social Stratification in Trinidad," *Social and Economic Stud-*

66 PERSISTENT POVERTY

In the plantation economies outside the New World, the influence of the plantation system on social organization and social structure in the national society was just as strong, even though there may not have been a legacy of slavery. Mauritius and Ceylon provide two good examples of this. Benedict, in his study of the plural structure of Mauritius, noted:

The pattern and nature of immigration to Mauritius produced a system of social stratification in which certain occupations tended to be the province of certain ethnic categories. The French were the estate owners. The British were the senior civil servants, the Creoles were the junior civil servants and artisans, the Chinese were the retailers and the Indians were the labourers. . . . in general the Mauritians did not amalgamate to form a homogeneous society. Each ethnic section preserved its own language, religion and social customs.[13]

The plantation influence on occupational and social status there seems clear. Benedict also indicated that the indenture system left a legacy of distrust and dislike between Franco-Mauritians and Indo-Mauritians and noted that attitudes and social structure prevailing in 1959 were similar to those noted by a Royal Commission of 1872. And in spite of the distrust of the two main plantation groups, there is this common bond of economic interdependence producing the same kind of dynamic social integration just noted for the New World plantation areas.

Slavery, as practiced in the New World and in Mauritius before Emancipation, had not been a part of the plantation history of Ceylon. Nevertheless, the character of the plantation there serves to color the over-all social organization and structure. The general

___

ies, October 1953; M. G. Smith, *The Plural Society in the British West Indies* (Berkeley and Los Angeles, 1965); and Elsa Goveia, *Slave Society in the British Leeward Islands at the end of the Eighteenth Century* (New Haven, Connecticut, 1965). For the Spanish Caribbean, see Charles Wagley and Marvin Harris, "A Typology of Latin American Sub-cultures," *American Anthropologist,* June 1955, and Julian Steward (ed.), *The People of Puerto Rico* (Urbana, Illinois, 1957). For Brazil, see H. W. Hutchinson, *op. cit.* And for the U.S. South, see W. E. Moore and R. M. Williams, *op. cit.,* and Morton Rubin, *Plantation County* (Chapel Hill, North Carolina, 1951).
13. Burton Benedict, *Mauritius: Problems of a Plural Society* (London, 1969), pp. 27 and 66.

social relations between the white European planter and the Indian Tamil work force on the plantation "can be summed up as a gruff paternalism, deepening often into respect and even affection on both sides; the planter, with perhaps 2,000 souls living a completely self-contained life on his estate, had to act towards them in the mixed capacity of commanding officer, labour manager, business adviser, peacemaker and Dutch uncle." [14] At present the general social structure in Ceylon consists primarily of four population groups which are defined basically in terms of the relationship of each to the land. In descending order, the social structure consists of (1) the white European commercial and planting community, (2) the native Sinhalese who are the officials, the lawyers, and the independent farmers, who rarely work on the plantations, (3) the Jaffna Tamils, old immigrants from south India, who are also independent farmers, and (4) the Tamils who make up the plantation labor force. The characteristic cultural pluralism, blended with social integration via a common European value system, is very much a part of the scene here as well. Everywhere else, the same basic pattern obtains.

3. Race, caste, and class

The predominant social characteristic of all plantation areas of the world is the existence of a class-caste system based on differences in the racial origins of plantation workers on the one hand and owners on the other. This is an inherent feature of the plantation system. In every instance, the system was introduced by white Europeans who had to rely on non-white labor for working the plantations. Race, therefore, was a convenient means of controlling the labor supply. Edgar Thompson, in his extensive studies of the United States South, argues that for the planter to establish continuing authority over the labor force, control must be founded on a "body of ideas and beliefs common to all. In the South such a principle of control was supplied by the idea of race the validity of which, once established, was denied by none, not even by mem-

14. T. M. Forrest, *A Hundred Years of Ceylon Tea* (London, 1967), p. 112.

bers of the subject race." [15] Thus we find that throughout the New World, race became the moral justification of slavery. At first, white people had justified slavery on the grounds that the black Africans were heathens. But when they had been converted to Christianity, that justification could no longer stand. And so the theory of the racial inferiority of black people was advanced.

Racial characteristics determined the caste line that separated masters from slaves in slave plantation society. And it is being argued here that, for all practical purposes, this caste line still exists in New World plantation society. It separates the superordinate white planter and commercial classes and other white people in these societies from the subordinate class of black people. All that has happened since Emancipation is that the caste line has shifted from a basically horizontal position which kept all black people more or less in the single class category of plantation laborers. Since Emancipation, increasing educational opportunities for black people and diversification of the structure of the plantation economies have made some modification in the class structure of these plantation societies. But in every instance race has been an important factor in the class divisions.

The proposition we have advanced concerning the persistence of a caste line in all the ex-slave plantation societies requires further discussion, particularly since there is some disagreement among scholars whether this is in fact so in all cases. The disagreement has arisen largely because of observed differences in the interaction of race and class in the United States on the one hand, and Brazil and the West Indies on the other. The real difference derives from the fact that the caste line is more rigidly defined in the United States than in the other two areas. In the United States, an individual is socially defined as black so long as there is an identifiable trace of Negro ancestry. In Brazil and the West Indies, the individual is defined as black only when his black ancestry is clearly evident from physical and social appearance. The differences between the two situations rests largely on whether one is concerned with race as a physical or genetic condition on the one

15. Edgar T. Thompson, "The Planter in the Pattern of Race Relations in the South," *Social Forces*, December 1940, p. 245.

hand, and as a social condition on the other. These two conceptual possibilities can be described as "physical race" and "social race." As concerns the first, there *is* a difference between the United States, and Brazil and the West Indies. But for the second, there is no difference at all. The situation in Brazil and the United States is described in what follows, as an attempt to illustrate the point.

For Brazil as a whole, Wagley informs us, the caste system of the slave plantation era has been supplanted by a system where social race is said to be one of a set of determinants which includes dress, manner of speech, education, income, occupation, family. Yet he observes that "it is still the general rule throughout Brazil that the people of the upper class are almost exclusively Caucasian in appearance, and the majority of the 'people of colour' are found in the middle and lower classes." [16] Wagley goes on to note that, in rural communities, competition for membership in the local upper class and for social ranking within it is intense, and that it is at this point in the social hierarchy that the criterion of race becomes most crucial in determining social position. Evidence is also provided to indicate that individuals have strong preferences for physical appearances that are closer to the European model and have derogatory attitudes to those that are like the African.[17] And, in a study of a sugar-plantation area of the Northeast, Hutchinson noted that race prejudice finds its strongest expression at the point of marriage into the upper class and concluded that whereas in the United States a distinct line is drawn between white and "Negro," in the Brazilian area studied this line is recognized rather than drawn. In his words, "A distinction between Negro and white is always kept in mind when classifying an individual. Everyone knows who is 'pure' white and who is not. Classification by color is one of the most important aspects of local culture. . . ." [18] The over-all picture for the Caribbean is identical to that described for Brazil.

16. Charles Wagley (ed.), *Race and Class in Rural Brazil* (UNESCO, New York, 1963), p. 145.
17. *Ibid.*, p. 149. On this last observation, see the interesting article by Errol Miller describing a similar situation in Jamaica, "Body Image, Physical Beauty and Colour among Jamaican Adolescents," *Social and Economic Studies,* March 1969.
18. H. W. Hutchinson, *op. cit.,* p. 117.

   As already hinted the situation is somewhat different in the United States, particularly in the plantation South. There, "social race" and "physical race" are identical, and the caste system is therefore more rigidly enforced. After Emancipation, the role of the planter simply changed from master to landlord. But the effect on black people was the same. Land then became important in social relationships and social organization in a different way than under slavery. And race was important in this connection. Monroe Work informs us that legal attitudes toward sharecropping and tenancy were strictly on the basis of race. For example,

It is dangerous for a Negro tenant to sue his landlord for non-settlement, and in some instances to even consider doing this.
   Negro farmers, owners and tenants, pay a higher average rate of interest than white farmers. . . . Negro tenants pay a higher rent than white tenants. . . . Negro tenants who paid cash rent averaged 10.3 per cent of the value of the land. Whites in the same districts paid cash rents that averaged only 6.9 per cent of the value of the land.[19]

He goes on to point out that, in addition, Negroes were discriminated against by crop settlements, lien laws and "more important than any of these the regulations compelling him to 'keep his place.' " These regulations include all kinds of laws concerning the social behavior and life of Negroes; these include regulations affecting their residence, education, and use of various public facilities and conveniences. The situation approximates the better known *apartheid* in South Africa.

   That the caste system is more rigidly enforced in the United States than in Brazil and the West Indies is the legacy of one important difference in the pattern of settlement of the plantation regions involved. In the United States South there were substantial numbers of white people who were not directly connected with the plantations. These were Europeans who had gone to the South to settle in independent subsistence ("yeoman") farming. In Northeast Brazil and the West Indies, on the other hand, such groups of poor white people were insubstantial. As a result, even before the

---

   19. Monroe Work, "Racial Factors and Economic Forces in Land Tenure in the South," *Social Forces,* December 1936, p. 214.

abolition of slavery, it was necessary for the planters in the U.S. South to emphasize the race-caste system. Because one sure way of keeping the poor whites on their side in the battle against those arguing for abolition was to indicate that the poor whites would suffer economically from job competition if the Negroes were freed. When Emancipation finally came, race continued to be emphasized in order to ensure that Negroes would continue to be available for plantation work. Both the planters and the poor whites realized that the caste system was essential for maintaining the status quo. And since the planters monopolized the legislature, it was easy for them to introduce appropriate regulations.[20] In the West Indies and Northeast Brazil, on the other hand, there was no potential competition between black people and an intermediate group of whites, so there was less need there for race to be given as much emphasis.

Another consideration in explaining the observed differences in the relative emphasis given to race is that, on account of the difference in settlement pattern, the sex ratio among white people in the U.S. South must have been more balanced than that in Northeast Brazil and the West Indies. So that miscegenation was more widespread in Brazil and the West Indies, resulting in relatively larger percentages of people of mixed ancestry. Since members of the white-planter class had parental links with the people of mixed blood, their attitude toward them was likely to be tempered somewhat and this may partly explain the lower tone given to "physical race" in those societies. Marvin Harris argues this point by indicating that in the Brazilian slave plantation society the white Portugese planters "were compelled to create an intermediate free group of half-castes to stand between them and the slaves because there were certain essential economic and military functions for which slave labor was useless and for which no whites were available." [21]

The conclusion we draw from this comparison between Brazil and the United States is that the caste line in the latter case is

20. Marvin Harris develops the thesis advanced here in his *Patterns of Race in the Americas* (New York, 1964).
21. *Ibid.,* pp. 86–87.

Figure 3.1. Diagrammatic representation of class, legal, and caste lines in slave plantation society

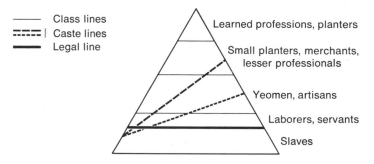

Source: Adapted from W. E. Moore and R. M. Williams, "Stratification in the Ante-Bellum South," *American Sociological Review*, June 1942, p. 349. The adaptation made here is the insertion of a more nearly vertical caste line than the one in the original diagram, to represent the situation in Brazil.

closer to being horizontal than that in the former case. Figure 3-1 summarizes the position for the two slave plantation societies. For the two societies today, the position of the caste lines in relation to each other remain unaltered. However, some modification of the over-all structure shown in the figure has occurred. First, the legal line is no longer relevant since slavery has been abolished. Second, the class designations have changed somewhat as the economies became more diversified; but only different labels are required in a few instances. And, third, *both* caste lines have made an equidistant swing toward the vertical, indicating that race is not so much of a barrier to higher occupational status as it was in slave society. The fact remains, however, that race is still an important factor in the determination of class in both cases. Harris summarizes the Brazilian-U.S. comparison in this way: "In both cases, the fundamental heritage of the slave plantation was the creation of severely handicapped minorities, darker in color than the rest of the population." [22]

An important aspect of the post-Emancipation evolution of class structure throughout the New World plantation areas is that

22. *Ibid.*, p. 64.

among the underprivileged black people, there developed within the caste group a class structure which placed those with most physical and cultural likeness to the superordinate white classes at the top and those with the least at the bottom of an internal class hierarchy. Consequently, within this group, race is supplemented by the degree of assimilation of white culture patterns in determining class positions.

Again, we find that in plantation societies elsewhere in the world race has been, and remains, an important factor in defining caste and class systems. Burton Benedict notes the correlation for Mauritius and informs us that class differences there grew up within each ethnic section of the population; these are "based on wealth and occupation, and followed by differences in behaviour. This does not necessarily diminish the pluralism of Mauritius. It can create an upper, middle and lower class for each ethnic section rather than single classes cutting across all sections." [23] In Ceylon, the caste line is between the white planter and commercial class and all other racial groups in the country, whereas the class structure is generally along racial lines with whites at the top, Sinhalese in the middle, and Tamils at the bottom. As elsewhere, however, racial class lines tend to be blurred slightly by other factors, such as occupation, income, education, family, and general life style. The over-all conclusion, it would seem, is that race has always been, and continues to be—along with color—an important determinant of class and caste in every plantation society in the world.

4. Political organization and distribution of power

As in other aspects of social life already considered, the nature of political organization in present-day plantation societies can be linked directly with the plantation. Political organization and state power are based upon principles of authority and control (law). So is the plantation. Again Thompson provides a good summary of the position when he states that "in no other way except through authority and law can a group whose members represent different

23. Burton Benedict, *op. cit.*, p. 2 *l*.

racial and cultural backgrounds be made to act as a unit. . . . In fact, the plantation is best defined not in terms of territory or of agriculture but in terms of the authority of the planter." [24] We have noted already that the individual plantation is an authoritarian institution in which power is centralized in the hands of the plantation owner or manager. This power involves decision making relating not only to production within the territory but also to all aspects of the life of those in the community. Consequently, in societies which consist largely of plantation communities, we should expect to find the same characteristics of political organization on the individual plantation reflected in the larger society. The thesis which this study advances in this connection is that all plantation societies have in common the following features: concentration of power among a small planter class and highly centralized political administrative structures (government).

This thesis can be substantiated by reference to the actual situation existing at present in the plantation societies of the world. But first it will be instructive to describe the evolution of patterns of political organization for one of the older plantation societies of the world. We draw here from the historical experience of the United States South. The earliest U.S. plantation colony was perhaps Jamestown. Under charter, the soil of Virginia had been given by the Crown to the Virginia Company and was held by the company at its disposal. The colony, "as maintained by Delaware and his deputies, had the following characteristics; absence of private property, agriculture as industrial basis, union of proprietorship with jurisdiction, government for economic ends chiefly, and discretionary administration." [25] The subsequent parceling out of land to colonists removed the "absence of private property" condition but the opening up of new company plantations is said to have given rise to colonial and local government structures designed to preserve political unity among the settlements in particular plantations areas.

L. D. Scisco, looking at the Virginia experience, points out:

24. Edgar T. Thompson, "The Plantation: The Physical Basis of Traditional Race Relations," *op. cit.*, pp. 192–93.
25. L. D. Scisco, "The Plantation Type of Colony," *American Historical Review*, January 1903, pp. 260–61.

The governments of the early plantation colonies had in them the elements of both general and local control, managing as they did the actual interests of single small settlements and yet holding the powers necessary for governing the whole region in which a settlement lay. At first these colonial governments were essentially local in nature. When settlements multiplied, the extensive powers of the several executives, which had been possessed from the beginning, were utilized to enforce political unity. The change brought no break in the sequence of colonial administration.[26]

This example illustrates a general phenomenon in the evolution of political administration of a plantation colony. Since each plantation unit is already a political entity in itself, it is natural that the political administration of a geographical region consisting of several plantations could best be effected by merging existing unit administrations—that is, all the planters in a region would administer the political affairs of the region. In like manner, political unity of these individual regions can best be effected by merging the existing centralized regional (local) administrations. In this way state power becomes concentrated in the hands of planters who already have authority and control over groups on their individual plantations and, at the local level, within plantation regions.

The Virginia pattern was more or less duplicated later throughout the plantation South of the United States. And this has largely influenced the present political organization and distribution of power, not only in the South but in the rest of the United States as well, for the demands of the South had to be met in order to secure the Union. The whole business of states' rights in the political organization of the United States emanated, in part, from the demands of the plantation South. What appears to be a well-developed system of local government for the federal territory as a whole reflects in part the system of strong central government in the plantation South, and this is directly linked to the plantation influence. Walter Wilbur summarizes this association, in reference to the slave period when the master of the plantation was ruler of his principality, in the following terms:

26. *Ibid.*, pp. 267–68.

There . . . developed throughout the South innumerable "indepen-
dencies," united by family and social ties but not by an interweaving
of functional economic relationships. Under such a system it was inevitable that the political bias of Southern leadership, vested almost exclusively in the "master" class, should be violently centrifugal. The
functions of state and local government were reduced to a minimum.
*The emphasis on state rights was in essence the fight to restrict the
unit of political authority to dimensions possible of local control. It
was not the sovereignty of the state, but the plantation . . . that was
at stake.* [27]

So long as political power was monopolized by individual plantation owners the scope of popular participation was limited. This is
an inevitable consequence of the fact that within plantation society, economic and social power is concentrated among a small
planter class and that, outside of the master's house, social organization within the plantation community tends to be poorly developed.

This legacy of the plantation persists everywhere we find plantation societies, and strong central government is characteristic of
all of these places. Given the distribution of economic and social
power, local government can emerge only if there is adequate social organization at the local level, but it appears that plantations
created loose and weak local communities everywhere they existed. The primary reason for this is that strong community organization tends to emerge only in situations where smaller units of
people are bound firmly together. The family is such a unit. But
the plantation system is generally not based on family units; indeed, if anything, the tendency is more toward family-less people.
The only unifying element within plantation community is the authority of the planter. Studies have revealed that Caribbean societies generally follow the pattern just described. The link with the
plantation system is summarized by Wagley as follows:

The lack of a strong and well-defined local community in the Caribbean region is the result of slavery and a plantation economy. The dec-

27. Walter Wilbur, "Special Problems of the South," *Annals of the
    American Academy of Political and Social Science,* November 1934,
    p. 50. Emphasis added.

imation of the Indians in the region precluded any possible aboriginal basis for local community life. The transferred population of African slaves from many tribes and nations were unable under conditions of slavery to form communities, although it is notable that escaped slaves in Jamaica and on the mainland found a basis for community organization. . . . While paternalism and common residence often united the slaves of a particular plantation into a neighborhood, they were unable to develop a full community life. Even after abolition the plantation system continued to exert an influence unfavorable to the development of a strong and cohesive local community. . . . Brazil, and to a certain extent the southern United States, share this historical heritage of the plantation and slavery and the resulting weak, divided, and amorphous community. *One is tempted to generalize that wherever the plantation and slave system were present, the rural community could not become an efficient and cohesive social unit.*[28]

We advance the hypothesis that the tentative conclusion reached by Wagley in the above applies not only to plantation societies with a legacy of slavery but to all plantation societies, for the reasons indicated above.

In spite of considerable diversification in the New World plantation economies since Emancipation, in spite of major constitutional changes in the political status of individual countries, and in spite of dramatic changes in procedures of selecting governments (involving the enfranchisement of black people who earlier had no vote), highly centralized government administration is in evidence everywhere. Part of the reason for this is that economic and social power has remained in the hands of the white-planter and commercial classes which more recently have been reinforced by industrialists of the same ethnic origin. Therefore, in those areas where full enfranchisement of black people has been delayed, legislatures still are predominantly comprised of people of the new planter class. Such is the case in the U.S. South and Brazil. For example, Taylor, in a study of a Brazilian sugar plantation region, notes: "In 1965, every one of Pernambuco's twenty-nine usineiro

28. Charles Wagley, "Recent Studies of Caribbean Local Societies," in Curtis Wilgus (ed.), *The Caribbean: Natural Resources* (Gainesville, Florida, 1961), p. 199.

families had a close relative or family member in *both* the federal congress and the Pernambuco assembly." [29]

Where full enfranchisement of black people came earlier and where these people make up the bulk of the population, there is a different pattern of racial composition of legislatures; but the basic structure of political organization remains the same. Since the 1940's black people in the West Indies have had the right to vote in government elections. At first, the white-planter class directly faced the electorate but it met with resounding defeat as the tide of the black vote overwhelmed it. The strategy then adopted was withdrawal from direct political involvement to an indirect role of providing financial backing for black political aspirants in what emerged as black political parties and trade unions. So today throughout the West Indies we find government administrations comprised of black people who essentially exercise authority and control on behalf of their financial backers—the white-planter, commercial, and industrial classes that remain for the most part in the background of political activity.[30] Given the terms of social mobility for black people in the system, as earlier described, the alliance between the dominant power group and the deculturated blacks has been easy and natural. For the deculturated blacks have as much contempt for the "unrefined" masses of black people as the dominant group.

The two patterns of racial composition of government administration described for the West Indies on the one hand, and Brazil and the United States on the other, are representative of the situation in all the plantation societies of the world at present. Wherever there is full enfranchisement, the subordinate racial group has its representatives in government legislatures but these representatives do not rely financially on the group they represent and have to depend on support from the superordinate economic and social group. This constrains their freedom to represent the inter-

29. Kit Sims Taylor, "The Dynamics of Underdevelopment in the Sugar Plantation Economy of Northeast Brazil" (unpublished thesis, University of Florida, 1969), p. 147.
30. This phenomenon and its development are described by Trevor Munroe in *The Politics of Constitutional Decolonization: Jamaica 1944–1962* (Mona, Jamaica, 1971).

ests of the subordinate group fully. Where complete enfranchisement has not been yet achieved, the superordinate groups still directly control the legislative process. The result in either case is
the same—real political and legislative power still resides with the
superordinate group among whom economic and social power is
concentrated. As in all societies, the distribution of real political
power is identical to the pattern of distribution of economic and
social power.

5. Plantation society: a synthesis

The structural features of plantation society, outlined in the foregoing sections, indicate sufficient uniqueness that it seems necessary to treat plantation society as a particular type of society.
Plantation society has properties which distinguish it clearly from,
say, peasant society, feudal society, urban society, and other such
types which social scientists have isolated for particular study. Its
own special type of social and political organization sets it apart
from other kinds of societies in the world today.

Plantation society is a plural society. It consists of different racial and cultural groups which are brought together only in the
realm of economic activity. This single common bond provides the
integrative element. The particular nature of this common economic activity determines the force and character of what social
integration exists. On the plantation itself the common economic
activity is production of the plantation crop. The plantation owner
or manager is the immediate embodiment of the superordinate
group in the wider society and the plantation workers of the subordinate group. The economic welfare of each depends on the
other. The two groups are therefore in a mutually dependent economic relationship. And since decision making resides with the
owner or manager, it is the plantation "great house" that symbol-
izes the integrating force. In addition, because the social structure
pyramids to the planter class, the social aspirations of lower status groups in the society are directed toward the social achievement of that class. One element of social integration in the society
as a whole is, therefore, to be found in the area of achievement
motivation.

Another element of social integration is nationalism. Plantation economy is dependent on metropolitan economy. The crop that binds different groups together in plantation society is destined for sale in metropolitan markets. Consequently, the fortunes of all groups in plantation society are bound up with relationships between plantation economy and metropolitan economy. Common attitudes concerning relationships with the rest of the world, and in particular with the relevant metropolis, are to be found among all groups that make up plantation society. Although the planter class monopolizes power internally, it needs to marshal the support of other groups to face any outside threat to its economic interest. And since its interests in this connection coincide with that of other groups, the society usually stands together in these matters.[31]

The elements of social integration in plantation society, then, are to be found in three main areas: economic production, achievement motivation, and nationalism. The question that now arises is whether the degree of social integration provided by these forces is strong enough to withstand the disintegrative elements that derive from social and cultural plurality. The answer to this must be equivocal: that it depends on the nature of the pressures on or within the society as a whole at any particular point in time. Whenever pressures emanating from outside are light, internal conflict is more likely to occur. But heavy external pressure may or may not stimulate the integrative mechanism; it all depends on the nature of these pressures. For example, a prolonged period of low prices for the plantation crop is likely to heighten workers' mistrust of the plantation owners; in addition, it makes their already low levels of living worse.[32] Internal social tension is likely to increase in such circumstances. All that we can say with cer-

31. An illustration of this is to be found in the present-day composition of national delegations to international commodity conferences. In most instances, the delegations from plantation economies are made up partly of people representing plantation owners and partly of those representing plantation workers.
32. The question of mistrust is important. Since plantation owners have such great power and control over plantation society, workers are not going to be easily convinced that these seemingly omnipotent people have no control over the prices they receive for the plantation output.

tainty is that plantation society will necessarily exhibit a condition
of underlying social tension at all times and that internal crisis
will be a recurrent feature in the development of this kind of society. These crises are also likely to involve racial divisions. This
follows from the particular grouping of production into castes as
well as from the consideration that as the society as a whole is
threatened with disintegration each component finds greater security within its own racial contingent.

Furnivall arrives at similar general conclusions in his study of
Indonesia, which he describes as a plural economy and society. He
notes that plural economy differs from homogeneous economy because (1) whereas social demand in homogeneous economy is
common to the whole society, there are two or more distinct and
rival complexes of social demand in plural economy; (2) production in plural economy is grouped into castes; and (3) in plural
economy, further sectionalization of demand follows when each of
the constituent social demands ceases to embrace the whole scope
of social life and becomes concentrated on those aspects relating
only to the separate province. The difficulty of achieving social integration is posed in the following way: "This distribution of production among racial castes aggravates the inherent sectionalism
of demand; for a community which is confined to certain economic functions finds it more difficult to apprehend the social
needs of the country as a whole." [33] Furnivall goes on to note that
the basic consideration is: "In a plural society . . . the community
tends to be organized for production rather than for social life."
As contrasted to the situation in a homogeneous community, this
results in abnormal conditions which create a kind of nationalism
in each section that "sets one community against the other so as to
emphasize the plural character of the society and aggravate its instability, thereby enhancing the need for it to be held together by
some force exerted from outside." [34]

The argument is heightened by the observation that nationalism
in plural society is itself a disruptive force which tends to disintegrate, rather than consolidate, the social order. It is instructive to

33. J. S. Furnivall, *Netherlands India—A Study of Plural Economy*
(Cambridge, 1944), pp. 451–52.
34. *Ibid.*, p. 459.

quote Furnivall at some length on this score because he highlights a fundamental problem confronting all plantation societies today.

Democratic principles imply that the preponderance of voting power shall be entrusted to the people; yet economic power remains with the other classes, and chiefly with the Europeans. . . . we have the economic rivalry of town and country, capital and labour, industry and agriculture, aggravated by racial difference; and with economic power on the one side and voting power on the other side, the future of the country under the accepted principle of Nationalism can hardly be envisaged with composure. The principle of Nationalism provides no solution in itself, for, in a plural society, nationalism is in effect internationalism.[35]

This generalization seems applicable to all plantation societies of the world today. This is not surprising because Furnivall arrived at these conclusions from a study of Indonesia which is one of our class of plantation society. In every such society, we find the recurrent feature of serious internal conflict existing alongside rampant nationalism. The conflict situations between Indians and Negroes in Guyana (and to a lesser extent Trinidad); Tamils and Sinhalese in Ceylon; Indians and Fijians, and Indians and the Colonial Sugar Refining Company in Fiji; Chinese, Malays, Indians, and Europeans in Malaya; Indians and Europeans in Mauritius; and between white people and black people throughout the New World are examples of the universality of this phenomenon among plantation societies.

Exceptions to this general phenomenon are to be found perhaps in those plantation societies where state ownership of the producing units is dominant—Cuba, for example. In such instances, the distribution of economic, social, and political power has been altered from the traditional pattern described in the present chapter. Because the state monopolizes power, sectional social demands are more likely to be integrated and internal conflict less likely to occur. Even so conflict can hardly be avoided. Much depends on the manner in which state power is manipulated. For example, if state power is used to redress the traditional distribution of power this will alienate the traditionally dominant group and thereby

35. *Ibid.,* p. 468.

generate internal conflict. This has been the case in Cuba and the former dominant group there has been forced into exile but continues to fan the flames of internal conflict in various ways. It seems then that every type of plantation society fits the general pattern of internal social conflict in spite of the presence of nationalism.

We must conclude, therefore, that the strongest elements of social integration in plantation society are to be found in the areas of economic production and achievement motivation. Individuals in every group are bound by their dependence on each other for economic survival. Their source of bread is the same. And they all want the same things in life. So they make common demands for social services, such as education and health, and common aspirations for material things associated with a Great House life style, such as housing and consumer durables. This level of social integration becomes tenuous during periods of crisis, but otherwise it provides a sufficient base for holding the society together.

The basic problem goes much deeper than this. The nature of social and political arrangements create several biases toward a continuous state of underdevelopment. Inherent social instability impedes investment; the rigid pattern of social stratification restricts mobility; the concentration of social, economic, and political power prevents the emergence of a highly motivated population; and racial discrimination inhibits the fullest use of the society's human resources. These and other aspects of the social economy of underdevelopment are considered in more detail in Chapter 7.

4

Changing scenes in plantation development

The rise of the modern plantation system can be divided into three phases. The first was the development of the New World plantations from the period of the great discoveries to the middle of the nineteenth century; the second was the establishment and growth of plantations in tropical Asia and the islands of the Indian Ocean and the Pacific from about the middle of the nineteenth century through the first two decades of the twentieth century, which was also the period of their establishment in parts of Africa. These two phases were linked directly with political colonization: imperial governments provided the foundations for European proprietary planters and companies to establish themselves in plantation production. The third and most recent phase was marked by the political and economic colonization of certain areas by the United States, and it was characterized by imperial political legislation and military might providing a cover for the flow of private capital to previous colonies of Spain and to constitutionally independent republics in Central America and Liberia.

Broadly speaking, the emergence of new areas of plantation activity have arisen in response to changes of one kind or another which have affected the competitive position of older established areas. Shortage of land at first led to the eclipse of the smaller Caribbean islands by the larger ones. Subsequently, shortage of labor in the New World as a whole after the abolition of slavery led to the introduction of the system to Asia, and this was boosted by improvements in ocean transport and shorter trade routes. And finally, as the growth of population in Asia limited further plantation expansion, the relatively empty lands of tropical Africa became inviting to the traditional plantation interests of Europe. Economic growth in the United States had by then generated sufficient surplus that overseas investment opportunities were eagerly being sought.

Certain changes in the nature of plantation operations have been associated with these phases of historical development. In the first phase, the individual proprietary planter was important throughout the seventeenth and eighteenth centuries. But certain major adjustments in the international economy during the nineteenth century resulted in the demise of individual planters and a corresponding rise in the importance of corporate capital. In the more recent phases direct investment by metropolitan corporate enterprise has been the major force in plantation expansion. These developments reflect changes in the world economic and political environment. Whereas up to the nineteenth century the pattern had been for temporary migration of planters to the Tropics, by the twentieth century economic maturity had arrived in the metropolitan countries and business corporations there were ready for direct overseas investment.

1. Overview of patterns of change

We can discern certain shifts in the concentration of capital in the production process throughout plantation history. For the first plantations the bulk of investments were tied up in the ownership of slaves. This was followed, after abolition of slavery, by a concentration of capital in machinery and equipment. Subsequently, in many places population pressure led to a rise in the price of land and land became an important aspect of investment. And finally there is the present stage in which elaborate processing of raw materials on the plantations and backward integration of production has increased the relative importance of processing and transportation capital (factories, steamships, railways, and the like). In addition, a continuous shortage of labor for plantation work has led more recently to an increase in the importance of machine capital for field operations. The trend has been toward relatively more capital intensive techniques of production resulting from the nature of technological change and the difficulty of securing labor supplies. Consequently, the individual proprietary planter has found it increasingly difficult to provide the necessary financing and has been largely replaced by modern corporate entities. The position of the planter became more precarious as a result of intensified competition in the production of plantation crops which caused wide fluctuations in output prices. And these price fluctuations encouraged backward integration by processing corporations. World trade has become increasingly complex and it demands a level of organizational skill normally beyond the capacities of the individual proprietary planter. Consequently, corporations dominate plantation activity throughout much of the Third World.

Labor and the problem of land have been inherently connected to the whole history of plantations. Compulsion and coercion were always necessary for plantations to secure labor supplies. First there was slavery, then indenture; in more recent times coercion has been exercised through plantation monopoly of land. This has been the pattern everywhere. It would appear that wherever people are able to provide their own subsistence they are not prepared to offer their labor services for subsistence wages. And so at present we find four general phenomena in all plantation economies: (1) concentration of capital in the form of land; (2) high unemployment (rural and urban) alongside expressed shortage of labor for plantation work; (3) increased mechanization of plantation field operations wherever this is technically feasible; and (4) high rates of emigration from plantation areas within a particular country and from the plantation economies to metropolitan countries.

The last of the above is particularly pronounced in the Caribbean where high rates of emigration from Puerto Rico to the United States and from Jamaica and other Commonwealth Caribbean countries to the United Kingdom have been characteristic of the post-World War II period. Whereas in the past the planters came from the metropolis to the plantation colonies, there is at present a reverse flow of plantation workers going to the metropolis. Rural people make up a high percentage of these emigrant groups. Within particular countries, the "push" effect resulting from plantation monopoly of the land has been greatest in Northeast Brazil and the U.S. South. In both places, this push effect and a "pull" effect, resulting from expanding employment opportunities in other regions of each country, have been responsible for large-scale out-migration of black people from the plantation regions.

Although the phase of heavy reliance on indenture and other forms of contract labor has passed, plantations in many places still depend on migratory contract labor. In the United States South contract labor is drawn from the Caribbean plantation economies which cannot secure enough of the same labor for plantation work at home. In some African countries, contract labor is usually brought in to the plantation areas from other parts of the same country. The same holds for Indonesia where Sumatra plantations bring in workers from Java. Elsewhere plantations rely to a large extent on labor services of peasant producers who use plantation work to supplement their own account production. If the early planters regarded their plantation ventures as temporary affairs to amass fortunes for their retirement at home in Europe, so did the plantation workers throughout history, whenever they could act according to their own free will. Whether it was indentured labor, other forms of contract labor, or peasant part-time labor, the worker always seems to have regarded plantation work as a temporary means of amassing certain sums of money to be used to secure his own independence.

The land situation has become increasingly tight in both Asia and the plantation sphere of the New World. Africa seems to be the only remaining area of relatively open resources and the question that naturally arises is whether the future will bring further plantation development there to create eventually a situation of closed resources, as has been the case in the other two areas. The answer to this will depend on two main considerations: the extent to which plantation enterprises still want to expand their operations, and the kind of receptivity that the new national governments in Africa provide for these enterprises in that event. By and large we would expect that metropolitan firms would want to avoid substantial new investment in countries over which they do not have political control. And that the colonial experience of the newly independent countries would be a sufficient deterrent to the encouragement of new penetrations of foreign capital. However

we find that the large plantation companies are able to exercise
political control over constitutionally independent governments in a
number of ways.[1] And the psychological legacy of colonialism has
created such a state of dependence in the minds of new national
leaders that we are unlikely to find many that will introduce policies deliberately to discourage foreign investment, although there
is increasing awareness of the need to safeguard the national interest.

In this last connection, we are likely to find a modification of
the existing pattern of outright metropolitan corporate ownership.
Many governments in the Third World are insisting on plantation
schemes based on joint ownership by metropolitan corporations
and either government or private share capital raised in the host
country. The metropolitan concerns themselves seem to welcome
this arrangement since it provides a kind of built-in insurance
against political risks. And several schemes of this kind have already been implemented in some of the African countries, Nigeria
for example. So far as concerns capital and management, then, the
history of plantations seems to be entering a new phase. And it
will be interesting to watch this development and to analyze the
significance of this arrangement at a later stage if it does become
an established pattern.

In the rest of this chapter, we provide a summary historical account of the patterns of adjustment and change that were associated with plantation development in different parts of the world.
This account provides empirical support for the generalizations we
have advanced; but, more importantly, it provides insights into the
dynamics of plantation development.

2. People, labor, and the land:
post-emancipation adjustments in the
slave plantation economies

The New World plantation system initially had been established
by grants of land by the imperial crowns to Europeans—either di-

---

1. The frequency with which revolutionary governments in the Third
   World have been deposed is part of the result of these operations.

rectly to individuals or indirectly to them through charter companies. The Portuguese Crown bestowed "captaincies" in Brazil to members of the nobility. In Virginia and the British West Indian colonies, settlement of Europeans was facilitated by chartered companies which were granted monopolies by the British Crown over wide geographical areas. And in the Spanish colonies of the Caribbean the *encomienda* system, which gave rights over certain large areas to Spanish individuals, was a precursor to the later development of the plantation system. The land was available for use by these early settlers only to the entent that they could overpower the indigenous Indian populations, and the establishment of plantations necessitated either putting these people to work for them or bringing in labor supplies from elsewhere. The European invaders did not have very great difficulty in overpowering the indigenous populations in the lowland island territories. The Indians in these areas did not have established settled communities and the relative sparseness of their population permitted a semi-nomadic type of shifting cultivation. The invaders first used forced Indian labor, but because these peoples were not accustomed to a regimented work existence and were unable to withstand the new diseases brought by the Europeans, they were soon decimated. By the end of the seventeenth century, practically the entire Indian population in the Caribbean region had been wiped out.

Subsequently, attempts to utilize indentured European labor proved largely unsuccessful for a number of reasons. The potential laborers had the alternative of settling themselves elsewhere in the Americas; and the indenture service of those who came under the system was a temporary and costly affair—after their period of service they had to be settled on land of their own. African slaves turned out to be the most suitable source of labor for plantation development. The Portuguese had already been using African slaves in plantation cultivation in São Thomé and soon brought the system to Brazil. Other European nations were quick to follow and a massive trade in African slave labor developed. It is claimed that the African slaves were better adapted to the plantation system than the indigenous Indian populations because of their previous cultural experience with the demands of field labor. Moreover, their earlier contact with Europeans had made them less susceptible to European diseases.[2] The system of forced African labor proved highly successful as the total labor supply was directed to production of the plantation staple—the slaves being allowed to practice subsistence cultivation on unwanted backlands only during periods when their labor power was not required for the plantation crop.

Emancipation of the slaves during the nineteenth century changed the scene drastically. It came first in the British territories in 1838. Immediately the slaves sought an independent existence and made it difficult for the plantation owners to secure their labor services for wages. But the extent to which the ex-slaves could divorce the plantation depended on the availability of land. In the smaller territories where land was in very short supply, as in Barbados, Antigua, and St. Kitts, the choice for the ex-slave was limited to continued work on the plantations and work in petty trades, services and fishing. The means for an independent existence were quite limited so that continued plantation work was generally the most realistic option. Consequently, in these islands the plantation managed to survive without much adjustment. In the larger territories where more land was available the ex-slaves were able to establish themselves in independent cultivation and the plantations had to introduce measures to secure their continued labor services on a wage basis. These measures included all kinds of legislation which made it difficult for black people to secure land and taxes which would force them to work for wages to secure cash for payment of the taxes.

In several islands a sharecropper system of production was introduced by the plantations. The sharecropper system was an expedient necessitated by the financial crisis which followed the withdrawal of protection on West Indian sugar in the British market in 1846. Woodville Marshall describes the system as it applied to the British Windward Islands as follows.

The planter was usually responsible for superintendance of the cultivation of canes and the manufacture of the sugar and for the provision of stock, carts, and machinery for the manufacture of sugar.

2. Marvin Harris, *Patterns of Race in the Americas* (New York, 1964), pp. 11–14.

Occasionally he also supplied pen manure and the plant canes. In return for these services he received half of the sugar (or a larger share when he supplied a field of ratoons) and in most cases, all the molasses and rum.[3]

He further notes that the general type of contract was oral and gave no firm guarantee to the sharecropper (metayer) of his rights of possession, security of tenure, and a clear claim to a share of the crop. Consequently there were numerous abuses of the sharecroppers who were in no position to object because of the absence of written contracts and the formidable expense of challenging planters in a court of law. In the West Indies the system of sharecropping was a short-term expedient which planters abandoned in periods of rising sugar prices. The pattern described for the British territories applied as well to the French West Indies after Emancipation in 1848.

In spite of the measures taken by the plantation owners, it still proved difficult to secure the labor services of ex-slaves (at least for the wages plantations were willing to pay). Consequently, the planters used their political power to secure a stream of indentured labor from India.[4] And this was the main source of labor until the Indian government terminated the scheme in 1917, after which the plantations had to resort to wage labor and intensified efforts for the mechanization of field operations. There was and still is some contract labor based on internal migration, but to a

3. W. K. Marshall, "Metayage in the Sugar Industry of the British Windward Islands, 1838–1865," *The Jamaican Historical Review,* May 1965, p. 36. It is interesting to point out here that the plantation monopoly on revenues from molasses and rum remains to this day. Cane farmers in the West Indies at the present time do not share in the benefits of molasses and rum production from the sale of their cane to the company estates and, as Chapter 5 indicates, the revenue derived from these products by the plantation companies is often greater than that derived from the sugar alone.

4. Again the need for indentured Indian labor was greatest in those islands where relatively abundant land made it more difficult to secure labor services of the ex-slaves. Thus Barbados, St. Kitts, and Antigua were not seriously involved, and the concentration of Indians in the present-day populations of Trinidad and Guyana (and to a lesser extent Jamaica) reflect the fact of an open-resource situation in these countries at the time.

large extent plantations must now rely on casual wage labor. The use of indentured Indian labor was also the basis for the development of plantations in Fiji and in the British colony of Mauritius after the slaves there had been freed at the same time as those in the British West Indies. Large numbers of the indentured Indians remained in the plantation colonies after their period of contract service. Today they make up a substantial percentage of the populations in certain places (see Chapter 3).

Elsewhere in the New World plantation areas, emancipation of the slaves came later in the nineteenth century and the pattern of adjustment was somewhat different, although everywhere the theme was the same: the plantation owners made it difficult for the ex-slaves to secure land of their own and introduced measures to force them to continue working on the plantations. In the United States South, access to what land was available was difficult and security of loans for purchase required the collateral of a white planter. According to James Allen, "All accounts testify to the fact that the Negroes demanded land, expected to receive it and, in a number of instances, armed clashes ensued when they attempted to seize land." [5] But the plantation owners completely controlled the first new state legislatures in 1865 and introduced the "Black Codes" which "were intended to assure a steadfast, thinly-veiled slave supply for the plantations." The "Black Codes" consisted of (1) the apprenticeship law which gave county authorities power to apprentice to employers all children under eighteen who had no visible means of support, and (2) the vagrancy law which affected all black people over eighteen who had no visible means of employment. These people, insofar as they did not meet the subjective visibility standards of the sheriff, would be seized and hired out. This was also the fate of those who could not pay the $1.00 poll tax imposed on all black people between the ages of eighteen and sixty.

This system of forced labor in the U.S. South gave the ex-slaves only a slim chance of escaping the dreaded fate of continued work on the plantations. In addition, the plantation owners seized the opportunity of avoiding to pay cash wages to this forced labor;

5. James S. Allen, *The Negro Question in the United States* (New York, 1936), p. 47.

they introduced the sharecropping system which has been a feature of the post-Emancipation plantation in that region ever since. In addition to sharecropping the planters introduced the system of "furnish" whereby they advanced food and clothing to workers, the cost of which was subsequently deducted from the croppers' share of plantation production. (These contemporary arrangements are described in detail in Appendix II. Here we simply note that the system militated against the escape of black people from the clutches of the plantation.) Crop-share arrangements were verbal and led to abuse; furthermore, advances to the croppers were recorded only by the planter whose final settlement account was not to be questioned by the croppers, most of whom could not read or write anyway. And so it is hardly surprising that the use of wage labor was not substantial until the last two decades or so. It is reported that in the Yazoo-Mississippi Delta, the heart of the plantation South, "before the advent of the Agricultural Adjustment Agency program, 78 per cent of the cropland was planted to cotton, 89 per cent of the farm land was operated under the plantation system, and 95 per cent of the farms were operated by croppers and tenants." [6]

Indeed, it seems hardly likely that wage labor and the associated trend toward mechanization would have emerged at all in the U.S. South without outside intervention by the federal government and the mushrooming possibilities for migration of black people to other parts of the United States in recent decades, especially during and after World War II. For there was little that black people could achieve within the "adjusted" plantation system and the plantation owners had no inducement to change things because, as Hesseltine puts it, "In truth, the old plantation system was re-established with the store account taking the place of the overseer's whip, the sheriff performing the duties of the ante-bellum 'patter-roller,' and the exploitation of men still furnishing the source of profits." [7] The choices which black people

6. Frank J. Welch, *The Plantation Land Tenure System in Mississippi* (Mississippi State College, Agricultural Experiment Station Bulletin No. 385, June 1943), p. 15.
7. W. B. Hesseltine, *A History of the South, 1607–1936* (New York, 1936), p. 651.

faced in the circumstances were: migration, continued work on the plantation in the condition of semi-slavery, and starvation. For the most part they opted for the first two but migration was costly and plantation work had kept them very close to starvation.

In Brazil and the Spanish Caribbean, there was yet another variation on the theme of adjustment to the abolition of slavery. The pattern of slave production had been somewhat different and this affected the adjustment process. In Brazil, mill owners had produced very little of the cane they milled during the slave plantation era. Independent planters (*lavradores*) grew the cane for the mills on a share basis. On a sharecropper basis *agregados* (or *moradores*) grew subsistence crops on exhausted or unused mill lands; they were not obliged to plant cane. The system of sharecropping, then, had been established at the time of slavery. After the abolition of slavery in 1889 this system managed to perpetuate itself because all the land in the region had already been claimed under the initial grants of "captaincies" (*sesmarias*). The former slaves were therefore forced by circumstance to remain within the orbit of the plantation by becoming moradores who were allowed to grow foodstuffs on plantation land, in return for which they were obliged to work two or three days a week for the plantation owner. "This system was known as *condicão* or *cambão* (literally, an ox-yoke). Whereas the *senhor do engenho* had previously been able to extract the surplus product from the laborer by virtue of his ownership of the laborer, he now did essentially the same thing by virtue of his ownership of the land." [8] This system of plantation labor still exists in the sugar cane region of the Northeast. In areas where sugar production has increased in recent times, however, wage labor has superseded the morador system of cambão because, as Taylor has suggested, the plantations needed more of the labor time of the morador. Before wage labor was introduced, the morador worked for the plantation owner only two or three

8. Kit Sims Taylor, "The Dynamics of Underdevelopment in a Plantation Economy: The Sugar Sector of Northeastern Brazil" (unpublished thesis, University of Florida, 1969), pp. 117–18. According to Taylor's estimates (in 1966) forty-six sugar factories and their associates, or about 150 individuals, own about 51 per cent of the land in the sugar zone of Pernambuco.

days a week, but without land he is now forced to work all week to earn his subsistence.[9]

The pattern of adjustment in the Northeast also set the stage for the type of labor regime that developed in the other plantation areas of Brazil. Coffee plantations had been established with slave labor early in the nineteenth century. After about 1850 most of the slaves in the coffee region were bought from the Northeast sugar region. After the abolition of slavery, the supply of labor from the Northeast was inadequate to meet the needs of coffee and cocoa expansion, and the nearer cocoa region managed to attract most of the internal migrants with the wage system that developed there. The southern coffee regions farther from the Northeast therefore had to rely on immigrant labor from Europe, mainly Italians, who found the relatively temperate plateau climate tolerable. After a brief period of experimentation with contracts for this immigrant labor, the *colono* system emerged as the most suitable. The plantation owners provided the immigrant (or colono) with a piece of land which he was obliged to clear and establish with coffee plants for the owner while growing his own subsistence crops in between. When the coffee plants reached maturity the land with the mature plants would be handed back to the owner for an agreed sum of money. The colono was then moved on to a new piece of virgin land to repeat the work. In this way, plantation owners in the coffee region managed to secure labor for establishing and cultivating coffee during the four-year waiting period for the first yield and they had a labor force on call for the annual harvesting of trees.[10]

The adjustment process in the Brazilian plantation system after the abolition of slavery can be summarized in the words of a re-

9. *Ibid.*, pp. 166–68. Taylor develops this thesis as an alternative to that proposed by Furtado that the plantation owners needed the land previously used by moradores for the postwar expansion of production. Taylor supports his thesis by reference to the fact that the morador system persisted into the 1960's only in those areas where production has not increased.

10. See P. P. Courtenay, *Plantation Agriculture* (London, 1965), pp. 36–37, and Manuel Diégues, Jr., "Land Tenure and Use in the Brazilian Plantation System," Pan American Union, *Plantation Systems of the New World* (Social Science Monographs, VII, Washington, D.C., 1959).

cent Committee for International Development (CIDA) report as follows:

. . . Large landowners have succeeded in maintaining to this day a cheap and dependable supply of labor which has several characteristics of slave labor. Many different types of farm workers have been, and still are, tied to the land through poverty, by lack of alternative opportunities or through contractual and informal arrangements with the land owners or their administrators. . . . the evolution of the *latifundio* system through to the present day can be viewed to a large extent as a continuous and clever effort of large-scale landlords to "attach" workers to their farms, but only in a manner whereby, probably in defiance of the law, no permanent or semi-permanent workers' rights or claims could originate or be enforced against them.[11]

In Spanish Cuba, Puerto Rico, and the Dominican Republic, the system that emerged in sugar plantation production was similar to the lavrador arrangement of the Brazilian Northeast but was described there as the colono system. Sugar mill owners processed the cane grown by the colonos for a share of the sugar, leaving the mill owners with the other share plus the proceeds from rum and molasses. The system still persists, apart from Cuba where the state has taken the place of foreign owners of mills.

It is clear from the foregoing that throughout the first-established New World plantation areas the basic pattern of adjustment to the abolition of slavery was the same: plantation monopoly of the land to prevent the ex-slaves from being independent of plantation work; legislation by planter-controlled governments to force the ex-slaves to continue working on the plantations; other measures to keep the ex-slaves "attached" to the plantations; and immigration of new laborers where all else failed. The question of land was intimately bound to the problem of securing plantation labor supplies and the degree of its availability materially influenced the fate of the former slaves. Where land was available, peasant production was established; and where it was not, laborers were largely forced to continue with plantation work until during

11. Inter-American Committee for Agricultural Development (CIDA), *Land Tenure Conditions and Socio-economic Development of the Agricultural Sector—Brazil* (Pan American Union, Washington, D.C., 1966), pp. 17–18.

the post-World War II period, when emigration from the clutches of the plantation became more feasible everywhere. Thus throughout the New World, high rates of emigration have been characteristic only of the plantation areas—internally for the sub-economies of Brazil and the United States and both internally and externally for all the plantation economies of the Caribbean. And with that the trend toward increased mechanization of plantation operations has been intensified.

3. People, labor, and the land:
patterns of change in the
new plantation regions

Although plantation development outside of the New World really blossomed after the abolition of slavery, the patterns of labor supply in those areas have much in common with that described above. Indenture of immigrant labor and coercion of one kind or another (and, to a lesser extent, land monopoly) were generally in evidence. This was the case even though the initial conditions in the new areas differed fundamentally from the open-resource situation of the New World tropical lowland region at the time of the so-called great discoveries. In much of Asia, the indigenous populations were well settled in systems of permanent agriculture and the density of population in some places, Java for example, approximated a situation of closed resources. It is important to note here that the plantation failed to make strong inroads into those countries of Southeast Asia which had the most highly organized societies prior to European penetration. Even in the lesser developed societies the plantation had to make an accommodation to established traditions and customs and could only gain a foothold by combining superior military might with negotiation with local chiefs and head men.

Java, in Dutch Indonesia, provides an interesting illustration of how the plantation system managed by accommodation to gain control. The Dutch East India Company, a Crown charter organization, had been the first instrument of colonization when the imperial interest was purely in trade. The company managed to secure export supplies such as spices through the village head men (*lurah*). Most of the land in the island was communally owned by members of various villages, so that when the imperial interest shifted from trade to production for export to the metropole a system of compulsory production of export crops by the Javanese people was necessary. Thus the introduction of the culture system (*cultuurstelsel*) in 1830, which involved "the remission of the peasant's land taxes in favor of his undertaking to cultivate government-owned export crops on one-fifth of his fields or, alternatively, to work sixty-six days of his year on government-owned estates. . . ." [12] In effect this transformed Java into a "mammoth state plantation." Technological changes in sugar production during the last half of the nineteenth century put strains on the culture system, which, according to Geertz, had been based on the substitution of Javanese labor for Dutch capital. At the same time the imperial government was withdrawing from direct production and encouraging private Dutch plantation development. So in 1870, the Agrarian Land Law was introduced. The law provided that all uncultivated "waste land" was inalienable state property which could be leased on a long-term basis to private plantation enterprises, and it made provision for long-term lease of communal village-owned lands to these concerns as well. The effect of this law was to make export-crop production a direct concern of the foreign-owned private plantations. In sugar, for example, whereas privately planted cane was about 9 per cent of total production in 1870, it was about 97 per cent two decades later.

The law made it possible for plantation enterprises to secure on good terms even that land which had been communally held by villages for a long time, and which was the basis of their subsistence rice production. Jacoby sums up the position this way:

The peasants, always in need of cash, became accustomed to lease their land for very modest advance cash rents on terms set by the company. Even in villages where communal land ownership with a periodic redistribution of *sawahs* (wet rice land) was still practised the *lurah* (head man) of the village, tempted by the high cash commission offered by plantations, would lease the village land even cheaper than

12. Clifford Geertz, *Agricultural Involution—The Process of Ecological Change in Indonesia* (Berkeley and Los Angeles, 1966), pp. 52–53. The rest of the discussion here on Indonesia draws from this source.

the individual peasant or, as frequently was the case, sell out the entire village to the company.[13]

And so the plantation system came to develop a stranglehold on the Indonesian rural economy. The plantation had to accommodate itself to this long-settled society but emerged on top in the end. Geertz describes the sequence of accommodation as follows: ". . . The Dutch moved from the institutional contrivances of adventurous capitalism in the eighteenth century, to those of state capitalism in the nineteenth, and to those of bureaucratic capitalism in the twentieth." [14]

Elsewhere in plantation Asia, the initial resource situation was not as closed as it was in Java. In Ceylon and Malaya land was available for capture by the invading Crown without seriously disrupting the settled or shifting agriculture of the indigenous people. And after capture the Crown made this land available on easy terms to British planters and companies. In Ceylon, for example, after the British conquest of the Kandyan Kingdom in 1815 all the vast areas of forest land in the central part of the island were taken over by the Crown; and when its suitability for coffee production was later established the Kandyan lands were sold to British investors and planters at five shillings an acre—the government defraying the cost of surveying and providing the infrastructure of roads.[15] In the Philippines the plantation system was superimposed on the *encomienda* legacy of Spanish colonization which had created large feudal land holdings but involved smallholders as well. The commercial plantation system led to greater concentration of land and elimination of the smallholdings. According to Jacoby:

Large land owners would frequently claim adjacent independent small holdings through the courts; more often than not they would win their case, because the incomplete titles to the small holdings could easily

13. Erich H. Jacoby, *Agrarian Unrest in Southeast Asia* (New York, 1961), p. 66.
14. Clifford Geertz, *op. cit.,* p. 50. The sequence describes the transition from the trading activities of the Dutch East India Company to that of the culture system and finally to that of the corporate plantation.
15. Donald Snodgrass, *Ceylon—An Export Economy in Transition* (Homewood, Illinois, 1966), p. 22.

be interpreted in their favour and the legal costs involved were way above the means of the peasants; "land-grabbing" contributed greatly to the elimination of small ownership and thousands of once independent and self-sufficient farmers were reduced to tenants and landless farm labourers.[16]

In Fiji the situation was much the same as that described for Java —a settled agricultural community with communal ownership of land in a closed-resource situation. And the basic pattern of plantation accommodation was similar to that in Java.

In the newest plantation areas of Africa and lowland Central America, plantation agriculture was established in open-resource situations somewhat similar to the first New World scene. Unused land was secured by plantation concerns on the basis of easy concessions which gave them access of vast areas of virgin country. Many of these concessions provided the basis for exploitation of natural (or wild) crops, as with oil palm in the Congo, but they also involved systematic plantation production which, in all cases, used only an insignificant part of the whole concessioned area. For the plantations in these cases, land was virtually a free input.

Whether the resource situation was open or closed, the second and third historical phases of the evolution of plantations were marked by the same problem of labor shortage that we described earlier for the first (New World) phase. In the open-resource situation of lowland Central America, the plantations had to rely on the labor of migrant black people from the older Caribbean plantation societies. In that of Africa, the concessions regime involved a slavery-style system of exploitation whereby the African peoples were compelled to collect produce for the imperial plantation interests. In the Congo, for example, compulsion took the form of a poll tax payable in rubber, or other forest products (and ivory of course). And during the Leopold regime, failure to produce led to inhuman acts of dismemberment and death.[17] Later in many parts

16. Erich H. Jacoby, *op. cit.,* pp. 200–201. The tenant arrangement was that of sharecropping.
17. The cruelty meted out to Africans under this system is well documented by Wolf and Wolf, *Rubber: A Story of Glory and Greed* (New York, 1936). The concession system which was used by most European governments in their balkanization of Africa is what the French called *cueillette* and the Germans *raubbau*.

of Africa, plantations had to organize contract migrant labor from nearby areas. In the relatively closed resource situations of Asia, labor supplies were secured by immigration of "coolie" labor from the nearby populous countries of India and China and by use of systems of sharecropping and share tenancy. Thus Ceylon, Malaya, and Fiji drew plantation labor supplies from South India and these Tamils now comprise substantial shares of the populations of those countries. In the Philippines, sharecropping and share tenancy by the dispossessed smallholders was the norm. In Indonesia, peasants became tenants on their own land in Java and plantation labor supplies for Sumatra came from the more populous Java. And Chinese, Japanese, and Philipino laborers were brought to develop Hawaii's sugar plantations.

In almost all cases indentured labor was secured by contractual arrangements which involved varying degrees of compulsion and coercion. Penal sanctions were the rule in many places and they always placed the migrant laborer in semi-servitude to the plantation. Lasker has suggested that there is an "organic relation of the indentured labor of the nineteenth century to the slave and serf labor that preceded it"—that it was the nearness of Southeast Asia to the labor reservoirs of India and China that made plantation production there competitive with that of the New World slave plantations. In his words:

Colonial economic enterprise usually started as collection of produce and from that developed forced production. During this second phase . . . began the herding of labor as a commodity for sale to users elsewhere. With the humanization of labor conditions in the nineteenth century, contract labor everywhere took the place of slave labor. . . . colonial and semicolonial types of enterprise were carried on with labor which, though nominally free, actually was under constraint once the laborer had been cajoled into signing a contract.[18]

When it is recognized that practically none of the migrant laborers could either read or write and that once they embarked on the program there was no way out, the similarity to slavery becomes more evident. The general pattern of plantation labor supply

18. Bruno Lasker, *Human Bondage in Southeast Asia* (Chapel Hill, North Carolina, 1950), p. 210.

which emerged in the newer plantation areas remained basically the same as that which applied to the first-established New World plantation system.

4. Growth and concentration of corporate capital: the fall of the planter class

While the plantation system was tightening the screws on Third World peoples after the abolition of slavery (conventionally defined), the system itself was being forced by external circumstances to make certain adjustments in the nature and organization of capital and management. During slavery the bulk of plantation capital was tied up in the ownership of slaves and land had been virtually free. The abolition of slavery created a new situation. Liquid capital was now needed to pay wages; or alternative arrangements involving money or commodity advances by financial intermediaries were necessary. This placed the proprietary planters in a difficult financial position. In addition, diminishing returns in the old plantation areas along with competition from the new areas induced technological change of a kind that could keep costs down. This involved the substitution of capital for labor which was now in short supply. Furthermore, technology in the plantation economies was affected by the spill-over of technological advance in the more advanced metropolitan economies. For example, the use of steam as a source of power became important and affected the plantations in terms of field transportation (that is, railways) and factory processing. Spill-over occurred as well in the area of business organization, for metropolitan business had by then proved the efficacy of the joint stock or limited liability companies for raising capital to finance production in their home environment. And it was a natural process to extend this to their overseas business interests. On top of all these developments, intensification of competition arising from the opening up of the newer plantation areas led to a loosening of long-standing policies of protected metropolitan markets for colonial trade and to recurrent wide fluctuations in the prices of plantation output. All of this set the stage for the general demise of the individual proprietary planter and contributed to the growth and concentration of corporate capital over the last hundred years or so of the history of plantations.

The decline of the planter class in the British West Indian colonies had been on its way prior to Emancipation. The main factors contributing to this were slave uprisings and unrest, soil exhaustion, absentee landlordism, independence of the American colonies which increased the cost of food and lumber imports, and general problems created by numerous wars in the Caribbean.[19] In the second half of the nineteenth century the situation was aggravated by three important events: first, Emancipation, which freed the slaves and raised the cost of labor and of production for the planter; second, the British equalization of tariffs which destroyed the monopoly position of West Indian sugar in that market; and third, competition from other New World cane producers still using slave labor (Cuba and Brazil, in particular) and from the newly developing beet-sugar production of Europe. These developments created a crisis situation which resulted in the bankruptcy of a large number of planters. Many estates were divided into small plots and sold to, or sharecropped by, the ex-slaves. Many were placed in receivership and those that remained in production were consolidated to set the stage for the emergence of the modern corporate plantation. The financial arrangements that had characterized the planter slave plantation and the phenomenon of absentee ownership helped to facilitate the change in ownership and organization.

The individual planter of the slave-plantation era had relied heavily on metropolitan merchants and factors for advances in respect of supply of provisions and for disposal of his sugar in the market. During the period of crisis, therefore, the planter became heavily in debt to these metropolitan financial intermediaries and the bankruptcy of the planter transferred ownership to the creditors. Not being interested in plantation activity as individuals, these creditors organized limited liability companies to raise share capital in the metropolis in order to salvage what was left of their assets in the West Indies. Share capital was easy to raise with the expanding wealth of England. The fact that many of the individual plantation owners were already residing in the metropole, and were therefore not really interested in planting, lessened the indi-

19. This is well documented in Lowell Ragatz, *The Fall of the Planter Class in the British Caribbean, 1763–1863* (New York, 1963).

vidual owners' incentive for salvaging the plantations. Ragatz informs us that non-resident ownership of plantations became the general rule in British America around the middle of the 1700's and was the norm thereafter. He attributes this to three factors: (a) plantation prosperity around 1750, which made possible the retirement of planters to Britain; (b) plantation property passed from 1775 to 1815 by inheritance to people in England; and (c) between the Napoleonic wars and Emancipation, property falling into the hands of creditors in England through the foreclosing of mortgages. Thus by the 1830's most of the Caribbean estates "were in the hands of new owners, almost none of whom had ever been beyond the Atlantic or had the slightest intention of going there." [20]

Technological change occurring during the period of crisis also made it difficult for individual planters to hang on, as the new technology was of necessity more capital-intensive. In the field, the plough and harrow were introduced to reduce the labor demands of holing and the introduction of the vacuum pan, centrifuge and steam power in sugar processing along with railway transportation for bringing cane from fields to factory gave rise to the central factory system.[21] The resulting increase in capital demands of sugar production in the new situation made it almost impossible for the individual planter to survive without dependence on a more capitalized plantation that could provide central factory processing. Corporate ownership of West Indian sugar plantations began to develop in the late nineteenth century and was further reinforced in more recent decades as metropolitan refining interests sought to establish their own sources of raw sugar supplies (see Chapter 5). There were of course variations among the West Indian islands for the general pattern just described. In some of the smaller islands of the Leeward group the plantations collapsed completely and the planters returned home. In St. Kitts, Antigua, and Barbados the crisis was not as pronounced because of the lim-

20. Lowell Ragatz, "Absentee Landlordism in the British Caribbean 1750–1833," *Agricultural History*, January 1931, pp. 7–13.
21. The first central factory in the British Caribbean colonies was established at Usine St. Madeline in Trinidad in 1871 by the Colonial Sugar Company.

ited opportunities confronting the ex-slaves, a lower incidence of absenteeism, and the smaller size of plantations. While in the French West Indies the last two factors and continued protection in the French market helped to maintain the status quo. Consequently in all these islands, the individual or family plantation has managed to survive to a greater extent than has been the case in Jamaica, Trinidad, Guyana, and British Honduras.[22]

The West Indian pattern was very similar in many respects to that which took place later in the United States South. There the sugar planter had also relied on merchants and factors in the towns for provisioning the plantations and disposing of the output. After the Civil War and Emancipation the planters were in difficulty. Although the prices of cotton and sugar were high, planters could not expand production because levees needed expensive repairs, costly new machinery was needed for sugar processing, and the Southern banking system had become insolvent. Technological change in sugar production similar to that described for the West Indies made things difficult for the individual planter. This gave rise to the development of family corporations. According to Roger Shugg:

Almost half the planters in 1869 bore names that slaveholding families would not have recognized. More and more estates were bought by partnerships and corporations, often with the help of Northern capital. . . .

The title to an estate often changed, but seldom its size, for every acre, all its equipment and crops were collateral for the credit necessary to work it.[23]

22. Antigua is a kind of special case. Drought has always been a chronic problem. In British Honduras, forestry, not sugar, was the plantation activity involved. The Belize Estate and Produce Company, Ltd., had been formed in London in 1875 "to trade over the assets of Hodge and Hyde, timber merchants, who had become indebted to the London banking firm, C. Hoare and Co." K. M. Stahl, *The Metropolitan Organization of British Colonial Trade* (London, 1951), p. 31.

23. Roger Shugg, "Survival of the Plantation System in Louisiana," *Journal of Southern History*, August 1937, pp. 319–20 and 325. See also J. C. Sitterson, *Sugar Country—The Cane Sugar Industry in Louisiana, 1753–1950* (Lexington, Kentucky, 1953), which states that incorporation was encouraged because "it was contended that when

But the individual or family planter in the U.S. South could manage to survive for a longer period than those in the West Indies
because the system of sharecropping made things easier for them.
However, the sharecropping-furnish arrangement still involved dependence of the planter on merchants in the towns, and whenever
periods of low prices came, there was the same recurrence of
planter indebtedness, foreclosure, and incorporation. During the
crisis of the 1930's this was particularly pronounced. Johnson *et
al.*, writing in 1935, claimed that the "South now is experiencing a
re-concentration of tenant farms under corporate ownership. . . .
It is estimated that areas amounting to 30 per cent of the cotton
lands of various states are owned by insurance companies and
banks." [24] In the post-World War II period the trend toward incorporation of plantations in the U.S. South has been further intensified by the shortage of labor and the need for capital-intensive mechanization of field operations.

The organization of wild-rubber gathering in Brazil had many
features similar to the planter-based plantation system in the West
Indies and the U.S. South. The *patrão* ran a provision store and
extended credit to his peons but the patrão in turn depended on
credit from the commercial houses on the coast which furnished
provisions and sold his rubber. Thus the pattern was set for the
acquisition of plantations by commercial houses when crisis bur-
dened the patrões with so much debt that they had to foreclose. In
the sugar-plantation region of Brazil, the planter class was also
shaken by the technological developments in sugar production.
The old engenhos with simple mills were transformed into mere su-

---

insolvency or death forced the sale of sugar plantations, they
brought low prices because there were few buyers for such large
pieces of property. Where the properties were incorporated, only individual stock ownership need be sold and the whole property would
not be sacrificed," pp. 262–63.

24. C. S. Johnson, E. R. Embree, and W. W. Alexander, *The Collapse
of Cotton Tenancy* (Chapel Hill, North Carolina, 1935), pp. 32–33.
Woofter claims that in the 1930's "about 10 per cent of the plantation land in the South was in the hands of large banks, insurance
companies, and mortgage companies which acquired it through fore-
closures." T. J. Woofter, *Landlord and Tenant on the Cotton Plantation* (U.S. Works Progress Administration, Research Monograph V,
Washington, D. C., 1936), p. xxii.

garcane planters as most could not afford the investment and expansion demanded by the new central (*usina*). A law of 1875 guaranteeing foreign loans for the construction of the new factories resulted in many factories being installed and operated by foreign corporations. But these were boycotted by the cane planters —the old engenho owners. Subsequently, the wealthier planters established factories to process the cane of several planters and family corporations in turn managed to extend their ownership of land at the expense of the planters. According to Hutchinson:

By refusing to mill the cane of the planter, or by taking his cane and then letting it sour, and by various other methods, the *usineiros* were able to force many planters into bankruptcy, after which the corporation bought the land. Also, many planters who continued to depend upon their own efforts, producing sugar in their old-style mills, gradually went into bankruptcy, since they could not compete with the improved product of the new factories.[25]

The extent to which this concentration has gone is indicated by the fact that by the 1960's, twelve Pernambuco family corporations produced 64 per cent of the state's sugar output.[26]

The decline of the planter class and an associated growth of corporate capital was taking place in other plantation areas of the Third World as well. Brookfield informs us that in Mauritius it was also the pattern that sugar planters received most of their financial capital requirements from a *bailleur de fonds* who was also a sugar broker. During the sugar boom of 1915–25 a heavy burden of fixed repayments had been taken on by the sugar planters, and this burden became insupportable during the subsequent depression, 1925–40. As a result "the *bailleurs de fonds* . . . became virtual owners and operators of many estates and small holdings." [27]

In Ceylon, Malaya, and Indonesia, the life cycle of the planter class was much shorter than that of the earlier New World planta-

25. H. W. Hutchinson, *Village and Plantation Life in Northeast Brazil* (Seattle, Washington, 1957), p. 42.
26. Kit Sims Taylor, *op. cit.*, p. 136.
27. H. C. Brookfield, "Problems of Monoculture and Diversification in a Sugar Island: Mauritius," *Economic Geography*, January 1959, p. 28.

tions. In that part of the world, much of the plantation development involved incorporation of firms from the beginning. But wherever individual planters had been involved we find similar forces leading to the fall of the planter class. In general, ownership by individual proprietary planters lasted for only one generation, after which the planter would become associated with an agency house that managed several plantations incorporated into the firm structure of the managing agency.

In Ceylon, this process accelerated enormously from the 1890's onward and has been described and analyzed by D. W. Forrest and N. Ramachandran. Forrest informs us that the marriage of agency-house capital with the managerial experience of proprietary planters provided the main foundation for the growth of corporate capital in the Ceylon tea industry and that the typical life cycle of the European planter there followed "a classical sequence: Planter—Visiting Agent—Partner in Agency—often with a final phase as Director of Tea Companies at home." Ramachandran notes that concentration of capital increased rapidly after 1939; by 1959, 58 per cent of the tea acreage in Ceylon was owned by limited liability companies.[28]

The development of the rubber industry in Malaya marked the decline in importance of individual planters and the growth of corporate ownership in that country. According to James Jackson, many rubber companies were floated in London by the large merchant houses of Singapore because individual planters "lacked the experience and contacts necessary to float their estates as companies." Because rubber was still largely a speculative business the long-established and well-known agencies and merchant houses were best placed to intervene in the raising of share capital and they "became the link between the plantations in Malaya and the sources of capital in Europe." [29]

A similar fate befell the planter class in Indonesia toward the end of the nineteenth century. Diseases affecting both coffee and

28. See D. M. Forrest, *A Hundred Years of Ceylon Tea, 1867–1967* (London, 1967), pp. 97–99 and 132, and N. Ramachandran, *Foreign Plantation Investment in Ceylon, 1889–1958* (Colombo, Central Bank of Ceylon, 1963).
29. James Jackson, *Planters and Speculators Malaya, 1786–1921* (Kuala Lumpur, 1968), p. 245.

sugar took their toll in the 1880's and the fall in prices of both these products brought on a general economic depression. Sugar was also passing through stages which affected its profitability everywhere: competition from European beet, technological change, and the like. Allen and Donnithorne inform us:

The slump had enduring consequences. The individual planter gave place to the limited company; the *cultuurbanken* [agricultural finance corporations] acquired greater control over the units which they financed; and the banks in turn passed under the control of financial institutions in the Netherlands.[30]

This trend, which continued until World War II, was further accentuated by the depression of the 1930's and involved increasing concentration of capital. Between 1929 and 1933, for example, the number of sugar factories in operation is said to have fallen from 179 to 45. The managing-agency business was as much a part of the scene in Indonesia as in Ceylon and Malaya; and it played a similar role in relation to the growth of corporate ownership in Indonesia's plantation industry as in the other two countries.

In Fiji we find much the same pattern as elsewhere. There European planters had been enjoying a boom in cotton prices during the 1860's but in the 1870's the tide changed and the subsequent fall in cotton prices cut the ground from under the feet of many individual planters. Gerard Ward tells us that during this time, ". . . Many of the planters who had borrowed money to buy land and machinery and to hire labourers were soon in difficulties. . . . From 1871 through to 1874 planters were abandoning their estates and considerable areas fell into the hands of creditors and trading firms."[31]

From the foregoing it becomes evident that in the plantation regions of the New World and of Asia and the Pacific there were a set of common forces at work which made it increasingly difficult for individual planters to continue to participate in plantation ac-

30. G. C. Allen and A. G. Donnithorne, *Western Enterprise in Indonesia and Malaya* (London, 1957), p. 27.
31. R. Gerard Ward, *Land Use and Population in Fiji* (London, 1965), p. 25.

tivity. If the trend had started before the middle of the nineteenth century it was accentuated and accelerated thereafter. Abolition of slavery, technological change, crop diseases, and violent price fluctuations all contributed to make the financial position of the individual planter precarious and set the stage for the rise in importance of corporate capital. However, lack of viability of the planters was not alone responsible for the growth of corporate capital in the world plantation economy. Positive forces were also at work in the metropolitan countries which served to reinforce the trend during the present century.

5. Growth and concentration of corporate capital: the new imperialism and the search for raw materials

Whereas the first stage of imperialism in modern world history was executed by metropolitan governments, the new imperialism of the twentieth century has been largely the work of metropolitan business corporations. Europe had reached a stage of mature capitalism with a considerable fund of financial capital seeking profitable overseas investments. And during this time many European firms involved in the processing of plantation output increasingly sought to establish direct control over their raw material inputs. Across the Atlantic the United States, fresh from its conquest over Spain in the Spanish-American War, was ready to embark on its own old-style government imperialism which provided a cover for private U.S. overseas investments. The major plantation developments of the present century have resulted from these factors which contributed further to the growth of corporate capital.

The rubber plantation industry of Asia was essentially a product of the forces mentioned above. From the start of the century, companies were organized to raise share capital in the metropolitan centers of Great Britain, France, Belgium, Holland, and the United States. Unlike tea in Asia and sugar and cotton in the New World, planter capital had not really paved the way for corporate capital in rubber (though this did occur to a certain extent). The rubber industries of Malaya, Ceylon, and Indonesia were largely established by investment trusts and syndicates established in the metropolitan countries expressly for the purpose of planting and growing rubber. And by the 1920's the major rubber-manufacturing companies in the North Atlantic began to get into the act themselves. In 1910 the Dunlop Rubber Company secured its first estate; by 1915 had formed Dunlop Plantations Ltd. and had the largest group of estates in Malaya. The United States Rubber Company also opened up extensive plantations in Malaya and Indonesia. So did Goodyear, Michelin of France, Pirelli of Italy, and so on.

Rubber-manufacturing firms were not the only metropolitan concerns seeking their own source of raw material (plantation) supplies. World prices of plantation output were increasingly subject to wide price fluctuations. And whereas periods of low prices forced individual planters out of production, periods of high prices served to induce the metropolitan processing concerns to secure their own sources of raw materials. Thus at all times there were forces contributing to the rising importance of corporate capital. There are numerous examples of processing companies and merchants establishing or acquiring plantations to provide their own supplies of raw materials. Since this aspect is due for further consideration in our examination of major plantation enterprises in Chapter 5, only a few examples are provided here. Unilever, the giant Anglo-Dutch combine involved in the manufacture of margarine and soap, was responsible for the development of coconut plantations in the Solomon Islands and of oil palm plantations in the Congo and Indonesia. Tate and Lyle, the British sugar refiners, began sugarcane and raw-sugar production in the West Indies in the 1930's. The Australian-based Colonial Sugar Refining Company established the sugar industry in Fiji early in the present century. And United States sugar refiners had done the same in Cuba, Puerto Rico, and the Dominican Republic. Some metropolitan plantation investment was made by firms involved in distribution, rather than processing, of plantation output. Sea captains who had been involved in the initiation of world banana trade in the late nineteenth century linked up with their associated distributors in the United States to establish the banana plantations of Central America. And distribution firms in Britain were getting into plantation tea production in Asia; Lipton Ltd., the English and Scottish Joint C.W.S., and Brooke Bond Ceylon Ltd. are examples of these.

A number of major plantation developments in the twentieth

century are associated directly with the emergence of the United States as an imperial power and the associated overseas investment of corporate firms in that country. The banana plantations of Honduras, Guatemala, Costa Rica, Panama, and Colombia were established as a result of investments of two large United States fruit companies—United Fruit and Standard Fruit and Shipping Company. These were really the efforts of private American initiative toward the end of the nineteenth century and involved concessions over wide areas of land and the establishment of railroads in the Central American republics. More directly linked to the new United States imperialism was the expansion of the sugar plantation industries of the Philippines, Hawaii, Cuba, Haiti, the Dominican Republic, and Puerto Rico. After the Spanish-American War all the countries named eventually came under United States control and their sugar industries mushroomed as a result of the inflow of capital from that country. Between 1898 and 1900, for example, $50 million (U.S.) is said to have been invested in Cuban sugar.

Cuba secured constitutional independence but became an economic colony of the United States. Political control over its colonies (Philippines, Hawaii, and Puerto Rico) provided the security for these plantation investments. Mention is usually made of the fact that the United States Congress had introduced legislation to limit the size of landholdings in its colonies. But the fact is that these have never had any impact on limiting plantation development. In Puerto Rico, the 500 acre law "was conveniently disregarded and, 40 years after its passage, 51 corporations controlled 249,000 acres of Puerto Rico's best land. One of these actually had over 50,000 acres." [32] The inflow of U.S. capital led to a dramatic increase in corporate ownership and in the concentration of capital in all these sugar industries. Data for Puerto Rico show that whereas in 1909 there were forty-eight mills of less than $5000 capital investment and only three of more than $500,000, by 1919 there were none in the lower category and thirty-two in the higher (most of these being over $1 million). Investment in individually owned sugar mills moved from $1.3 to $3.3 million be-

32. R. C. West and J. P. Augelli, *Middle America—Its Lands and Peoples* (Englewood Cliffs, New Jersey, 1966), p. 130.

tween the two dates while that of corporate mills moved from $13.1 to $45.9 million.[33]

The United States was also involved in the twentieth-century development of plantations in Haiti and Liberia, two constitutionally independent republics that were within the colonial orbit of the new U.S. empire. Although sugar had been produced during and after the French colonial period in Haiti, it was during the American occupation of that country between 1915 and 1934 that modern centrals and plantations were developed. The U.S. government set the stage for the penetration of American capital by its repeal of a Haitian law which forbad the ownership of land by foreigners. And so much of the scarce coastal lands came to be owned by U.S. plantation corporations. In Liberia, the U.S. government provided the necessary assistance which gave the Firestone Rubber Company a foothold in that country and led to the establishment of company plantations there in the 1920's.

The major twentieth-century plantation ventures which have resulted from direct metropolitan corporate investment are the rubber and oil palm industries of Asia and Africa; the banana plantations of Central America; and the expansion of sugar plantations in certain Caribbean, Pacific, and Asian countries. There are a few countries and places where plantation development can be attributed almost exclusively to this phenomenon. Central America has been mentioned already; the Congo, Liberia, and, to a large extent, Malaya are other examples. So is British Honduras and almost all the plantation activity in Indonesia's Sumatra. The new imperialism has therefore materially contributed to the growth of corporate capital in the world plantation economy during the twentieth century.

33. S. W. Mintz, "Cañamelar: The Sub-culture of a Rural Sugar Plantation Proletariat," in J. H. Steward *et al., The People of Puerto Rico* (Urbana, Illinois, 1956), p. 339.

5

The dynamics of growth and the nature of metropolitan plantation enterprise

Once metropolitan corporate enterprise got involved in plantation production, the stage was set for subsequent cumulative growth of these enterprises without any significant corresponding growth of plantation economy. This association of growth on the one hand without stimulus on the other derives from certain "economies" that arise from modern plantation production and which individual firms are in a position to secure. However, because metropolitan plantation enterprises are normally multinational in character, the benefits of these economies do not accrue as much to any single country as to the firm itself. The economies of firm expansion have become cumulative over the past few decades, so that within the Third World at present, plantation investment is highly concentrated among a small group of large corporations.

Everywhere in the plantation world proper, we find that metropolitan enterprise is predominant in production and trade. The only exceptions are the sub-economies of Brazil and the United States, and the state plantation economy of Cuba. British enterprises account for the bulk of West Indian sugar production and trade; United States enterprises for the bulk of sugar output and trade in Puerto Rico, the Dominican Republic, Haiti, and the Philippines; U.S. rubber companies for almost all of total output in Liberia; U.S. companies for close to the total banana output and trade of the Central American republics; an Australian company for all the raw sugar in Fiji; and American, British, Dutch, and other European companies for most of the rubber, tea, and oil palm and for the trade in Ceylon and Southeast Asia.[1] Some of the names of these enterprises are better known to the people of plantation society in many countries than the names of their government prime ministers or presidents. United Fruit Company in Honduras, Guatemala, Costa Rica, and Panama. Tate & Lyle in the West Indies. Firestone in Liberia. Unilever in the Congo ("Huilever") and the Solomon Islands. Harrisons and Crosfield in Ceylon, Malaya, and Indonesia. Brooke Bond in Ceylon. Socfin in Malaya and the Congo.[2] The Colonial Sugar Refining Company in Fiji. These companies are all household names in the respective countries, and they represent a vision of great power and authority in the minds of people living in plantation society. They should, therefore, be examined carefully.

How and why did these giant enterprises gain an ascendancy in the plantation world? How big are they really? How are they organized and what is the structure of decision making like? What do all these enterprises have in common? And what role are they likely to play in influencing development or underdevelopment in plantation economies now and in the future? These are some of the basic questions that are dealt with in this chapter. The answers are not all that easy to come by. One reason is that much of the information required for a full analysis is not generally available to the public. The companies concerned guard certain information

1. Three books which provide more detailed information on the importance of metropolitan enterprise are Kathleen M. Stahl, *The Metropolitan Organization of British Colonial Trade* (London, 1951); N. Ramachandran, *Foreign Plantation Investment in Ceylon, 1889–1958* (Colombo, Central Bank of Ceylon, 1963); and G. C. Allen and A. G. Donnithorne, *Western Enterprise in Indonesia and Malaya—A Study in Economic Development* (London, 1957).
2. The British-owned company of Harrisons and Crosfield Ltd. "controls nearly 2 million acres under rubber, oil palm, coconuts, tea, coffee, cacao, and abaca, with estates in Malaya, Sabah (North Borneo), Indonesia, India, Ceylon, and East Africa. Several other British organizations are almost as large, as is the Franco-Belgian giant Socfin, which operates the world's largest oil palm estate and has properties in Vietnam, Cambodia, Malaya, Cameroon and both Congo republics"; see D. W. Fryer, *World Economic Development* (New York, 1965), p. 87.

very closely. During the course of this study, the author asked several firms about the extent and nature of their plantation activities and the contribution of these activities to the relevant plantation economies. Several firms co-operated somewhat, but several were extremely reticent. One tea company responded as follows: "In our opinion the scope of the study on which you intend to base a book is so wide that it could only be misleading for us to attempt to assist you in correspondence." [3] The United Fruit Company indicated that they do not break down their operating figures in a way that would readily indicate the degree of vertical integration of the enterprise nor their profits by country of operation; and added that some of those figures are regarded as "classified" information.[4] Unilever indicated that whereas they do not "reveal all," their subsidiaries in "major [metropolitan] countries" provide more public information on operations than their plantation subsidiaries located in Third World countries.[5] These two responses describe a general condition that merits discussion here.

Since this study is concerned with the welfare of people living in plantation economies, it requires a particular kind of company information to inform the analysis. The fact that United Fruit does not break down their operating figures in a way that would throw light on the questions asked here suggests that they have different perspectives from this one. That is understandable, for their interest is that of the company, while ours is that of the people in plantation society. And it is likely that the two may not coincide. But not being able to secure the desirable breakdown, we are not in a position to determine the degree of divergence between the two interests. We shall offer some qualitative judgments on this score in subsequent analysis. Like United Fruit, Unilever frankly admits that it does not "reveal all." But Unilever's policy is bent a little—to reveal more—in what it regards as "major

3. Letter to the author dated 19 November 1969 from James Finlay & Co. Limited, Secretaries of the Consolidated Tea and Lands Company.
4. Letter to the author dated December 22, 1969, and signed by Webster Lithgow, Assistant Director of Public Relations, United Fruit Company.
5. Letter to the author dated 10 February 1970 and signed by D. U. Gregg, Public Relations Manager, Unilever Limited.

countries." The company states explicitly that this does not include the plantation countries.

It seems necessary for us briefly to consider the reason for acting according to such "double standards." One possible explanation is that the company, on its own initiative, reveals more in some cases because it is in the company's interest to appear not to be withholding. That is to say, if the company is operating in a country where the public is generally accustomed to asking questions about business performance and receiving answers, it is a sensible strategy for the company to reveal more than it would in a country where the public is generally uninformed. Another possible explanation is that governments in the plantation countries demand less company information than governments in the so-called "major countries." Companies will go only as far as they are allowed. And as far as the people of plantation society are concerned the responsibility for protecting their welfare rests squarely on their own governments. It would appear that, at present, these governments have failed to bear this responsibility adequately, with the result that companies like Unilever are able to treat them as "minors." The fact that the infrastructure of public communications media is less developed in plantation society than in the advanced countries, and that people in the former have low literacy skills, increases the need for government intervention of a kind that will force companies to provide more information than they currently give. This is a matter of top priority.

1. The dynamics of the growth of enterprise

Metropolitan firms engaged in the processing or marketing of plantation products first get involved in plantation production either because they want to gain control over raw material supplies in order to control or influence input prices for metropolitan processing, or because market restrictions on further expansion of processed output limit investment opportunities at the processing level. In either event, the enterprise is induced to engage in this activity by the prospect of greater profits in the long run and/or less variability of profits in the short run. Once the enterprise embarks on plantation production a chain of events follows, leading to further expansion. First, plantation investment normally involves the creation of social infrastructure (roads, ports, schools, hospitals, and so forth) and this creates *external economies* which make other activities profitable (for example, company stores, internal transport services). The external economies deriving from plantation investment serve to reduce the marginal cost of setting up these activities.

Second, interindustry linkages come into play and stimulate further enterprise expansion into related fields in order to secure *inter-industry economies*. This explains the pattern of entry into such activities as shipping, wharfage, and stevedoring. It also explains why the enterprise will begin to produce plantation inputs, such as sugar machinery. Third, the interindustry linkages become reinforced as the enterprise enters the field of heavy industry involving engineering skills, and further expansion becomes necessary to maximize returns from these skills which it now possesses. It therefore embarks on allied engineering works to utilize fully the available skills—*skill economies*. Fourth, because engineering and other such skills are not product-specific, the firm is in a position to expand further, this time into non-plantation-related areas, and so is able to secure *economies of diversification*. Technological change will influence enterprise expansion in additional ways not yet considered. Fifth, increasing capital-intensive technology reinforces the advantage of the integrated firm already producing the capital goods for plantation operations and makes weaker plantation companies prey to it. This is the effect described as technologically induced *economies of scale*. It accounts for the concentration of plantation capital in individual countries and the expansion of the vertical combine at the expense of smaller less-integrated firms. Sixth, certain fixed capital assets are not product-specific and once these have been installed the enterprise can expand into new lines and secure *fixed capital economies* resulting in further diversification away from pure or allied plantation types of activities. Such is the case, for example, with bulk shipment equipment and bulk storage facilities. Seventh, there are *market infrastructure economies;* once the enterprise has established marketing outlets and has experienced sales staff covering wide areas in the world, it is relatively simple to introduce new product lines into the existing framework. Contacts with wholesalers and retailers have already been established, advertising campaigns well seasoned, and buildings and transport equipment already on location. Such economies are likely to lead to diversification and to reinforce the expansion process.

The considerations surrounding decision making in connection with the growth and expansion of metropolitan plantation enterprises indicate that decision makers in these organizations have been always fully aware of the economies described and have, in every instance, been guided by the prospect of increasing profits by expanding to secure these economies. Some indication of this is provided by the following examples. On the acquisition by Tate & Lyle of United Molasses, the following pronouncement was made:

The T. & L. Group . . . has been the largest group in the world concerned with sugar production and refining, but nevertheless lacked its own facilities for the handling and distribution of molasses, the most important by-product of sugar manufacture.

In its trading activities the U. M. Company acquires large quantities of molasses from producers and refiners all over the world, including the molasses output of the T. & L. Group; at the same time it deploys a worldwide storage and distribution organisation. Both companies are operating in the same countries; molasses depots exist in cane sugar areas where T. & L. have interests; both companies are shipowners, with the Sugar Line fleet of bulk sugar carriers and the Athel Line fleet of tankers.

The acquisition may be seen as the logical extension of a worldwide sugar organisation.[6]

Recognition of interindustry economies is clear in the above statement. An example of recognition of fixed capital economies leading to diversification is provided by the 1968 decision of United Molasses to enter the field of alcohol trade. According to the company's 1968 *Report and Accounts,* "the United Molasses Group entered into a new realm of commodity trading by establishing themselves in the international field of alcohol. This new business is complementary to the international trading, shipping and storage divisions" because the bulk storage equipment and bulk ship-

6. *Tate & Lyle Report and Accounts 1965* (London), p. 4.

ping equipment are capable of handling a variety of liquid products, "from a complete range of petroleum products to highly toxic or flammable chemicals—from edible oils and fats to sensitive latices." According to the managing director of United Molasses, the group had to diversify for further growth because its preeminent position in every molasses market of the world gives the company such a large share of the total molasses trade that the opportunities for further expansion in the principal commodity have been limited. But expansion into new areas "will derive from allied skills in trading, product handling, storage and shipping." More precisely, "Promising lines of development, therefore, lie in expanding into new trading areas at the same time benefiting from our international network of offices, storage facilities and ships." [7]

There are numerous other examples that could be given to substantiate the claim that company decision makers are constantly aware of the various types of economies noted above. A look at company reports will confirm this. One question that arises is whether in point of fact these decision makers are necessarily always guided by prospects of increasing profits by decisions to expand the enterprise. In earlier days, there was evidence that the company pioneers were not necessarily always guided by the prospect of greater profits. For example, Charles Wilson tells us that Lever's plantation adventures were motivated by the dream of empire building.

Lever was held by the sheer fascination of the scene. The great colonial enterprises of the seventeenth and eighteenth centuries had never been "business" in its narrow sense; they were the work of adventurers as well as of city men. In Lever the two types combined. . . . Expanding business brought not merely bigger profits but more opportunities for adventure.[8]

Today these corporate enterprises are run by boards of directors who are not likely to have the same kind of individual spirit of

    7. G. W. Scott, "Expansion by Diversification," *Tate & Llye Times International,* July 1969, p. 5.
    8. Charles Wilson, *The History of Unilever,* Vol. I (London, 1954), p. 187. Wilson, quotes Lever as saying "One can go to places like the Congo, and organize, organize, organize, well, very big things indeed. But I don't work at business only for the sake of money. I am not a lover of money as money and never have been. I work at business because business is life. It enables me to do things."

adventure as Lever had. Nevertheless, there is some indication that they are not always necessarily guided by considerations of profit maximization. The power of individuals is enhanced if they are involved in managing large enterprises, and this may be a consideration leading to continuous enterprise expansion. And there may be other factors as well which make decision making by corporate boards of directors inconsistent with the profit maximization ideals which the shareholders, whom they are supposed to represent, may have. Ramachandran has provided several examples of the occurrence of this in his study of foreign plantation investment in Ceylon.[9] The facts of the matter are simply that the process of decision making is such that shareholders in corporate enterprises today have very little say in what companies do.

On balance, it seems reasonable to speculate that considerations of power may often be influential in decisions concerning the expansion of enterprise. A company's share of the market can be decisive in determining levels of profits in the long run. It is therefore not inconceivable that boards of directors may forego short-run profits in favor of enterprise expansion. If in the earlier period of metropolitan plantation activity the important consideration was control of raw-material supplies, at the present time control of the market is perhaps of even greater significance. This has resulted largely from changes in the technology of distribution involving an increasing degree of product differentiation. Brand names have come to be of great importance in the trade of final products derived from plantation output. Chiquita and Cabana bananas, Lyle's Golden Syrup, Mr. Cube, C and H Sugar, Lipton Tea are only a few of the consumer household names in various metropolitan markets. Product differentiation emphasizes the importance of market occupancy; and enterprise expansion is guided by this consideration.

We can conclude, therefore, that the dynamics of expansion of metropolitan plantation enterprise derive from two main considerations. One is the need for increasing and maintaining market shares in increasingly differentiated product markets. The other derives from inherent cumulative economies that begin to arise once the enterprise starts plantation production.

9. N. Ramachandran, *op. cit.*

2. The ascendancy of metropolitan enterprise in plantation production and trade: two case histories

As we noted earlier, metropolitan enterprise got into the act of plantation production in the quest for raw materials, as a corollary to long-established trading in plantation products, in the default of the proprietary planter to withstand price fluctuations and other uncertainties, and under the cover of a new imperialism. This was all toward the end of the nineteenth century and during the early decades of the twentieth century. Since that time metropolitan enterprise has consolidated its position and at present these companies control the bulk of world plantation production and trade. The factors contributing to the growing relative importance of metropolitan enterprise derive mainly from the generally hospitable political environment in plantation societies, certain interindustry economies which these firms have managed to secure, technological change creating scale economies which they are best placed to capitalize on, and generally volatile product markets which have served continuously to eliminate weak competitors. To illustrate these influences, we need to look briefly at the historical development of some of these enterprises.

UNILEVER

The best documented company history available at present is that of Unilever.[10] This case will therefore be used to illustrate what seem to be some of the trends. According to Charles Wilson's account, Lever, as a soap maker, was from the very beginning sensi-

10. Reference here is of course to the three-volume work of Charles Wilson, *The History of Unilever*, 2 vols. (London, 1954), and *Unilever, 1945–1965* (London, 1968). On the history of some other companies, see Kathleen M. Stahl, *op. cit.*; Charles D. Kepner, *Social Aspects of the Banana Industry* (New York, 1936); Charles D. Kepner and J. H. Soothill, *The Banana Empire—A Case Study in Economic Imperialism* (New York, 1966); Alfred Lief, *The Firestone Story—A History of the Firestone Tire and Rubber Company* (New York, 1951); and "A Brief History of Tate & Lyle Limited," *Tate & Lyle Times International,* January 1969–January 1970, quarterly issues.

tive to the problem of foreign raw-material supplies. "Round about the turn of the century, the fear of being 'squeezed' for these materials by the merchants and brokers became almost an obsession with him, and in the projects for winning raw materials that followed there was probably a large element of defensive strategy." Lever managed to secure a ninety-nine-year lease from the British government for 51,000 acres in the Solomon Islands and incorporated Lever's Pacific Plantations Limited in England in 1902. Thus Lever started in coconut production; but that was not the end of the matter. Wilson informs us: "It soon became evident that the undertaking was going to involve commitments of quite a new kind. Trade between the Islands and the transport of copra to Sydney necessitated a ship, and Lever Brothers bought the S.S. *Upolu*." And later "As the estates came into bearing it became necessary to increase the Company's fleet: in 1910 and 1911 four ships were built or bought." [11] Land acquisition posed no problem in the Pacific as the company was able to secure freehold or leases of 999 years but, as usual, labor was difficult to get. By 1913, the company's land holdings in the Solomons had increased from the original 51,000 acres to 300,000—3 per cent of the islands' total area. In addition to coconuts, the company had 1500 head of cattle in its territory, "each of which could do two men's work in keeping down the grass, besides ploughing and draft work."

The Solomons were only a small beginning for Lever. From the start, Africa was his target for large-scale plantation development. Lever himself is said to have confessed: "Our task in the Solomons is child's play to our task in the Congo Belge." There, an inexhaustible supply of palm oil and palm kernels was available from natural groves waiting to be exploited. The British government turned a cold shoulder on the company for the acquisition of land in its African territories. But the Belgian government was more than hospitable. Lever Brothers signed a convention with the colonial government of the Belgian Congo in 1911 which created Huileries du Congo Belge. Ratification by the Belgian parliament gave the convention statutory force. Under the convention the company's operations were to be carried on in five areas of palm-

11. Charles Wilson, *The History of Unilever*, Vol. I, pp. 159–63.

bearing "domainal land"; and it had an option on a maximum of 200,000 hectares in each area provided that the total area held in all areas did not exceed 750,000 hectares. Payment of ground rent would give the company freehold possession. And the company was given power and authority over the concessioned areas. Wilson paints a true picture when he states that "Lever . . . undertook a task which was little less than the reorganization of a principality."

The convention had provisions which gave the company responsibility for "safeguarding the physical well-being and cultural development" of the Congolese people. And other provisions ensured that production and trade would benefit the Belgian economy. Another historical event was to take the company into another related line of activity. Because British policy prevented Lever from securing land in British West Africa, he was compelled to buy palm fruit and kernels from Africans there. And "He had, therefore, to enter the ancient and none-too-reputable Coast Trade." Although Lever then had no experience in merchandise trade, his need for produce was decisive. According to Wilson, "he was impelled to enter the trade by his conviction that the only solution to the soap maker's difficulties lay in the increase of the world's resources of oilseeds. That conviction was shared by many others in the oils and fats industries." [12] So Lever first acquired a Liverpool firm, trading mainly timber in Nigeria; and after that another firm trading in Sierra Leone and another in Liberia. These firms managed to secure him kernel supplies by bartering textiles with the Africans. Thus began Lever's merchant trading activities. Having started in this line in British West Africa, the company soon expanded its operations in the Congo to include merchant trading, with its prospect of quick returns. "This was the genesis of the Société d'Entreprises Commerciales du Congo Belge (SEDEC for short) which from 1917 proceeded to make handsome profits out of the purchase and export of palm kernels, and the sale in the Congo of European merchandise." [13]

Further expansion of Lever's African operations came from the

12. *Ibid.,* p. 180.
13. *Ibid.,* p. 235.

company's involvement in shipping. The West African merchant trade was a highly profitable business during World War I, as produce could be bought cheaply on the Coast and sold dearly in England. But sea transport was scarce and expensive. In addition, the West African sea route was dominated by one company— Elder Dempster's.

By 1916 Lever's had made up their minds to go into shipping themselves. Their first move was to bring their steamer the *Kulambangra* from the Pacific for the Coast trade, but they had much larger future plans than that. If Lever's were to be independent of Elder Dempster's, four or five steamers would be necessary. Ships were expensive to buy but the profits on shipping were very high. Over and above any immediate profits, however, Lever's would be assured of carrying capacity to deal with their exports to Africa and their raw material imports from Africa.[14]

Lever's discounted the risk that Dempster's would retaliate by entering the soap-making business; and thus secured six ships for the West African trade. After only eighteen months of operation the venture was judged to be highly successful financially and was fully complementary to other established Lever activities. According to a company spokesman, the fleet enabled the company to secure raw materials that would not otherwise have come forward; and thus helped to keep down the prices of raw materials. And company warehouses on the Coast which had been blocked up before acquiring the fleet were thus able to continue with their trading activities.

All along, competition among metropolitan processors for oils and fats had been quite intense as in addition to the soap makers, margarine manufacturers were "bidding furiously" for vegetable oils. The Dutch firm, Margarine Unie, had also started its own plantation production and trading activities on the Coast. The United Africa Company was the product of a merger of the major firms trading on the Coast; and after the metropolitan merger between Lever's and Margarine Unie to create the present Unilever, Unie's West African interests became a part of United Africa

14. *Ibid.,* p. 237.

Company. This company served to eliminate previous intense competition that characterized West African trade and its more or less monopoly position gave it a great advantage in establishing new lines of activity. Soon the company was engaged in a wide range of activities which "included shipping, river and motor transport, oil palm and rubber plantations, mining royalties, cold storage depots, automobile and agricultural machinery agencies, bakeries, cotton ginning, tank installations, and timber concessions, not only in Africa but elsewhere." According to Wilson, the company's "management scorned no area and no decent business which would help its profits." [15] These came to be a substantial part of the Unilever enterprise. In the early years after World War II when manufacturing in Europe was slowly recovering, the company's plantation and trading subsidiaries "were providing between one-third and one-half of Unilever's total profits, and perhaps one-quarter of total turnover." [16]

The post-World War II period has marked a new phase in the company's activities in the plantation economies, as a result of changes associated with political developments. In West Africa, the company lost its trading importance as the governments in many countries set up statutory produce-marketing boards. In the Congo, the company's plantations suffered from the political turmoil there. And so "legislation, competition and social change combined to demand new policies for the United Africa Company." The result was further diversification of its activities. In British and French West Africa, the company has entered new areas of production and services (timber in Nigeria and Ghana, for example) where it could supply needed capital and skills or where it could supply capital and its own knowledge of marketing conditions in partnership with other European firms with technical knowledge for manufacturing commodities (like beer, stout, and cement). The company's own Niger River Transport is now a common carrier for government agencies and other firms in addition to carrying company raw materials. And its Palm Line ships carry competitive freight of timber and produce of the government

15. *Ibid.*, Vol. II, p. 324.
16. Charles Wilson, *Unilever, 1945–1965*, p. 214.

marketing boards to Europe and elsewhere. The same general pattern has been in evidence in East Africa as well.

As the political climate in the Third World has changed, Unilever has expanded metropolitan investment at a faster rate than it has its investment in Third World countries. And today "The proportion of Unilever's total capital invested in the developing countries is small compared with that invested in Europe. Even so, in absolute terms, the volume is large." The company's plantation activities are still quite substantial. In 1965 it had a total of 224,217 acres under cultivation and employed 37,000 people in plantation work.[17]

The history of Unilever reveals some of the factors, at the firm level, accounting for the ascendancy of metropolitan enterprise in plantation production and trade. We saw that the political environment was critical in the establishment of plantations in the Congo, in the company's decision to undertake trading activities in West Africa, and in the diversification out of trading in the postwar period. From the beginning when the decision to engage in plantation production resulted from high prices for raw materials and fear of being squeezed by middlemen, volatile markets and elimination of weak competitors have been important at various points along the way. And interindustry economies stimulated the company's shipping, river and road transport, and other directly allied activities at first; more recently, they led to partnership ventures with other European firms into less allied activities.

Similar forces have been at work in the histories of other metropolitan plantation enterprises, as is revealed in the story of United Fruit, the Firestone story and that of other rubber manufacturers, in the development of metropolitan raw-sugar production, and in the evolution of tea production and trade in Asia.[18] The general pattern emerging from the interplay of historical forces has been one of increasingly large concerns becoming more

17. *Ibid.*, p. 268.
18. See Charles D. Kepner, *op. cit.*; Alfred Lief, *op. cit.*, Chapters 11 and 21; and H. and R. Wolf, *Rubber—A Story of Glory and Greed* (New York, 1936), pp. 238 and 241–48; and *Tate & Lyle Times International.*

and more vertically integrated at first and diversifying into new activities later.

TATE & LYLE

Technological change and corresponding scale economies have reinforced for certain enterprises the pattern of vertical integration and diversification. This was not so obvious in the Unilever example but was important in sugar and banana production and trade. Tate & Lyle, the giant British sugar-refining concern, resulted from the amalgamation of two family refining companies "to cease competing and to fight the foreigner by forming the biggest sugar company of the day. . . . One raw sugar buying department eliminated competition and permitted the carrying out of considerably bigger deals." [19] In the metropolis, the firm subsequently cashed in on the transporting of sugar after the packet sugar trade began in 1924. Similarly, as the refining business expanded, the firm acquired lighterage companies. "Prior to this all lighterage had been contracted out and, as tonnage had been increasing, it was felt that it would be to the Company's advantage to have some measure of control over this side of the business." [20] Limitations of market size after a while made further expansion of refining increasingly difficult and this led to raw-sugar plantation production in the West Indies beginning in the 1930's. By the 1950's, the company had acquired so much experience in internal distribution in the United Kingdom that it entered the general transport business.

During this time also the technology of bulk shipment had arrived on the scene. And this affected the company in two ways. The rapid growth of delivery of bulk and liquid sugar resulted in the acquisition of a fleet of specially designed road tankers for distribution in the United Kingdom. And the transition from bag to bulk shipment of raw sugar led the company into the shipping business for the first time: "bulk carriers were specially built for Sugar Line and the service that they provided exceeded expectations." In the 1950's too, the company acquired control of sugar-

19. *Tate & Lyle Times International,* January 1969, p. 5.
20. *Ibid.,* April 1969, p. 7.

refining interests in Canada. As a vice chairman of the company recently said, "We are a classic example of a company which, having the vitality to grow, has been forced into overseas investment if it is to expand in its own line of business." [21] As the company's raw-sugar plantation investments expanded, it found it profitable to acquire engineering firms for the manufacture of sugar machinery. In addition, a technical services company was established "firstly designed to serve the refineries and other parts of the Group, but rapidly giving promise of its later development into a world-wide service for sugar interests everywhere." [22] And more recently, since 1965, an even higher stage of vertical integration was reached with the acquisition of United Molasses, an established company one-third the size of the previous group with worldwide control of molasses trading. Soon after, the firm acquired Farrows Ltd., leading specialists in irrigation, whose know-how "will undoubtedly complement future projects throughout the world which T.L.T.S. hopes to tackle." [23]

In the plantation economies, Tate & Lyle's expansion of plantation activities was largely a result of technological change in raw-sugar production but also of interindustry economies. Increasing capital demands of modern factories for processing raw sugar gave an advantage to firms with subsidiaries engaged in manufacture of factory equipment and eliminated many obsolete factories and companies operating these. In 1937, the year after Tate & Lyle began sugar production in Trinidad, there were eleven factories owned by nine different companies in that country. Since that time the Tate & Lyle subsidiary, Caroni Ltd., has absorbed most of these companies and at present there are only two small sugar producers other than Caroni—one being a government-owned estate. Caroni now cultivates some 25,000 hectares of cane and produces 200,000 tons of sugar—92 per cent of total Trinidad output—in four factories.[24] In addition, the company is engaged

21. Sir Peter Runge, "The Case for Overseas Investment," *Tate & Lyle Times International,* October 1969, p. 7.
22. *Ibid.,* p. 4.
23. *Ibid.,* January 1970, p. 4. T.L.T.S. stands for Tate & Lyle Technical Services which was mentioned earlier.
24. Jean-Claude Giacottino, "L'économie trinidadienne," *Les Cahiers d'Outre Mer,* April–June 1969, pp. 125–26.

in allied activities such as bulk storage and shipment of sugar, wharfage, and rum manufacture.

The Tate & Lyle experience is simply an extension of the general dynamics of enterprise growth revealed by the more detailed history of Unilever. In sugar manufacture and trade, the significance of technological change was very pronounced during the last few decades. Because this technological change was highly capital-intensive and involved considerable economies of scale, the larger metropolitan concerns were able to eliminate weaker competitors in plantation production and to secure certain linkages associated with that production. This experience can be generalized with the hypothesis that the growth of metropolitan plantation enterprise is enhanced by rapid rates of technological change in plantation production and trade.

3. Size, organization, and structure of modern plantation enterprises

Many metropolitan plantation enterprises are very large concerns. The dynamics of growth which they have enjoyed in the past and which continues at present has resulted in giant complexes which in many instances dominate the economies of particular plantation economies. We saw earlier that much of the growth which these enterprises have achieved was linked in one way or another with their initial engagement in plantation production. It is, of course, impossible to determine how much of their growth derived from this source because of the lack of data and the general impreciseness of the linkages we have identified. Nevertheless it seems reasonable to speculate that a substantial share of the expansion they have achieved was stimulated by plantation activity.

Some appreciation of the size of some of these enterprises can be gained by comparing their annual sales and profits with relevant national aggregates of associated plantation economies. This is done in Table 5.1, on the following page, for selected companies and countries. The table gives data on national income, value of total exports, and the value of plantation exports for each of six countries in a recent year in comparison with data on sales and net profits before taxes for four associated enterprises. A word of

Table 5.1   Big companies and small countries: A comparison of company activity data and national aggregates for selected plantation economies, 1967–68 (*millions of dollars*)

| | Company | | Country | | |
| | *Annual sales* | *Net income* | *National income* | *Exports* | |
				Total	*Plantation*[a]
Firestone	2,131.4	127.0			
Liberia			175.0	85.0	38.0
Booker	198.6	11.5			
Guyana			162.5	108.2	31.8
Tate & Lyle	549.2	27.1			
Jamaica			787.2	219.5	44.9
Trinidad			569.0	466.2	24.2
United Fruit	488.9	53.1			
Panama			634.0	95.2	55.6
Honduras			649.0	181.4	85.4

Source: All Country data except Liberia from International Monetary Fund, *International Financial Statistics*, January 1970. Liberia data are from various official sources. Company data are from respective company annual reports.
[a] Plantation exports refer to exports of the commodity produced in the particular country by the relevant metropolitan enterprise.

caution seems in order before proceeding to comment on the table. Sales and net income of companies relate to their total operations (in all countries) and these total operations are not simply a direct derivative of plantation activity in the respective countries. In like manner, the national income and exports of a particular country are not simply a direct derivative of the relevant company's operations in a country, although this may be the case for plantation exports in some instances. Finally, the choices made have been to some extent guided by the desire to dramatize; even so, we have tried to use a representative range of company sizes —varying from the large Firestone complex to the medium-sized United Fruit and Tate & Lyle to the relatively small Booker McConnell organization.

The general impression given by these data is that the metropolitan enterprises are at least as large as, if not larger than, the individual plantation economies. The first two cases show the relative position of two company plantation economies. We describe Liberia and Guyana in this manner because in both these countries, much of the national economic activity (as reflected in national accounts) emanates from the presence of a single metropolitan plantation enterprise. Again it is difficult to ascertain, in any reliably quantitative fashion, what share of the national income of these countries is attributable to company presence, directly and indirectly. What is clear is that each company is of sufficient importance that changes in its operations in the relevant country are bound to affect materially the level of national income. "If Bookers sneezes, Guyana catches a cold," someone has said. The same is true of Firestone and Liberia; Colonial Refining and Fiji; and Unilever and the Solomons. The degree of dependence of these countries on a single company is one thing. The other is the fact that each company is larger than its satellite country. The companies are of course engaged in activities elsewhere (in the metropolis and in other plantation economies) and in more than just plantation activity; indeed, plantations are only a small part of the companys' over-all operations. Hence the annual turnover (sales) of each enterprise exceeds the national income of its satellite plantation economy. Firestone's annual sales are over ten times the national income of Liberia. And in spite of its large bauxite industry, Guyana's national income is a good deal less than the relatively small-sized Bookers.

In the West Indies and Central America the relative positions of countries to companies is a little more balanced. The national economies of Jamaica and Trinidad generate slightly more income per year than the revenue generated by the Tate & Lyle complex. In these cases much of the difference derives from mining activity. Without the enclave foreign-owned bauxite-alumina industry in Jamaica and the similarly placed petroleum industry in Trinidad, both these countries would fit easily into the pocket of Tate & Lyle which dominates their sugar production. Finally, in Central America, United Fruit Company comes dangerously close to being on par with Panama and Honduras in terms of annual value of economic activity. Costa Rica, for which data are not provided, has about the same level of national income as Panama. When it is realized that another metropolitan enterprise, Standard Fruit

Company, is present in Honduras and Costa Rica, the position of these economies relative to metropolitan plantation enterprise is somewhat worse than is suggested by data shown in the table.

The size of these enterprises relative to the plantation economies poses many important problems. The question of negotiating strength in government-company dealings and transactions is an obvious one. Another is the problem of the pricing of intra-company transactions, as occurs when Firestone takes rubber out of Liberia or United Fruit "exports" bananas from Central America.[25] An associated difficulty is the question of the appropriate assessment of taxes payable to government in the plantation economies. As Norman Girvan recently pointed out, size is not the only problem to be considered; equally important is the asymmetry of dependence reflected in the inordinate dependence of one country on a single company but not of any one company on a single country. These and other related problems have a fundamental bearing on the development capacity of individual plantation economies.[26]

Some indication of how metropolitan plantation enterprises have achieved the size they exhibit at present can be gained from an examination of the extent and nature of their activities. Tate & Lyle is used here to illustrate the general case. It is a good example of what was originally a metropolitan firm concerned with processing plantation output—in this case sugar refining—up to just over thirty years ago. The decision of the firm to engage in plantation sugar production in the late 1930's subsequently sparked its activities in shipping, engineering, molasses trading, and much else. The complexity and range of its activities at present have to be drastically summarized to fit into Table 5.2.

25. The latter case has been examined by R. A. LaBarge, "The Imputation of Values to Intra-Company Exports—The Case of Bananas," *Social and Economic Studies,* June 1961; and the IMF Country notes in the IMF, *International Financial Statistics* indicate that the Fund regards the official banana-export values of these countries as undervalued.

26. See Norman Girvan, "Multinational Corporations and Dependent Underdevelopment in Mineral-Export Economies," *Social and Economic Studies,* December 1970; and, on the general problem of size, Dudley Seers, "Big Companies and Small Countries: A Practical Proposal," *Kyklos,* Vol. XVI, Fasc. 4, 1963, pp. 599–608.

Table 5.2 The Tate & Lyle group holding company: Tate & Lyle, Limited (London)

A. U.K. subsidiaries

Subsidiaries	Activities
1. *Sugar Refining*	
Tate & Lyle Refineries Limited	Sugar refiners, London and Liverpool
John Walker & Company (Sugar Refiners) Limited	Sugar refiners, Greenock
Merton Grove Company Limited	Syrup and treacle manufacturers, Liverpool
Millwall Sugars Limited	Manufacturers of industrial sugars, London
2. *Transport and Handling*	
Greenock Bulk Handling Company Limited	Raw sugar handling, Greenock
Huskisson Transit Company Limited	Raw sugar handling, Liverpool
Tate & Lyle (Ulster) Limited	Refined sugar distributors, N. Ireland
Tate & Lyle Transport Limited	Road haulage
John Walker Sugar Transport Limited	Road haulage
Silver Roadways Limited	Road haulage
3. *Shipping*	
Sugar Line Limited	Shipowners (11 bulk sugar carriers)
Silvertown Services Lighterage Limited	Lighterage contractors
Sugar Line Terminals Limited	Bulk sugar loading installations, W. Indies
Kentships Limited	Ship brokers and agents
Athel Line Limited	Shipowners (21 tankers, bulk carriers and liners)
Athel Marine Insurance Company Limited	Shipping insurance

Source: Adapted from *Tate & Lyle Report and Accounts, 1966* and supplemented with data and information in subsequent annual reports. Except those indicated, all companies are wholly owned subsidiaries of Tate & Lyle Limited.

Subsidiaries	Activities

4. Molasses Trading

The United Molasses Company Limited	Molasses purchase, shipping, storage, and distribution; shipowners; alcohol manufacture and distribution

5. Engineering

A. & W. Smith & Company Limited	Sugar machinery manufacture and engineering
Foundry Plant & Machinery Limited	Selling agents for A. & W. Smith & Company Limited
R. G. Ross & Son Limited	Selling agents for A. & W. Smith & Company Limited
The Tills Engineering Company Limited	Bulk storage and pneumatic conveyor installation
Richards (Shipbuilders) Limited	Shipbuilders
W. J. Yarwood & Sons Limited	Selling agents
Mirrless Watson Company Limited	Sugar machinery manufacture and engineering

6. Miscellaneous

Tate & Lyle Technical Services Limited	Technical consultants
Galban Lobo (England) Limited	
Tate & Lyle Farms Limited	Arable farmers, sugar beet producers, and developers
Tate & Lyle Investments Limited	Holding company for overseas investments

B. Overseas subsidiaries

Subsidiaries	Country	Per cent holding	Activities

7. Sugar Refining

Subsidiaries	Country	Per cent holding	Activities
Canada & Dominion Sugar Company Limited	Canada	56.42	Sugar refiners, beet processors
Rhodesia Sugar Refineries Limited	Rhodesia	50.13	Sugar refiners
The Zambia Sugar Company Limited	Zambia	57.81	Sugar refiners
Tate & Lyle (Nigeria) Limited	Nigeria		Refined sugar distributors

Table 5.2   (Continued)

Subsidiaries	Country	Per cent holding	Activities
8. Raw Sugar Production			
The West Indies Sugar Company Limited	Jamaica	90.63	Sugarcane, raw sugar, and rum products
Caroni Limited	Trinidad	70.59	
Chirundu Sugar Estates Limited	Rhodesia	90.03	
Belize Sugar Industries Limited		99.99	
Plantations Limited	British	99.99	
The Colonial Agricultural Development Company Limited	Honduras	99.99	
Zambia Sugar Company Limited	Zambia	57.81	
9. Molasses Trading			
Pacific Molasses Company	U.S.A.		Molasses purchase, transport, storage, and distribution
Canada West Indies Molasses Company Limited	Canada		
Caribbean Molasses Company Limited	Guyana		
Caribbean Molasses Company (Jamaica) Limited	Jamaica		
Caribbean Molasses Company (Trinidad) Limited	Trinidad		
Companhia Exportadora de Melacos Limited	Mozambique		
Pure Cane Molasses Company (Durban) (Pty.) Limited	South Africa		
Nederlandsche Mélasse Handel Maatschappij N.V.	Holland		Molasses purchase, transport, storage, and distribution
Mieles Del Pacifico S.A.	Mexico		
Pacific Molasses Transport Company	U.S.A.		
S.A. Tank Installation de Mélasse Continentale (Tameco)	Belgium		
The Indian Molasses Company Private Limited	India		
P. T. Java Transport & Trading Company	Indonesia		
Compagnie des Mélasses S.A. (Comessa)	Switzerland	51.00	
The Mauritius Molasses Company Limited	Mauritius	66.67	
Societé des Mélasses du Niari	Republic of the Congo	51.00	

Subsidiaries	Country	Per cent holding	Activities
10. *Miscellaneous*			
Tate & Lyle (Norway) A/S	Norway		Selling agency for Tate & Lyle Limited
Eastern Sugar Trading Corporation	U.S.A.	94.50	Trading on commodity exchange, N.Y.
Unital (Trinidad) Limited	Trinidad	70.59	Import and export agents for Caroni Limited
Wisco Wharves Limited	Jamaica	90.63	Wharf owners, lighter men, and shipping agents
Sugar Marketing (Pvt.) Limited	Rhodesia	42.10	Sugar marketers and distributors
Storage Limited	British Honduras		Wharfingers, lightermen, and shipping agents
European Sugars S.A.	Belgium	66.67	Sugar refining, Europe
11. *Associated Companies*			
The Bagasse Products Company Limited	United Kingdom	34.59	
East African Storage Company Limited	Kenya	50.00	
Panelboard Pty. Limited	Australia	50.00	
Paktank Storage Company Limited	United Kingdom	50.00	

There we see an agro-industrial complex that engages in numerous production and service activities related directly or indirectly to plantation production. It manufactures inputs for plantation production, processes and distributes the plantation output and by-products, and provides supplementary services of all kinds. The image is one of a vertically integrated combine operating in numerous countries of the world, with its headquarters in the United Kingdom.

The relative importance of the various activities of the company can be gauged from the following tabulation which shows turnover (sales) and profits before taxes in thousands of pounds sterling for 1968:[27]

	Turnover	Profit
Raw-sugar production		
West Indies and British Honduras	20,669	98
Refining and distribution		
United Kingdom	127,166	3,121
Canada	18,672	3,691
Africa	6,064	402
Molasses trading, storage,		
and distribution	36,835	1,923
Shipping	11,652	3,820
Engineering and miscellaneous		
United Kingdom	9,708	313
Overseas	2,484	53
TOTAL	233,250	13,421

Because of the degree of vertical integration of the complex, the profit earned on any one activity may be inversely related to that of another. For example, a low profit on raw-sugar production resulting from low prices for raw sugar may result later in a higher profit on refining, for which raw sugar is an input. What data are available suggest that a change in profit on raw sugar in a given year is associated with an inverse change in profit on refining in the following year. But the association is tentative and is complicated by several considerations, such as government intervention and stocks.[28] For judging the relative importance of activities, the

27. From *Tate & Lyle Directors' Report and Accounts 1968* (London), p. 9.
28. In explaining the 1964 fall in the U.K. refining profit, for example, the chairman of the board reported to shareholders that "the behaviour of the raw sugar market in 1964 did not exhibit the features which in 1963 gave exceptional opportunities for profitable trading. In the Home Trade sector a heavy carry-over of trade stocks from 1963 resulted in reduced sales and as operating margins were held substantially unchanged the profit reflects considerably higher costs" (*Tate & Lyle Report and Accounts 1964*, p. 8).

turnover figures are more appropriate. Still, plantation activity does not exceed very much the shipping and engineering and miscellaneous categories to which it gave rise, and it is substantially less than the complementary molasses trading, storage, and distribution recently added. The fact is that although plantation production stimulated engagement in other activities, at present this aspect of the firm's operations is relatively small. It reminds us of the familiar agriculture-economic development relationship in the growth of an economy: agriculture may be important in stimulating the growth of an economy but declines in relative importance once the stimulus takes effect.

It remains now to consider how such a large and varied complex, spread over so much geographical space, is actually held together for purposes of management. The answer is simply that the board of directors of the parent company makes all important long-term decisions relating to each subsidiary company and the group of companies as a whole. But the day-to-day running of each subsidiary is left to its own board of directors. The general position for this type of complex has been described by the chairman of the parent board of Booker McConnell:

. . . Responsibility for the management of each operating company is placed fairly and squarely upon the shoulders of its own Board. . . . But in fact these are not independent Public Companies. The members of the Group Parent Board have to remember that . . . they, and they alone, are ultimately responsible to Bookers shareholders—the owners of the business—for the stewardship of their property and for the success or failure of the business.

Therefore the Group Parent Board explicitly retain authority in certain vital matters. These are the appointment, dismissal and emoluments of Directors of Subsidiary companies; the sale or purchase of assets other than in the normal course of business; capital expenditure; borrowing powers; the objects of the business; and the broad policy and ethics of the business; also—as an umbrella—"any matter thought by the Directors of the Subsidiary Company concerned significantly to affect the interests of shareholders." [29]

29. J. M. Campbell, "Postscript," to *Bookers Sugar,* Supplement to 1954 Accounts of Booker Brothers-McConnell and Co., Ltd., pp. 87–88. For a more detailed description of the administrative organization of similar enterprises, see Alfred D. Chandler, Jr., *Strategy and Struc-*

Basically, then, decisions about growth and expansion of any individual subsidiary and the group of companies as a whole rests with the directors of the parent company and cannot therefore be made by those responsible for the enterprise's activities in the plantation economies with which we are here concerned. This is worthy of special note because of a recent trend to appoint nationals of plantation societies to directorships of these plantation companies, and the impression given by the firm's public relations agencies is usually that more discretion and control is being transferred to the people of plantation society. From the above quotation, it is clear that nothing could be further from the truth.

4. Political and economic aspects of enterprise operations

The characteristics of multinationalism and vertical integration noted above in the Tate & Lyle example are typical of all metropolitan plantation enterprises. The size and multinational character of these firms give them great political power and influence, not only in the plantation economies but in the metropolis and international spheres as well. Numerous examples of the exercise of this power can be cited. In Fiji the Colonial Sugar Refining Company is regarded as "the other government." The Liberian government was in hock to Firestone for forty years until recently when it liquidated a loan by the company. And we know that "he who pays the piper calls the tune." In addition, the United States government turned to Firestone when it wanted to establish an airfield in Liberia to provide it with a link to the war theater of Europe during World War II. The company obliged. Unilever plays an important part in Congo affairs. The term "banana republics" applied to the Central American countries is a reflection of the political power of United Fruit in that area. The United States government is said to rely heavily on that company for information on the Central American republics; and, in at least one instance, has intervened to depose a government which threatened to nationalize

---

ture: Chapters in the History of Industrial Enterprise (Cambridge, Massachusetts, 1962). The economic and administrative organization of individual plantation subsidiaries are described in detail in Appendix II of this study.

the company's assets. That was the Arbenz government in Guatemala in 1956. Bookers has been, and continues to be, very influential in the political destiny of Guyana.

Tate & Lyle had sufficient political power to mobilize British opinion against the Labour government's proposals to nationalize sugar refining in that country during the period 1949–52. "Mr. Cube," the company's symbol depicting a David and Goliath encounter, emerged from his campaign with greater political power than the British prime minister. Some idea of the bankruptcy of political leadership in plantation society is given by the fact that in this battle with metropolitan government, metropolitan enterprise was able to win the support of colonial government in plantation society. In a review of its history, the company boasts that "the head of the Jamaica Labour party, Mr. (now Sir Alexander) Bustamante, weighed in with a cable threatening to call strikes throughout Jamaica if we were nationalised." [30] At present, Tate & Lyle still wields considerable political power in the constitutionally independent dominions of Jamaica and Trinidad. In 1969 a threat by the company to close down its Jamaican operations forced the government there to accede to the company's earlier unheeded demands for greater mechanization of field operations and the establishment of bulk loading facilities. And official West Indian delegations to international sugar conferences are partly led by Tate & Lyle personnel.

The general pattern, revealed by these examples, is one which provides metropolitan enterprise with full information about, authority over, and control of government policy and administration in plantation society and which in return keeps the people and government of plantation society ignorant of metropolitan enter-

30. "A Brief History of Tate & Lyle: Part III—Mr. Cube's Campaign," *Tate & Lyle Times International,* July 1969, p. 4. On the same page there is a reproduction of a newspaper column "Commonwealth Commentary," with the headline HANDS OFF OUR SUGAR by W. A. Bustamante. Mr. Bustamante may have had shares in Tate & Lyle; if so, the "our" would be appropriate in his private personal capacity. The impression given, however, is that "our" meant the people in Jamaica, for he was writing as the "Jamaican Minister of Communications and veteran West Indies labour leader" which is the way the article describes him. In that event, his imagination can be described only as wild.

prise activity, with no control over it. This is the typical balance of power between plantation society and metropolitan enterprise.

The multinational character of these enterprises derives from the geographic spread of their operations and the typical pattern of management control. The normal pattern is one with the main company head-quarters in a metropolitan country where product elaboration and distribution are carried out and where allied high-value production and service activities are located; plantation and some allied operations in the Third World countries; and other product elaboration and distribution in other metropolitan countries. This multinational dimension gives these enterprises a kind of United Nations character in the sphere of international relations and politics. Metropolitan governments rely quite heavily on them in framing and implementing economic and political policies relating to the Third World countries. After all the enterprises have an infrastructure for marshaling knowledge about these countries which metropolitan governments are able to utilize at little cost. The enterprises have been in the Third World since long before these countries gained "independence."

Vertical integration arose naturally in the growth of metropolitan plantation enterprises. Their initial involvement with plantation products took them "backward" to plantation production and, subsequently, further backward to manufacture of plantation inputs and forward to allied activities like shipping. The degree of vertical integration varies from one enterprise to another and is difficult to measure precisely in the absence of data. Although the output at one level of enterprise activity may be used as an input at another level, the total output at a lower level may or may not enter as inputs at higher levels as part or all may be sold to other firms. In these instances, profit maximization at the lower level is viewed as an end in itself. This is often the case with plantation output and metropolitan processing. Examples of this are Unilever's plantations, which produce such a small share of oil requirements for processing by the company that its plantation output is normally sold in the open market. On the other hand, the output at lower levels may go entirely as inputs at a higher level. This is normally the case with shipping, where the company is geared to carrying its own raw materials, and with metropolitan distribution, where the transport and marketing network is geared directly to moving company produce. In these instances, profits at higher levels in the farm-consumer chain depend ultimately on the flow of product from lower levels.

Tate & Lyle and Booker McConnell are somewhat representative of the two general cases just described. Booker McConnell does no processing of plantation output, so that much of its activities relate to production and distribution tied directly to its plantation output. These include manufacture of rum and other spirits, shipping, engineering, and, to a lesser extent, shopkeeping. The firm evolved from initial merchant activity and got involved in plantation production by the acquisition of sugar estates from planters indebted to the early merchant enterprise. The shopkeeping operations are therefore somewhat independent though these have benefited from extra sales generated by plantation activity. In 1968, shopkeeping accounted for slightly more than half of the annual turnover of £83 million; and the company reported that inter-group transactions for the complex as a whole were of the order of £12 million. This means that about one-seventh of the total business of the enterprise was generated by demand within the complex itself. If we exclude shopkeeping from the total turnover, the share of inter-group transactions would be close to one-third. This reflects a high degree of internal interdependence between different levels of enterprise operations. The same pattern applies to firms like United Fruit and Standard Fruit for which shipping and distribution are tied directly to plantation production. But where there is a high degree of metropolitan product elaboration, as with Unilever and Tate & Lyle, the degree of internal interdependence is likely to be much less.

The nature of operations of these enterprises is reflected in their asset structure. We need briefly to examine the structure of enterprise investment because it strongly influences decisions concerning production and resource use. Unfortunately, we were not able to get data which would show the patterns for the two kinds of vertically integrated enterprise that have been identified. Some aggregative type data are available for Booker McConnell and United Fruit but not for any of the firms with a relatively low degree of internal interdependence. Table 5.3 shows the available

Table 5.3   Booker   McConnell   Ltd.:   distribution   of   capital   employed and profits, by operations and territory, 1968 (*thousands of pounds*)

	Capital	Profit
A. Operations		
Tropical agriculture (mainly sugar)	18,925	956
Shopkeeping (wholesale, retail and mail order distribution and related manufacturing)	11,042	1,641
Rum and other spirits (distillation, manufacture and marketing of rum, liquors and other spirits)	6,183	800
Shipping (ocean and coastal shipping, trawling in Caribbean, wharehousing, and stevedoring)	3,921	738
Engineering (sugar machinery, mining equipment, hydraulic presses and pumps)	6,072	416
Other operations	6,037	853
Total	52,180	5,404
B. Territories		
Caribbean (plantation economy) (mainly Guyana, Jamaica, and Trinidad)	29,330	2,631
Zambia	2,665	794
Canada	1,658	146
Britain (metropolis)	18,526	1,710
Total	52,179	5,281

Source: *Booker McConnell Report and Accounts, 1968*, pp. 20–21.
Profit figures are before interest and taxation. Totals in (A) and (B) may differ owing to omission in (B) of "other overseas."

data for Booker McConnell. It indicates that enterprise investment in plantations and in plantation economies is a high percentage of total investment. In terms of operations, plantations account for about 37 per cent of total investment, whereas in terms of territory, 56 per cent of capital employed is located in the plantation economies. It is not surprising that such an enterprise would want to have political control of plantation society, given the fact that such a high percentage of its investment is tied up there. And for the company as a whole, a high percentage of profits are earned on its Third World operations—about 65 per cent of the total.

The available data for United Fruit Company are summarized in the table below which gives investment in fixed assets and the book value of these (net of accumulated depreciation) for 1967, in thousands of U.S. dollars: [31]

	Fixed investment	Net book value
Lands	10,722	6,484
Houses and buildings	61,927	26,355
Cultivations	63,005	29,755
Equipment	96,651	42,878
Railways, tramways, and rolling stock	38,174	9,583
Wharves, boats, etc.	7,222	4,186
Sugar mills and refineries	18,631	8,539
Steamships	116,646	58,289
Total	412,978	186,069

These data give us an indication of the relative importance of various operations in the United Fruit complex. The figures are too aggregative to show the share of direct plantation activity in the total asset structure. Lands and Cultivations fall clearly in that category. So would a part of Houses and buildings and a part of Equipment, and if we assigned half the values of each of them to plantations, the resulting plantation share of total investment would be over one-third. It is worthy of note that Steamships alone account for some 28 per cent of total investment; and if we include the associated figures for Wharves, etc., and Railways, etc., the share of transporting plantation produce to metropolitan markets rises to almost 40 per cent, which is more than that invested in direct plantation activity. This means that insofar as the company relies on its own plantation production to provide car-

31. From *United Fruit Company Annual Report 1967* (Boston), p. 24.

goes for its transportation network, production on the land must be geared to utilize fully this capacity for the investment to pay off.

This leads naturally to consideration of the pattern of landholding and use. The table below summarizes the position on this in 1967 for each of the four Central American countries where United Fruit operates plantations: [32]

	Total land owned or leased by UFCO (thousand acres)	Total cultivation (bananas, etc.)
Costa Rica	261,500	73,900
Guatemala	78,200	9,600
Honduras	216,400	43,400
Panama	125,700	44,000
Total	681,800	170,900

On average, cultivated land represents only 25 per cent of the total land owned or leased by the company. This high rate of underutilization is no doubt a reflection of the low cost of holding land, and of the need for maintaining as much flexibility as possible for output adjustment at the plantation level, in order to guarantee a product flow adequate for full capacity utilization at the transport level where much fixed investment is concentrated. More of this in the next chapter.

The last economic aspect of enterprise operations to be examined here is the general pattern of distribution of value-added between the plantation economies on the one hand and metropolitan economy on the other. Again, only approximations are possible because data are not available in a form directly useful to us. The best data we have are from United Fruit Company reports. Total sales of the company in 1968 were of the order of $510 million (U.S.) but not all of this was from the sale of bananas. We have added the figure for bananas ($322 million) and that for transportation ($39 million) to arrive at a sales figure of $361 million, which is, more or less, directly comparable with the value of total

32. United Fruit Company, *The United Fruit Company in Middle America* (Company leaflet, Boston, n.d.), p. 1.

company payments in Third World countries of $160 million. All of these countries together, therefore, received only 45 per cent of the disposal value of the commodities produced with their resources. The value-added accruing to the company, and by extension to metropolitan economy, is greater than that accruing to plantation economy. Table 5.4 shows how company payments were distributed among Third World countries, by type of payment, in 1968. Each country gets a little bit but on the whole none seem to get very much from a business whose sales in the same year stood at $510 million (U.S.). On average, payments to governments in all were only about 11 per cent or so of total payments in these countries. This looks like a very small percentage indeed. About one-third or so of the total payments go to labor as wages and one-fifth or so represents company purchase of materials and merchandise in the plantation economies.

We cannot ascertain how well the United Fruit example represents the general plantation-metropolitan shares of value-added. But we suspect that it may overstate the plantation economy benefits for some cases, particularly those where more elaborate metropolitan processing is involved, for example, sugar, and oils and fats products. Much more research is needed in this area to determine more precisely how much of the development potential deriving from plantation activity is leaked out of Third World countries because the distribution and elaboration of plantation output is controlled by metropolitan enterprise. But for this research to proceed, Third World governments will have to demand more company information than is now available.

5. A summary view and glimpses of the future

From our examination of the historical process of growth of metropolitan plantation enterprise, we identified dynamic elements deriving from the cumulative effect of at least seven identifiable economies. These seven types of economies come into play at various stages in the development of the enterprise, and most tend to be automatic once a decision is made to engage in a major activity. The thesis presented here is that the most critical decision is the one to engage in plantation production and that once this deci-

Table 5.4 United Fruit Company: payments to governments, employees, and suppliers in third world countries, 1968 (*thousands of U.S. dollars*)

	Co-lombia	Costa Rica	Guate-mala	Hon-duras	Pana-ma	Jamaica Nicaragua Mexico Salvador Ecuador British Honduras (combined)	Total
Payments to governments in 1968							
Income taxes		2,554		6,233	5,238	57	14,082
Import duties	15	478	92	217	251	81	1,134
Export duties		208	130	180	172		690
Other federal and municipal taxes	43	340	107	820	120	542	1,972
Railway transportation and wharfage			40				40
Total	58	3,580	369	7,450	5,781	680	17,918
Payments to employees and suppliers in 1968							
Payrolls							
Ordinary wages	455	13,048	4,770	20,038	14,076	3,627	56,014

Social benefit payments	354	1,794	1,334	3,510	1,755	620	9,367
Workman's compensation	2	316	172		262		752
Retirement fund contributions	7	72	47	236	112	26	500
Purchase of agricultural products							
Bananas	15,601	505	696	3,744	7,345		27,891
Other (cacao, sugarcane, plantains, cottonseed, palm oil, livestock, etc.)		4,160	13	201	106	1,633	6,113
Merchandise and materials purchased	6,371	2,443	4,193	3,817	10,115	3,850	30,789
Transportation							
Railway		48	532	430	180		1,190
Air and other	32	87	149	284	186	130	868
Rentals including aerial spray							
Contracts	317	243	117	282	379	73	1,411
Utility services	24	167	23	47	130	109	500
Other miscellaneous payments	1,711	1,748	292	161	848	1,583	6,343
Total	24,874	24,631	12,338	32,750	35,494	11,651	141,738
Grand total	24,932	28,211	12,707	40,200	41,275	12,331	159,656

Source: The United Fruit Company, *The United Fruit Company in Middle America* (Company pamphlet, Boston, n.d.), p. 2.

sion is made and implemented, successive rounds of the economies described pile up and stimulate a seemingly never-ending enterprise expansion. None of the economies described are new in the sense that they are being noticed here for the first time. Development economists have long been aware of these complementarities in the growth of an economy. What is new is that we here recognize, perhaps for the first time, that part of the growth potential of the plantation economies has been canalized by metropolitan enterprises and has resulted in a growth of metropolitan enterprises to a stage where at present many of these have a larger annual turnover than the total output of many plantation economies.

The size of many of these enterprises is such that they wield great power and influence in political affairs, not only of plantation society but of metropolitan and international as well. The nature of their operations is such that they profoundly influence resource use and the welfare of people in the Third World. These are matters which the next two chapters explore at some length. The rest of the present chapter looks into the future, through the eyes of spokesmen for these companies, to see what can be expected in relation to further growth of these enterprises and the presently skewed balance of power between them and the Third World.

A vice chairman of Tate & Lyle Ltd. speaks:

We are conscious of having an international expertise in sugar which nobody else can approach. . . . But our expertise is slowly but surely broadening and is being extended into other fields. . . . in my view . . . our excursions into this or that field will result in one or two major new activities which will form, as it were, additional boughs to the sturdy tree that exists already. . . . we shall prosper.[33]

And the chairman of the board of the same company, in his 1968 annual statement, looks at the future thus:

To supplement the modest growth prospects in sugar refining we are aiming to exploit other sources of growth. . . . we are applying the

33. Sir Peter Runge, *op. cit.*, p. 7.

trading and distribution skills resident in the Tate & Lyle Refineries and United Molasses Groups to analogous businesses. . . .

We shall continue to acquire diverse businesses that complement existing ones as opportunity offers.[34]

It is interesting to note here that while the same company is seeking to diversify because of the "modest growth prospects" for sugar, company spokesmen have been successful in convincing West Indian governments that they should not seek to diversify those plantation economies because sugar is a better bet than anything else. Ironically (though not surprising in view of our analysis of plantation society in Chapter 3), this has now been accepted as official policy by these governments which all devalued their currencies in 1967 in order to "save the sugar industry." [35]

But the best is yet to come. Let us listen carefully to the president of United Fruit Company delivering an address in Brussels in 1968: [36]

In the world food and fiber economy, the inescapable fact is that people are reaching farther back in the areas of production for sources of raw material and reaching out in more distant markets for the sales of finished food and fiber products.

. . . Within just a few years the multinational corporation may well emerge as one of the dominant business institutions of the world. . . .

. . . *World corporations will have to find somehow their own legal, political and commercial framework within which they can operate more effectively.*

Now listen further to his obvious contempt for the governments and peoples of the Third World. And to plans for further canalization of the development potential of these countries.

34. *Tate & Lyle Directors' Report and Accounts 1968* (London), p. 8.
35. In addition to diversification, Tate & Lyle is also gearing itself to switching to beet sugar processing in the event Britain joins the EEC and Commonwealth cane sugar thus runs into difficulty. But West Indian governments are meanwhile increasing their subsidy of the sugar industry.
36. Herbert C. Cornuelle, "The Enormous Future: An Outline to the Challenge of the Multinational Corporation," *United Fruit Company Annual Report, 1968* (Boston). Emphasis added.

Among the most important reasons for the internationalization of the multinational corporation is to increase its utility in the developing world of Latin America, Asia and Africa. *Its role in the development process becomes more urgently clear every day, as we witness the limitations and handicaps of local governments.* . . . even if local governments were strong and assistance to them plentiful, *the fact is that the enormous complexities of the development process require abilities and attributes which are as natural to the multinational corporation as they are unnatural to government.*

This sounds as if God has ordained powers and ability to the multinational enterprise which Third World peoples and governments could never achieve themselves. For if the multinational corporations have achieved these "abilities and attributes" through experience (that is, by doing), why can't Third World peoples do the same? After all United Fruit is only just over sixty years old! Finally, on enterprise and politics the United Fruit president reminds us:

There remains the question of the political impact of a large world corporation in a country such as Honduras. The United Fruit Company, for example, last year provided 11.2% of the country's taxes, 6% of its foreign exchange and 6.98% of its gross national product. It would be foolish to pretend that the company is without influence in Honduras.

And that's the way it is from the point of view of metropolitan plantation enterprise as we enter the 1970's.

The question that remains is: what is the point of view of Third World governments and peoples? Is there any evidence that they intend to counter the offensive of these enterprises so as to retain more of the benefits of development and thereby improve the material welfare of Third World peoples? The answer to this seems, on the whole, to be in the negative. If anything the trend seems to be toward making the environment as hospitable as possible for further enterprise penetration in the plantation economies.[37] We

37. In a few Third World countries economic nationalism has gained an ascendancy more recently. But there are as yet only a small number which have implemented policies in this direction, to any significant degree.

can expect, therefore, that short of revolutionary change in these societies the economic, political, and social power of metropolitan enterprise will increase and plantation society will remain dependent on them for what little development is possible within the framework of the existing institutional arrangements. Such development possibilities as are inherent in the present structural environment are considered in the next two chapters.

6

Social costs of plantations: resource misallocation in plantation economy

How resources are used in any society will influence the welfare of people who live in it in important ways. The stock of resources at any point in time, and additions to this stock over time, are a constraint on the capacity of the society to produce the goods and services desired by consumers. But, in general, shortage of resources (in the sense of physical scarcity) has not been an important constraint on development in the Third World. More important have been constraints governing how available resources are used. The analysis in the present chapter indicates that institutional factors play an inportant part in determining patterns of production and resource use in plantation economies and that, more often than not, these patterns are not representative of the best deployment of resources for the people of plantation society. By and large, the patterns of resource use that obtain in the circumstances fit best the private objectives of plantation owners but do not seem to be the best allocation for the society as a whole. To put it differently, specific distortions in the use of available resources within plantation economy are of such a kind that they result in the impoverishment of the society.

1. Considerations regarding the efficiency of resource use

At the level of any individual unit of production, certain basic decisions have to be made about what and how much is to be

produced, how to go about doing it, and when and where to buy
and sell. Decisions about these matters are influenced to a large
extent by the objectives of the decision maker—that is, what it is
that he is trying to achieve. It is indicated in the discussion of the
economic organization of plantations in Appendix II that different
types of plantation owners are likely to have different objectives
—that we would expect company plantations to be more influenced by motives of profit maximization than, say, family plantations for which family welfare and security may be more important considerations. Such differences are bound to be reflected in
the patterns of production and resource use. That the plantation
subsidiaries of metropolitan enterprise are constrained by the
product requirements of the complex as a whole and that this influences production decisions in a specific way are also indicated
there. The case of the Jamaican company plantation discussed in
Appendix II illustrates this point. We see there that requirements
of the parent company dictate that the choice of product mix at
the plantation level be restricted to sugarcane and that the objective be to maximize profits on sugar production. Similarly, we find
that on tenant plantations, the owner decides the product mix and
how factors are combined to produce a certain level of output.
Sharecroppers and share tenants in this situation make no decisions and are as closely supervised in their work as are wage laborers.

The question of efficiency of resource use can be raised at several levels. One is the degree to which plantation owners or
managers succeed in achieving the objectives they set themselves,
that is, efficiency at the narrow level of private achievement. Another level is the extent to which the actual pattern of resource use
meets the social needs of the community as a whole; it is this aspect that concerns us. A few brief considerations will set the stage
for subsequent discussion. Plantations are an important part of the
agricultural sectors of all plantation economies. But, given our
terms of reference, concern must be with allocative efficiency
within the agricultural sector as a whole, not with allocative efficiency of the firm as a firm. What is good for the firm is not necessarily good for the country where it produces. Indeed, the general
thesis advanced here is that efficient resource allocation on indi-

vidual plantation units coexists with inefficient resource allocation within plantation economies.

We can begin by setting out briefly the general efficiency conditions for the agricultural sector, in the conventional way economists do, as follows: resources are allocated most efficiently when (1) allocation within each farm equates the marginal value productivities of the resource services—that is, a unit of labor or capital should not be used to grow sugar if it can produce a greater value product in livestock; (2) resources are distributed between farms and farming areas so that marginal value productivities are equal; (3) resources are distributed between farming and other productive activities to equalize marginal value productivities; and (4) resources are allocated over time so that their discounted value products are equal. However, the problem is not quite so simple. For where we are dealing with an economy in which resources are not fully employed and where perfectly competitive systems do not exist, there will be product and factor price distortions which complicate the calculus. In all plantation situations these distortions are likely to be quite excessive. Monopsony in the labor market, imperfections in the capital market deriving from the metropolitan connections of company plantations, and monopoly of land are characteristic on the factor side of the picture; intra-company transfers, government intervention, and international and bilateral commodity agreements create distortions on the product side.

These distortions result in a divergence between private values and social values. From the point of view of the economy, the relevant value productivities to be equalized at the margin in order to achieve a socially efficient pattern of resource allocation are the social marginal value productivities. To arrive at these it is necessary to correct both input and output prices for distortions arising from the social-private divergences of values mentioned above. Normally, with plantations these divergences are quite substantial. In looking at this problem in the case of the Jamaican sugar plantation industry, for example, Brewster has argued:

The *net returns to the social economy* (as distinct from the private) from the sugar industry is its gross private return *less* repatriated profits, *less* payment for imported materials and imported equipment, *less* the net diseconomies, *less* the effective subsidy. This figure has to be even *further reduced* by discounting for the risk element.[1]

From his considerations Brewster concludes that "the true social returns are considerably smaller than the private earnings of about £18m. . . . Upon it will hinge what figure we get for income per man, income per acre and income per unit of capital invested. I suspect they will all be very, very low." [2] Thomas also has considered the question of the cost to Jamaican society of maintaining the sugar plantation industry; he indicates that this appears to be substantial.[3]

It seems not unreasonable, judging from the Jamaican experience and considering the structural dimensions of plantations as outlined in previous chapters, for us to offer the hypothesis that in general plantations create situations leading to sharp divergences between private and social values and costs. Everywhere in the plantation world we can expect to find external diseconomies arising from government services to plantations, distortions arising from the pricing of foreign exchange, problems associated with the opportunity costs of investible funds, unused land and underutilized labor, and the problem of discounting for risk and uncertainty in export trade. In earlier discussions we have referred to the universal phenomenon of shortage of land for peasant production in all plantation settings and to the general tendency for mechanization in societies with high unemployment. All these phenomena are an expression of the social-private value divergences which are characteristic of plantations. In the rest of this

1. Havelock Brewster, "The Social Economy of Sugar," *New World Quarterly*, Vol. 5, Nos. 1–2, 1969, p. 34. The net diseconomies referred to include social and economic costs of preserving the industry of which the government's decision to devalue the national currency is cited as an example.
2. *Ibid.*, p. 35.
3. Clive Thomas, "Diversification and the Burden of Sugar to Jamaica," *New World Quarterly*, Vol. 5, Nos. 1–2, 1969, pp. 43–44. Among the costs listed by Thomas are (1) the imperfections created in the capital market by plantations, (2) the indirect subsidy of plantations by peasant farmers, (3) the proliferation of government fiscal incentives to the plantation sector, and (4) the high percentage of government administrative costs attributable to the sugar industry.

chapter we shall deal specifically with a number of distortions that inhere in the plantation system. We have introduced a general discussion of these here in order to emphasize the difficulties confronting any analysis which attempts to quantify the extent of allocative inefficiencies in plantation economy.

The approach we adopt in the circumstances is one which makes a pragmatic examination of different types of plantations. The analysis is concerned with how the characteristics of each type are likely to influence the pattern of resource use, particularly in relation to the creation of product and factor price distortions and the limitations in product and factor substitutability that inhere in the system. We repeat that our concern is with efficiency of resource use for plantation economy, not for plantations.

2. Company plantations and resource-use distortions

Several aspects of company plantation operations tend to induce distortions in resource use in plantation economies. The chief ones considered in this section relate to production objectives, the high degree of specificity of fixed capital inputs, rigidities inherent in company structure, product and factor market imperfections, risk and uncertainty, and the patterns of land use.

PRODUCTION OBJECTIVES

It is generally assumed that profit maximization is the chief production motive of company plantations. We need at once to question this assumption. There at least two important reasons why profit maximization may not always be the operative principle. The first derives from a divergence of interests between directors (the decision makers) and shareholders (the owners). The second is related to the vertically integrated structure of certain plantation enterprises.

On the first, Ramachandran's studies of foreign plantation investment in Ceylon provide some useful information:

The sterling tea and rubber companies . . . nearly always had a large and scattered membership, and shareholders' control has therefore been weak. Furthermore, shareholders do not appear to have a deep insight into the operations of their companies. These are managed, for the most part, by agent-directors whose commissions vary with the quantity of tea or rubber produced. *They therefore appear to favour maximum output even if the cost of winning it is high, i.e., they seem to maximize production rather than profits.*[4]

In another connection, Ramachandran informs us that other aspects of the personal interests of directors adversely affected decisions relating to plantation production. In their capacity as agents many company directors receive secretarial fees and sales commissions which vary with sales revenue rather than with profits. Besides, many agent companies are also involved in sales of inputs and consumer goods to the plantations they manage and their profits on this business are unrelated to plantation profits. Another consideration is that "it is necessary to distinguish between the returns which a company makes on its employed capital and the returns accruing to an investor who purchases the company's shares. It is quite possible for a company to make low profits on realizable asset values, and concurrently for its shares to be good investments." [5] Because overseas plantation investment is relatively risky, these shares can usually hold their own as investments. Apparently this has been the case with Ceylon tea plantation companies, many of which should normally have been dissolved were it not for this and for the tendency to pay out an excessively high percentage of profits as dividends.

On the second point, where plantation production involves a farm-factory combination, profit maximization at the farm level is constrained by requirements at the factory level. In such circumstances we find that maximization of farm output is important to ensure an adequate raw-material flow to the factory. But there is yet another consideration here for cases with an even higher degree of vertical integration. It is that, insofar as the firm draws heavily on raw material supplies other than its own at higher levels of production and marketing, lower profits at the plantation

4. N. Ramachandran, *Foreign Plantation Investment in Ceylon 1889–1958* (Colombo, Central Bank of Ceylon, 1963), p. 170. Emphasis added.

5. *Ibid.,* p. 108.

end may result in higher over-all profits for the complex as a whole. These relationships are indicated in the following schematic representation of, say, the Tate & Lyle situation.[6]

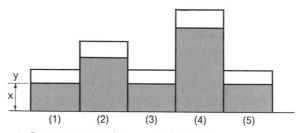

1. Sugar-cane growing   4. Refining
2. Raw sugar production   5. Distribution
3. Shipping

Each block represents a different level of operation in the integrated enterprise. Costs (x) are indicated by shaded, profits (y) by unshaded areas. Blocks 1, 2, and 4 are directly related. Block 1 shows costs and profits of the firm's subsidiaries on farming (growing of sugarcane) in the West Indies. The firm also produces raw sugar in the West Indies at stage 2 from its own supplies of sugarcane plus that purchased from independent cane farmers. The imputed price of its own cane output is therefore equal to the price at which it buys from cane farmers $(x + y)_1$. This plus a margin for factory costs sets the cost level at stage 2—i.e. $(x)_2$. At stage 4, the firm refines its own plus purchased supplies of raw sugar at going prices.[7] So that its costs at this level are $(x + y)_2$ plus shipping plus refining costs leaving a refining profit of y_4.

Insofar as changes in output prices at various levels affect levels

6. The diagram has been simplified by omitting certain by-product operations, like rum, molasses, and alcohol production.
7. In actual practice, the Commonwealth preferential system for West Indian sugar places Tate & Lyle in a unique position. The raw-sugar output from its West Indian factories is sold along with other sugar produced in the West Indies to the British Sugar Board at a special negotiated price which is usually in excess of the world market price. The Sugar Board is, however, obliged to sell British refiners at the world market price. So that normally this firm sells its raw sugar at one price and buys back the same sugar (for refining it) at a lower price.

of profit, the firm is in a position to hedge losses at one stage against gains at higher stages of production, so long as the final disposal (consumer) price does not change proportionately with changes in the prices of primary and intermediate outputs. For example, the lower the price of raw sugar purchased for refining (stage 4), the lower will be profits on the West Indian operations (stages 1 and 2); and the higher will be profit on refining, since the value of x_4 has been reduced. The upshot of the foregoing is that the maximization of total profit for the firm as a whole is not dependent on profit maximization for its agricultural activities. The importance of agriculture in this connection depends in part on the share of agriculture in the firm's total investments. The smaller this share, the lesser will be the need for using the profit maximization principle on its agricultural operations.

Since the agricultural operations of plantation enterprises are located in the Third World economies with which we are here concerned, this observation has implications for agricultural resource use in these economies. Changes in the structure of output prices (for the whole range of agricultural products which can be grown in these countries) which offer more profitable opportunities than the particular plantation crop do not induce a shift of resources from production of those crops because the profit horizon of the plantation enterprise (which controls these resources) extends beyond these purely agricultural opportunities. Even in the long run, the adjustment process tends to be limited to output adjustments for the particular crop rather than to a more flexible deployment of resources over the range of production possibilities in line with differential marginal value productivities.

CAPITAL SPECIFICITY

One of the outstanding characteristics of plantation enterprises is that the capital stock of these firms is highly specific to the production and processing (including marketing) of particular crops. In addition to specific capital investment on the agricultural side (for example, sugar factories and tea factories), complementary investments at other levels tend to be specific to the plantation commodity. For example, bulk terminals, special bulk sugar vessels, and refining equipment for sugar; and specially designed ships for bananas. This high degree of capital specificity produces further inflexibility in the pattern of agricultural resource use. The more integrated the firm structure, the stronger the limitation. For this means that the firm also has investments outside of agriculture which are geared to the particular crop.

The degree of specificity tends to be least at the actual farming level. Equipment, field labor, and land used in cultivation can be used for the production of any number of crops. But the capital required for processing (in the farm-factory and elsewhere) and shipping is quite specific. For example, sugar mills cannot be adapted to processing vegetables and banana boats are specially designed to their task. In the vertically integrated structure of the firm, it is these specific non-farm investments that help to create rigidities in resource use on the plantation. For capital specificity in related non-farm operations of the firm makes it less profitable to undertake crop switching or diversification at the farm level.[8]

Once ancillary investment commitments have been made, the firm is constrained to a short-run production possibilities curve with a limited scope for switching resources to alternative products.[9] This is illustrated on page 163. The first diagram shows the long run production possibilities for combinations of two crops, sugar and bananas, with a given set of resources. This is denoted

8. Certain factors at the farm level tend as well to be highly specific; for example, laboratories and managerial functions. It has been suggested that these rigidities in output adjustment may derive as much from the circumscribed entrepreneurial horizons of firm managers as from the existence of capital specificity in a physical or engineering sense. Firm managers who have established themselves as "sugar men" or "banana men" are unlikely to contemplate crop changes which would erode their established authority. Although this is a factor which is of relevance, it does not really set plantation operators apart from other types of agricultural producers. This same kind of "psychological attachment" to crops can be found among peasant farmers. It seems therefore that the degree of capital specificity is the more important consideration.

9. The set of production possibilities at the farm level is not influenced by ancillary non-farm investments in a technical sense but are affected indirectly by the resultant relative profitability of alternatives once specific commitments have been made.

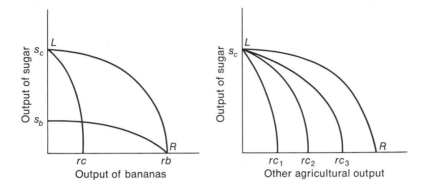

by the curve LR. Once the firm commits itself to specific investments relating to one or the other crop, the long-run production possibilities (opportunity) curve is no longer relevant. If the investments are specific to sugar production, the operative opportunity curve then becomes $s_c r_c$, while if they are specific to bananas it is $s_b r_b$. The degree of flexibility for product-product combinations is reduced as a result of the specific commitments.

The second diagram shows different degrees of capital specificity for a set of firms involved in sugar production. The more resources the firm has tied up in activities linked to sugar the greater the degree of inflexibility. Thus in the case of West Indian sugar producers, if rc_1 represents the position of Tate & Lyle subsidiaries, Bookers would operate on a curve to the right of this, say rc_2, since the latter does not have sugar-refining investments; while a simple farm-factory combine (sugar estate) without shipping and refining investments would operate further to the right, on say rc_3.

The greater the degree of vertical integration the lesser will be the flexibility of adjusting resource use to changing production opportunities across the range of agricultural commodities which can be produced with available resources. This is one factor contributing to inefficient resource allocation within the agricultural sectors of plantation economies. Even in the case of the simple farm-factory combine, the fact that profits on factory operations are normally greater than those on field operations contributes to a tendency for maximizing output rather than profits in the field. Brookfield, in an examination of the distribution of net profits between field and factory of estate companies in Mauritius, concludes:

The milling process demands large capital costs but low running costs: marginal return from increases in the quantity of cane handled is therefore at a maximum when the mill is large and running at full capacity. . . . For the estates with factory this . . . means that it is most profitable to capitalize cultivation so as to expand the throughput of the factory.[10]

These considerations constrain the efficiency with which resources are allocated at the farm end.

RISK AND UNCERTAINTY CONSIDERATIONS

The heavy capitalization and the crop specificity of investments expose plantation enterprises to an inherently high degree of risk and uncertainty—particularly in respect of crop losses from natural or other (political, for example) causes and of price fluctuations. This induces at least two counter-measures which affect resource allocation within the plantation economies.

The first is the exploitation of market imperfections. On the product side, this is expressed in enterprise control over disposal prices. United Fruit Company achieved this so effectively in the United States banana market that it had to face a Consent Decree of the Department of Justice to divest itself of part of its capital for the formation of another smaller company. In any event, United Fruit Company will still be able to maintain its position of price leader in the trade. Tate & Lyle subsidiaries on the other hand achieve this through industry collusion in the West Indies (that is, sugar manufacturers' associations) and political lobbying in the United Kingdom for preferential pricing arrangements. In matters relating to other overseas sugar markets it is normal practice in the West Indies for industry leaders to "speak for the governments." The consequence of this counter-measure is to distort

10. H. C. Brookfield, "Problems of Monoculture and Diversification in a Sugar Island: Mauritius, " *Economic Geography,* January 1959, p. 32.

artificially the structure of output prices for the range of farm products that can be produced in the plantation economies, and thereby to bias resource use in favor of the plantation crop. On the factor side, market imperfections arise from control over supplies of inputs produced within the vertically integrated structure of the firm and from the normally monopsonistic position of the plantation in the labor market. The latter derives from the fact that the land area covered by the plantation enterprise is so vast that it is usually the only source of employment within fairly wide areas.

The second counter-measure is the geographic dispersal of the firm's plantation operations. This minimizes the risk of crop losses. In addition to losses from weather and disease, this measure is a hedge against unfavorable changes in the political and economic situation in individual countries and it increases the flexibility of output expansion for the firm itself. It also leads to perverse supply responses for individual countries. For although the firm may increase over-all acreage and output in response to an increase in the relative price of its output, it may, in the process, contract acreage and output in a particular individual country.[11] The firm is concerned with efficient resource allocation between its different areas of agricultural operations. And this often results in inefficient resource allocation within a particular plantation economy. Because of the multinational character of plantation enterprises efficiency conditions tend to be met on the over-all operation—that is, between plantation sectors of national states but not within the agricultural sectors of individual nation states.

LAND USE

The farm-factory operations of plantations are located in the Third World plantation economies. Where the factory for processing

---

11. In a recent study of banana supply functions for each of four Central American countries, the author could find no correlation between changes in planned output (using acreage as an index) and changes in relative prices for bananas. But some significant correlations were derived when acreage data for each of two companies (United Fruit and Standard Fruit) were aggregated for all four countries and plotted against relative price over a number of years.

plantation output represents a substantial capital investment, the firm is concerned that adequate supplies of raw material be available for utilizing factory capacity in a reasonably efficient way. Sufficient land must, therefore, be acquired to produce the desired flow of raw material.[12] Even where raw-material supplies are available for purchase from independent farmers, the firm would be in too vulnerable a position if it relied exclusively on such supplies. This means that the plantation enterprise will try to secure sufficient land to produce some, or all, of its raw-material requirements and to allow for some degree of flexibility of output adjustment over time in response to changing market opportunities.

The land area required by a plantation will be influenced by several factors: the price of land, the size of factory investment, the ratio of factory investment to total farm-factory investment, the availability of raw-material supplies from other sources (preferably contract suppliers), and expectations re future market possibilities which influence desired flexibility of output adjustment. The actual land area acquired by plantations will depend on the resources of the firm, the cost of land, and the scale economies of processing particular crops. Given a particular scale of plant, the minimum area then required would be determined by the level of output required to cover fixed costs in processing where nonplantation supplies are available. Where these are not available a larger area will be necessary to make processing profitable. The same argument applies to shipping.[13]

Normally, plantations would try to secure land well in excess of the technical minimum. Price expectations and the cost of land would mainly determine the maximum area. The lower the cost of

12. The argument applies as well to enterprises which have shipping capacity, such as in the banana case where although no elaborate processing is done shipping is an important part of the firm's operation. By producing its own bananas United Fruit has greater control over utilization of its shipping capacity.
13. For example, for bananas "there is a certain minimum area required to justify the specialized shipping facilities that the trade demands. United Fruit Company usually specifies that at least 5,000 acres of first-class land . . . be available in one block before a farm can be established." (H. B. Arthur, J. P. Houck, and G. L. Beckford, *Tropical Agribusiness Structures and Adjustments—Bananas* (Boston, 1968, p. 48).

land and the brighter the long-term market expectations, the greater would be the area secured for plantation production. Because historically the establishment of plantations has been associated with the opening up of new territory, low-cost land has been usually available and this has led to the alienation of vast areas even beyond expected requirements at the time of establishment. Kepner in his study of the United Fruit Company indicates that that company and others acquired more land than they could possibly use for banana production for a number of reasons: (1) continuity of the plantation tract, (2) control of right of way to other favorable areas, (3) marginal land (that is, grade or location) may have profitable future use, (4) speculation, (5) keeping out competitors, and (6) the fact that bad land goes with good.[14] In addition, we might expect further inducement for excess landholdings to derive from the following considerations: (1) land ownership increases political power; (2) land increases the flexibility of accounting since its valuation can be used to raise the value of the capital stock, thereby adjusting the profit *rate;* and (3) land can be a hedge against political risks of nationalization if going market prices are part of compensation arrangements.

The land area actually in use at any particular point in time is a function of the price of output, the cost of production, the technical requirements of plant scale, and the price at which the firm can obtain independent supplies of the raw material. High rates of profit are characteristic of the early stages of development of plantations as a result of the natural fertility of virgin land. But over time, profits get squeezed as diminishing returns and rising costs set in. This stimulates technological improvements to raise the productivity of land (for example, new improved varieties, irrigation, fertilizers). As technology changes, some lands previously in production may become marginal but the plantation will keep these in reserve since future favorable changes in output prices may justify their use at a later date. In Central America, for example, United Fruit for several years maintained possession of thousands of acres which had been abandoned in the wake of Panama disease and the company was able to bring these areas back

14. Charles Kepner, *Social Aspects of the Banana Industry* (New York, 1936), pp. 86–87.

into production quickly during the 1960's with the advent of the disease-resistant "Valery" variety and favorable market prospects.

There is therefore a tendency toward underutilization of land in plantation agriculture. The extent of underutilization (that is, size of acreage reserve) will depend on the cost of securing land and of holding it. So we would expect smaller acreage reserves in countries which are short of land than in land-abundant plantation economies.[15] Underutilization of land is one means of providing for flexibility of output adjustments over time. Though this may represent an efficient pattern of resource use for the firm, it creates inefficiencies in allocation within plantation economies. This is most acute in situations where land is generally in short supply.

3. Distortions of resource use with tenant plantations

The major distortions in resource use with tenant plantations arise from the inherent conflict between the interests of plantation owners and those of the tenant workers.[16] This conflict derives from the fact that each of the two parties is utilizing inputs that belong to the other. As a result each may consider the inputs owned by the other to have a zero price; the tendency therefore is to use the other party's inputs up to the point where their marginal product is zero. Thus the plantation owner is induced to use the tenant's labor to a point where additional labor services bring no return. And the tenant is induced to use additional land so long as the value of the marginal product of the land is greater than zero. With the traditional temporary tenure associated with plantation

15. In Central America, for example, United Fruit Company normally has only one-third of its total owned acreage in bananas, whereas the share of estate land in sugarcane in the West Indies is generally about 80 per cent. However, population density may work in the opposite direction. Strong competition for land will lead to a secular rise is land prices which would encourage the holding of idle land for speculative purposes. David Edwards informs me that there is evidence that this has been the case for certain sugar estates in Trinidad and Antigua.

16. See Appendix II for a description of how tenant plantations are organized and for definitions of different types of tenant workers. The discussion there also provides precise definitions of the terms "sharecropper" and "share tenant," as these are used in the present study.

sharecropping this situation is seriously aggravated and soil erosion is usually the stark evidence of this conflict of interests.

The basic economics of sharecropper arrangements can be illustrated diagrammatically as in Figure 6.1. The figure contrasts the situation of an owner-operator or cash tenant with that of sharecropper production. The underlying assumption in both cases is that the producer seeks to maximize profits which in terms of the diagram means producing up to the point where marginal cost is equal to marginal revenue—that is, the cost of producing one more unit of output is equal to that unit's contribution to revenue. We can assume that for farm production the marginal revenue is equal to market price since one more unit of output from the individual unit cannot depress market prices. The marginal revenue curve (MR) is therefore represented by a horizontal line at the going market price. The marginal cost curve (MC) rises in the normal way. Now for the owner-operator or cash tenant the operative curves would be MR_1 and MC_1; and the most profitable output in that event would be OB. The sharecropper who pays half the crop as rent receives only half the marginal revenue that the

Figure 6.1.—Production effects of sharecropper arrangements on tenant plantations

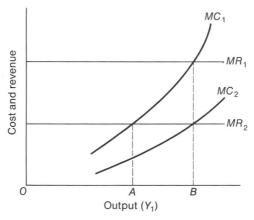

Source: C. Bishop and W. Toussaint, *Introduction to Agricultural Economic Analysis* (Chapel Hill, North Carolina, 1963), p. 159.

owner-operator or cash tenant receives; so the operative marginal revenue for him is MR_2. If the plantation owner does not share variable costs with the sharecropper, the sharecropper's operative marginal cost remains at MC_1, and the most profitable output in that event is OA. From this it can be seen that sharecropping can result in a lower level of output than would otherwise obtain.

In the case of share tenancy where the plantation owner shares variable costs with the tenant worker, although the marginal revenue curve for the tenant worker is MR_2, the costs met by him are now one-half what they were in the former case, as shown by the curve MC_2. And OB once more becomes the most profitable level of output. For this case the same level of output is produced as for owner-operators and cash tenants; this is so only if the sharing of variable costs is in exactly the same percentage as the sharing of revenue. This is the ideal case of a partnership arrangement. However plantation share tenancies are quite far removed from any concept of partnership. Checking with Appendix Table II.1 which gives the picture for the U.S. South, we find that there fertilizer is the only variable cost shared by the plantation owners with share tenants. The rest of variable costs—labor, seed, and feed for stock—are met fully by the share tenant. For sharecroppers we see there that the plantation owner meets half the fertilizer costs and other variable costs and the cropper contributes all the labor input. Since labor represents the bulk of variable costs in plantation production, it is obvious that for both sharecropping and share tenancy the tenant workers bear a heavier share of variable costs than the share of revenue accruing to them. Consequently, levels of output that obtain in these two instances are less than those that obtain for similar owner-operated or cash-tenanted farms or plantations.

The insecurity and shortness of tenure on tenant plantations are yet another source of distortion of resource use. In our discussion of the organization of such plantations in Appendix II, we indicate that the contracts of both sharecroppers and share tenants with plantation owners are verbal and insecure. In consequence of this, tenant workers produce only those commodities which involve short periods of production. Whether plantation owners permit it or not, long-maturing crops and livestock (except perhaps for poultry and other small stock) are ruled out by this consideration. This constraint on choice of product limits the choice of product mix, leading to inefficient resource allocation in the first instance and to diminishing of resource (land) quality in the long run. Furthermore insecurity and brevity of tenure create a situation wherein tenant workers have no inducement to invest in long-maturing capital assets, such as buildings, fences, and conservation measures. And plantation owners have little incentive to make improvements for which they receive little or no direct return. The poor state of housing and farm buildings on tenant plantations are a reflection of this.

One more general proposition we can advance in regard to tenant plantations relates to the choice of plantation crop. Labor is an important part of all plantation production: it is generally hard to get and its cost is a high percentage of total costs. The plantation owner must therefore devise means to hold what labor he can get and to utilize what is available efficiently. And so we find in the U.S. South, for example, that because labor is a larger factor in cotton than it is with other crops it is to the plantation owner's advantage to produce cotton with the labor contributed by sharecroppers and share tenants. Numerous studies of the plantation South have revealed the same pattern: the percentage of land in cotton is higher on tenant plantations than on plantations utilizing wage labor. Although plantation owners concentrate production on the most labor-intensive crops, the system nevertheless is unable to utilize fully what labor is available because of seasonality of labor requirements of the plantation crop, and the landlord-tenant conflict in relation to supplementary tenant production that might in some way compete with the labor needs of the plantation crop. Studies in the U.S. South have indicated:

Devotion to the single cash-crop and the fact that food crops mature during the same season as cotton, make it virtually impossible under the system to raise subsistence crops. Because the growing of household produce does not fit into the economy of a cash-crop, it is not encouraged by landlords, whose prerogative it is to determine the

Figure 6.2. Labor use and availability on sharecropper tenant plantations in the United States South

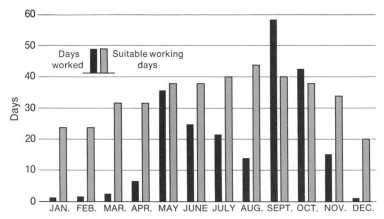

Source: E. L. Langsford and B. H. Thibodeaux, *Plantation Organization and Operation in the Yazoo-Mississippi Delta Area* (U.S. Department of Agriculture, Technical Bulletin No. 682, Washington, D. C., May 1939), p. 44.

crops grown. As a result the diet is limited largely to imported foods, made available through the commissaries and local stores.[17]

These constraints on resource use inherent in the tenant plantation system result in the misuse not only of land but of labor as well. Studies of the U.S. South confirm this. One study carried out in the Mississippi Delta indicates that the high percentage of crop land used for cotton "results in a poor distribution of labor in which rush seasons alternate with long periods of idleness, and in a limited number of work days per worker during the year." [18] The pattern observed is indicated in Figure 6.2. The data were derived from a sample of twenty sharecropper farms on plantations in the Yazoo-Mississippi Delta over the five-year period 1932–36.

17. C. S. Johnson, E. R. Embree, and W. W. Alexander, *The Collapse of Cotton Tenancy* (Chapel Hill, North Carolina, 1936), p. 16.
18. E. L. Langsford and B. H. Thibodeaux, *Plantation Organization and Operation in the Yazoo-Mississippi Delta Area* (U.S. Dept. Agriculture, Technical Bulletin No. 682, Washington, D. C., 1939), pp. 43–44.

These data show that the heavy demand for labor occurs from May to mid-July, when cultivating and hoeing are in progress, and again from late August to late November, when the cotton crop is harvested. During the rest of the year the sharecropper family of three workers is idle most of the time unless employment can be found elsewhere. The same studies concluded that diversification would increase the volume of production of these tenant plantations and would raise the level of returns per worker, although probably at a lower return per acre of land.[19] This finding confirms our earlier theoretical analysis which indicated that plantation owners with sharecropper tenants would aim to maximize returns on *his* inputs (that is, land) rather than that of the tenant (that is, labor). In the calculus of social costs and social returns the system is clearly inefficient.

Evidence can be brought to bear on all the propositions relating to distortions of resource use which have been advanced earlier in this discussion of tenant plantations. Studies in the U.S. South on the effects of insecurity of tenure indicate that since tenants have no legal claim on improvements they make on the farm they have no interest in conserving or improving land or buildings. On the contrary, it is to the tenant workers' advantage to mine the soil, burn rails and fences for firewood, and so forth. In fact, it is suggested that any tenant who tries to improve his holding is merely inviting the landlord to raise the rent or give him notice in order to secure a higher rent from another tenant.[20] Several surveys have revealed very little production of home-use foods because (1) the tenant's credit for obtaining subsistence and other goods is based on cotton production, (2) production of livestock is ruled out because of shortage of capital and pasturage (pasturage because plantation owners assign acreage on the basis of what *cotton* acreage the tenant family can handle), (3) the lack of security of tenure and corresponding high mobility of tenant workers, and (4) the absence of refrigeration and preserving facilities demands that food be consumed fresh.[21] Every survey also indicates that share-

19. *Ibid.*, p. 46.
20. C. S. Johnson, E. R. Embree, and W. W. Alexander, *op. cit.*, pp. 20–21.
21. See, for example, H. W. Blalock, *Plantation Operations of Landlords*

croppers receive the lowest returns of the different types of tenant farmers, and conversely that the plantation owner makes better money himself when he rents his land on some system of shares, particularly during periods of low cotton prices. Indeed, the tendency is for tenant plantations to move away from crop share arrangements whenever output prices are on the increase.

Looking at the tenant plantation system as a whole, Brannen concludes that it offers very limited prospects for improving the material welfare of tenant workers because of limitations in size of acreage assigned, constraints on the cropping pattern inherent in the system, the special nature of the credit system that keeps tenant workers tied to plantation owners, limitations on ex-plantation employment opportunities due to distance and lack of transportation, and other factors which in addition to these serve the interests of plantation owners but not those of the tenant workers. The inflexible nature of the system "is evidently suitable and economic from the point of view of the plantation" but from the tenants' point of view serves only "to restrict economic and social advancement." [22] We must conclude, therefore, that in social terms, the tenant plantation system creates outstanding inefficiencies in resource use and produces very low social returns for plantation community as a whole.

4. Brief comments on family plantations

Family plantations have their own special limitations which restrict the effectiveness of resource use in plantation economy. Perhaps the most important among these are absenteeism, tradition, and family social security. The plantation family is in social isolation within the plantation community and needs to go elsewhere for social intercourse. This generally leads to urban residence with occasional visits to the plantation. However, the worst incidence of absenteeism usually arises when the plantation is inherited by

and *Tenants in Arkansas* (University of Arkansas, College of Agriculture, Agricultural Experiment Station Bulletin No. 339, Fayetteville, Arkansas, May 1937), p. 28.

22. C. O. Brannen, "Limitations of the Plantation System as a Basis for Progress of the Tenants," *Southwestern Social Science Quarterly*, December 1942, pp. 260–62.

successive generations of the family. Having grown up mostly in an urban environment the heirs normally have little interest in, or knowledge about, plantation activities and the quality of management tends to decline. Choice of crop enterprises is limited to possibilities that are least demanding of management, and owners resort to various forms of renting—including sharecropping and share tenancy. What is even worse is that the new owners may regard the plantation more as a source of speculative investment or of social prestige than as a means of generating income through production; in this event, we find plantations are allowed to deteriorate and gross under-utilization of land results eventually.

Somewhat related to the question of absenteeism is the influence of family social security on plantation owners. Everywhere ownership of large tracts of land is important in determining the social status of individuals within a plantation society. Families are therefore reluctant to sell plantations even if they do not have the capacity to manage them as productive units, and they are prepared to tolerate underutilization because of the benefits derived from the social prestige that ownership provides. For the heirs who maintain interest in plantation production this consideration finds expression in the tendency to invest continuously in land from whatever surpluses are generated on the plantation. The social prestige and political power associated with land ownership induces over-investment in land beyond the managerial capacity of the family and over time the rate of underutilization of land increases. This is a phenomenon revealed by numerous studies of family plantations in Brazil. In addition, the social dimensions of land ownership create imperfections in the market for land, and these imperfections restrict ownership by people in the society who have the managerial capacity to operate farming units. Consequently, we find a characteristic under-utilization of the managerial resources of plantation economy.

Tradition plays an important role among all plantation families. Whether heirs remain on or off the plantation, basic decisions relating to what is produced and the techniques to be used are guided more by what the family has been doing for generations than by anything else. This element of tradition introduces a certain degree of inflexibility in relation to choice of crop enterprises and creates a strong element of resistance to technological change and scientific practices. The result is constant misallocation of resources and limited development possibilities over time. Harry Hutchinson has documented some of these aspects of family plantations in an interesting comparison of the family-owned sugar industry of Northeast Brazil with the corporate-owned industry of the Brazilian Center-South. He concludes the comparison by indicating that the backwardness of the industry in the Northeast in relation to the more advanced Paulista industry can be attributed to the value orientations of the planter class in the Northeast. Among the values are (1) urbanism and anti-technologism, reflected in strong preferences for urban residence and an anti-scientific tradition; (2) their view of human nature which places a premium on secrecy, thus preventing the accumulation of data with which to evaluate the efficiency of existing techniques; (3) a traditional concept of time and change which attributes more powers for change to the supernatural than to human intervention; and (4) the human relationships that serve to keep plantations within the extended family.[23] In addition, we may add that the strength of tradition is reinforced wherever plantations produce income sufficient to support desired levels of living of their owners or where monopoly of the land is secure. In the first instance there is no incentive to change things while in the second there is no pressure to do so since there is no competition.

The comments we have offered here are intended to apply generally to family plantations. To be sure there are many instances in the world which do not conform to these generalizations. In more recent times especially, new generations of plantation heirs the world over have availed themselves of university training in scientific agriculture and have returned to plantations to apply these principles. Even so, they must fight the resistance of others within plantation community whose co-operation they need to implement the new ideas. These exceptions relating to traditionalism in technology do not alter the basic fact that in family plantation situations generally, social aspects of land ownership, absenteeism,

23. See H. W. Hutchinson, "Value Orientations and Northeast Brazilian Agro-Industrial Modernization," *Inter-American Economic Affairs,* Spring 1968.

and tradition create distortions which result in resource misallocation and limited development prospects within plantation economy.

5. Resource underutilization alongside underconsumption and poverty

Each type of plantation considered in the preceding sections has
its own inherent characteristics that create social diseconomies in
plantation society. But a general pattern seems to emerge. In all
cases the social diseconomies find ultimate expression in a rather
unique combination of resource underutilization alongside underconsumption and poverty among the majority of people in plantation society. This is a characteristic feature of the plantation system everywhere in the world at present. Earlier, we argued that
inherent in the plantation system is the tendency toward monopol-
ization of land by plantation owners as a device to deprive the
majority of people access to an independent livelihood and therefore to ensure the plantation of labor supplies. But the nature of
plantation work is such that it cannot fully utilize all available
labor all of the time; and independent use of labor by the plantation work force is prohibited by the land monopoly situation. So we
find in all situations that resource misallocation is starkly expressed in the occurrence of gross underutilization of labor and
land. At the same time the economic power of plantation owners
and their need to exercise control over the labor supply create a
situation which provides limited economic advance for the majority of people; and underconsumption and poverty is their perpet-
ual legacy.

The inescapable conclusion is that the plantation system, as a
type of economic and social organization, creates the following social diseconomies: (1) persistent and expanding unemployment;
(2) relatively low levels of national income; (3) a most unequal
distribution of what little income is produced; (4) gross underutilization of land; and (5) extreme underconsumption generally. Underconsumption is perhaps most acutely reflected in a widespread
occurrence of protein malnutrition in the very presence of abundant agricultural resources.

It has been suggested that underutilization of land is directly correlated with the underutilization of labor in plantation economy. For example, in a study of Brazilian Northeast, Taylor expressed the view that underutilization of land is one means by which plantation owners as a class are able to maintain control over the supply of labor and are able to make labor available for plantation work at close to subsistence wages. For if workers had access to the means of independent subsistence they would withdraw their services from plantations or make these services available only at higher than subsistence levels of wages. To paraphrase Taylor, plantation owners have a vested interest in securing as much available land as possible, not so much to use it, as neo-classical economics suggests, but rather to withhold it from use, thereby ensuring their perpetuation as a class and the plantation system as a whole.[24] The association between underutilization of land and labor is evident everywhere in the plantation world, as our earlier empirical observations seem to indicate, and our analysis strongly suggests causality of the type indicated by Taylor.

The important conclusion we wish to draw is that unemployment and underutilization of land in plantation economies are structural phenomena that inhere in the system itself. This has hardly been recognized anywhere in the abundant literature on unemployment and underemployment in underdeveloped countries. Yet it is as important as most of the currently accepted causes of unemployment in these countries. The most frequent causes advanced are rapid population growth, inappropriate technology, limited labor absorptive capacity of industry resulting from the normally capital-intensive technology associated with manufacturing, low agricultural productivity in peasant agriculture, rural-urban population drift, and sometimes simply that people in these countries have nothing better to do with their time. These are all somewhat superficial explanations which require further exploration. We need to ask why, for example, people have nothing better to do with their time when their present consumption falls so short of what is clearly desirable from their own point of view as well

24. See Kit Sims Taylor, "The Dynamics of Underdevelopment in the Sugar Plantation Economy of Northeast Brazil" (unpublished thesis, University of Florida, 1969), Chapter VIII.

as by nutritional standards. Why, for example, agricultural productivity among peasants is low although there is every indication
that peasants aspire to higher incomes. For plantation economy
the answers to these questions are to be found in the nature of the
system itself.

Our analysis indicates that for every type of plantation organization we have examined, the resource situation is fractured. That
is to say, the system ensures that the supply of resources is structurally unadjusted to the demand for their use. Thus the supply of
land is largely limited to the small planter class and the demand
for the *use* of land (as distinct from the social function of ownership) is largely concentrated among the landless plantation workers and peasants who have managed to secure minute parcels.
Likewise the supply of labor is available among the landless and
peasant classes, but the demand for labor resides largely with the
planter class which controls the land on which labor services can
be applied. It follows from this that "people have nothing better to
do" than to be unemployed not because they just like having nothing better to do but because they have no access to land and other
resources with which to apply their labor services. We have already explained why the people of plantation society place such a
low premium on plantation work and are willing to pay the price
of unemployment and underemployment in order to be as independent of plantations as possible (see Chapter 4). The existence
of open unemployment and underemployment as revealed in peasant production and the petty trades in all plantation economies is
a reflection of a structural condition that inheres in the system. No
policies to restrain population growth and to introduce "appropriate technology" can deal with this situation.

In like manner the existence of low agricultural productivity
among peasants in plantation economy is due more to a reflection
of the poor quality and insufficient quantity of land which these
farmers are forced to work with than it is to their use of "traditional" techniques of production (as is popularly claimed). Again
we saw earlier that everywhere in the plantation world at present,
plantations have forced peasants on to the most marginal land
available in every country. In the nature of the situation created
by plantations many peasants engage in crop production for ex-

port. And in most instances their performance in this endeavor is at least as efficient as that of plantations in the same country. This has been recognized by some studies, such as those relating to rubber production in plantation Asia. One of the reasons why economists have failed to recognize that this is more often than not the case is because comparisons have been based for the most part on physical yields per unit of land. Physical yields are an inappropriate index of relative productivity, and usually the error is further compounded by the fact that comparisons are not made on the same base line. More specifically, plantations normally grow crops in pure stands while peasants mix export crops with other things. The density of export crop population per unit of land is therefore not the same. If adjustments are made for this and physical productivity per plant (or some such measure) is used, physical productivity on peasant farms becomes respectable, if not better than that of plantations. Even when value productivities for the enterprises as a whole are used, economists fail to account for distortions in values arising from product and factor market distortions which always favor plantations in those economies under consideration.

We have made a brief but necessary digression from the point we started to establish. It is that low productivity among peasants within plantation economy is really a consequence of the fact that peasants are denied an opportunity to exercise their obvious managerial and entrepreneurial abilities because the plantation system creates a situation which gives them limited access to the necessary co-operant resources of land and capital. Labor and entrepreneurship are bottled up within the peasant sector while land and capital are monopolized by the plantation sector. That there is usually excess entrepreneurship in the peasant sector is reflected by the fact that the adjusted physical and value productivities are so respectable *in spite of the fact that peasants work inferior quality land with limited capital.*[25] Low productivity in the peasant

25. By "excess entrepreneurship" in the peasant sector we mean excess in relation to cooperant resources of land and capital. For more discussion of this theme in relation to the Caribbean experience, see G. L. Beckford, "Towards Rationalization of West Indian Agriculture," *Papers presented at the Regional Conference on Devaluation,* Institute of Social and Economic Research, University of the West Indies, Mona, Jamaica, February 1968.

sector of plantation economies is the inevitable result of the structural deficiency of land and capital in the peasant sector. Policies designed to "modernize" peasant farming and to provide credit in the circumstances are doomed to failure because additional capital inputs will yield close to zero return on the poor quality land now held by peasants. The low productivity problem can be meaningfully tackled in this context only by making more of the high quality plantation land available to peasant farmers who, unlike plantation owners, have the economic incentive to make that land productive. The same increments of capital now being injected into peasant farming will yield far higher returns once good quality land is made available to peasants.

Apart from unemployment, underutilization of land, and low agricultural productivity, there are several other social costs which people in plantation economies have to bear on behalf of plantations. Some have been mentioned in the first section of this chapter. There is one which should be elaborated on further: the diseconomies generated by government assistance to plantations the world over. This is an important subject for consideration because it is one of the few areas where discretion can be exercised to correct an already socially imbalanced situation. Everywhere in the plantation world at present and in the past the state has acted on behalf of plantations in several ways. Examples are imperial preference systems, international commodity arrangements, public research programs geared to plantation crops, labor legislation, crop assistance programs, subsidies of one kind or another, devaluation of currencies, and so on and on. In every instance it is plantation society as a whole which bears the burden of maintaining the plantation system even though, as we have seen, the system itself offers the majority of people very little in return. Some of the subsidies borne by plantation society are less direct than others and become hidden. For example, the impression is usually given that imperial preferences are borne by the metropolitan treasury. It is seldom recongized (and never officially stated) that the plantation economies give *quid pro quo* preferences to manufactured goods coming from the metropolis and that as a result people in plantation society have to pay higher prices for manufactured goods than they would need to in the absence of the preference system. So that the plantation subsidy really comes from plantation society itself and, in fact, from that section that can least afford it. The general point to be made here is that the high social costs inherent in the plantation system proper are everywhere further accentuated or heightened by government policies which essentially soak the poor to help the rich within plantation society. It is not surprising, from the analysis of the characteristic social and political organization in this volume, that this happens to be the case.

To sum up, it is clear from the analysis presented that the plantation system generates serious resource misallocation in plantation economies, with resulting high social costs to the societies concerned. The question that remains for us to consider is whether it is really worth it—that is to say, whether the benefits to the society are greater than these costs.

7

The dynamics of underdevelopment with plantation agriculture

We need now to consider how the structural characteristics of the plantation system influence the pattern of development in plantation economies. The main thesis of this book is that development possibilities in all countries are determined chiefly by institutional factors that ultimately influence the more proximate growth variables, such as resources, capital accumulation, technological change, and human capital. In the plantation economies of the world these institutional factors derive their flavor from the plantation system, and the discussion in preceding chapters has served to reveal this. Now we must determine how these institutional (or structural) factors affect the pattern of development. There are several obvious ways in which plantations contribute positively to economic development, but there are also several ways in which the system inhibits economic development in Third World countries. The analysis so far in this study suggests that, on balance, the underdevelopment biases tend to outweigh the development impact, and this explains the equilibrium of underdevelopment that characterizes all plantation economies of the world at present.

1. The economic development impact of plantations

The most obvious development impact of plantations on any country, and perhaps the most important, is the opening-up effect which derives from the entry of plantations into previously uncultivated areas. The opening-up effect normally results in the creation of substantial social and overhead capital. Third World countries have undoubtedly benefited from the plantation-induced supplies of roads, railways, ports, telecommunications, water supplies, electricity, schools, clinics, and hospitals which now exist in places that otherwise would certainly be without these amenities. These amenities have contributed to economic advance in many ways: the media of communication have brought previously inaccessible areas into productive use and have provided outlets to the outside world for subsistence producers, thereby extending their production possibilities and introducing new consumer goods to stimulate increased production for markets. In this way subsistence economies have been transformed into money economies which have greater development possibilities than those that existed before plantations came in. Thus, communications contributed to an increase in over-all production and income. Provision of water supplies and electricity further stimulated increased production. (Clean and reliable supplies of water for household use and irrigation are important for every society. Irrigation increases the control of water supplies to growing crops and makes possible the production of crops that otherwise could not be grown.) And the introduction of schools, clinics, and hospitals helped to improve the skills and health of people in plantation society, thus contributing further to increased production and income.

The second obvious development impact is, of course, the expansion of production and income resulting directly from plantation activity. The output of plantations made a significant gross addition to the domestic output of plantation economies and resulted in a sizable increment to national income. And because of the export-orientation of production, the plantation output earned foreign exchange which otherwise would be unavailable. This permitted the importation of capital goods and new consumer goods. The former contributed to an expansion of the capital stock in plantation economy, thereby raising the long-term development potential; the latter introduced new wants among the people of plantation society and induced higher levels of productive effort as a result.

A third development impact of plantations comes from contributions to technology in underdeveloped countries. On the whole plantations have for some time practiced scientific agriculture based on considerable investments in research.[1] Such research has produced new varieties of high-yielding crops, new techniques of production that raised the yields of established varieties, new methods of processing that have increased the product yield from given supplies of raw material (as in sugar, palm kernel oil), and new techniques of distribution that have expanded consumer demand for final products of plantation raw materials. These improvements in technology have all served further to expand output and income in plantation economy.

A fourth development impact derives from the demonstration effect of plantation production on the output and income of peasant producers. Everywhere in the plantation economies of the world peasants have come to participate in the growing of export crops which were introduced by plantations. Very often these new crops could be introduced into the subsistence production regime that previously existed without diminishing that output. So that the plantation influence contributed initially to increased peasant output. Over time as well, this influence continued as peasant producers would adopt improved practices introduced by plantations. New varieties of seed developed by the plantations became available to them and other technological improvements spilled over to the peasants growing export crops. Much of the increase in peasant output and income in plantation economies can be attributed in many instances directly to demonstration effects created by plantations.

A fifth immediate development impact is what economists call the multiplier effect. This follows the increase in investment, output, and incomes generated in the first round. Part of the increases in income resulting from plantation activity are subsequently spent within plantation economy on goods and services produced there, and this results in further increases in output and incomes for those supplying these goods and services in the second round. This

---

1. This is more true of company plantations than of tenant and family plantations. Indeed, in the last chapter we pointed out that the family plantations have an inherent bias against science and technology.

process goes on in the third and subsequent rounds to create a total incremental income which is some multiple of the original plantation investment. The size of this multiplication depends, in large measure, on the propensity of people to spend their increased incomes on goods and services produced within plantation economy itself. On the whole this propensity has been sufficiently great to add materially to the indirect contribution of plantations to income growth in underdeveloped countries.

The five major development impacts just described have together undoubtedly made a net contribution to the growth of national income and output in plantation economy. However, the argument so far has considered only the gross impact. The direct effects of plantations on production have been quite substantial and it is perhaps fair to say that the net impact of these effects was almost equal to the gross impact. This hypothesis derives from the consideration that in almost all instances plantation production did not displace previous production and that peasant production of plantation crops was more often than not grafted on to subsistence production without any significant diminution, if any, of subsistence production. Java is perhaps the only notable exception to this general observation. Apart from this case, plantation agriculture everywhere became established initially in open-resource situations. The divergence between gross and net impact is greatest in connection with the indirect effects on national output and incomes in plantation economy. The three main causes of this divergence are the foreign ownership of plantations, the high import content of plantation investment, and the relatively high consumer import propensity. Each contributes to significant leakages from the stream of income generated by plantation activity and each exists because of the nature of plantations.

Foreign ownership results in the diminution of the surplus which becomes available for reinvestment in plantation economy because a part of this is paid out as interest and dividends to investors outside the economy. Payments for capital goods which are imported (like factories, machinery and equipment, and building materials) do not form part of the investment benefits accruing to plantation economy in terms of the multiplier effect but rather give rise to increased incomes in the countries from which the goods are imported. The same applies to expenditure on imported consumer goods, where the production regime of all plantations is such that there is a characteristic heavy reliance on imported food supplies in all plantation economies. In consequence, the development impact deriving from the multiplier effect is considerably dampened.

These limitations apply as well to the contribution of plantations to foreign exchange earnings. The net contribution here is what remains after we deduct from the incremental income created the value of imported inputs, factor incomes going abroad and consumer expenditure on imports. On balance, then, the net direct contribution to export earnings and the net indirect additions to output and income resulting from plantation production are significantly less than suggested earlier in considering gross development impacts.

Economists usually consider the growth of income per capita as a better index of development than the growth of total output and income. The argument is simply that if total output or income is rising at the same rate as population, over time the average person in the society is getting no better or worse off in material terms. If population rises at a slower rate the average person is becoming better off, and if at a faster rate, worse off. In rounding off our discussion of the development impact we need, therefore, to consider the effects of plantations on population growth. Two observations can be made in this connection. First, the introduction of social capital of certain types serves to reduce mortality and raise the population growth rate. The clearing of swamps and the introduction of preventive medicine associated with hospitals and clinics brought in by plantations served everywhere to reduce the incidence of epidemics and communicable diseases which previously kept mortality rates at high levels. Eradication of diseases like malaria and yellow fever have often been associated with plantation development. So in this respect we find that plantations have contributed to increases in population growth rates in many countries. The second observation is that the immigration of labor for plantation work brought about a rapid increase in population, far beyond rates of growth previously resulting from natural increase.

These two observations lead us to conclude that the effects of plantations on population growth have been very substantial. Therefore, the net development impact in terms of contributions to the growth of per capita income in plantation economies is substantially less than can be inferred from considerations relating simply to the growth of national output and income.

Impact connotes a kind of once-and-for-all effect. This is really not quite the case for the development effects considered so far. Most of these are legacies which plantation economies still have and they continue to influence development. However, there are several other, more dynamic effects that inhere in the plantation system and which serve to retard the development process. These are the subject of later discussion; but before turning to these it will be useful first to consider briefly certain aspects of the general dynamics of agricultural development and economic growth in order to assess what has been said so far and to set the stage for subsequent analysis.

2. Conditions of agricultural development and economic growth: some neglected issues

Agriculture plays a fundamental role in the economic development of any country. It often initiates the growth process and is always crucial in sustaining the process once this has started. Initiation of the process of modern growth in any country may result from one of three events: an increase in agricultural export production (as with plantation production or peasant export production such as happened in West Africa); some fortuitous non-agricultural occurrence—often discovery and exploitation of mineral resources or the development of tourism; or an increase in agricultural production for the home market. For most of the Third World countries the first two events have been the most important. And it has been suggested that we can almost rule out the third possibility because it is unlikely that such development could for long be sustained since the inelastic demand for food would make farmers bankrupt if other sectors remained stagnant and since this would require an almost impossible rate of movement of farmers out of agriculture.[2]

For the growth process to be sustained a continuous increase in agricultural output and productivity is essential.[3] If the growth induced by non-agricultural activity is not soon accompanied by an increase in agricultural output, food prices will rise and discourage further non-agricultural expansion or food supplies will have to be imported. In either event the growth process is impeded. The same result is obtained where growth is initiated by agricultural exports. Without responsive food production the export earnings will just be frittered away on food imports, and whether the country is better or worse off will depend on the terms of trade between exports and food imports. An increase in agricultural output for consumption in the home market is therefore essential no matter how growth is initiated.

There is a voluminous body of literature on the role of agriculture in economic development and on the subject of agriculture and structural transformation.[4] On the first, the main considerations are that the agricultural sector is the chief source of food and of factor supplies for the growth of other sectors, that it provides the main market for the output of those sectors, and in many countries it is an important earner of foreign exchange. On the second, the chief observation is the secular decline in the relative importance of agriculture, in terms of output and employment, as the economy develops. On the whole the available literature tends to gloss over certain matters which are crucial to understanding the development process. Among these are the desirable output mix that is required of the agricultural sector, linkages between agriculture and industry that provide certain spread and feedback

2. See W. Arthur Lewis, "The Shifting Fortunes of Agriculture: The General Setting," *Proceedings of the Tenth International Conference of Agricultural Economists* (London, 1961).
3. We wish to ignore here the semantics of the "balanced growth" debate which is not really concerned with balance vs. imbalance at all, but with the question of timing. Everyone agrees that some kind of balance is essential for sustained growth.
4. For a recent summary of much of this material, see Bruce F. Johnston, "Agriculture and Structural Transformation in Developing Countries: A Survey of Research," *The Journal of Economic Literature,* June 1970.

effects, the problem of factor-supply rigidities and leakages, and the terms of trade adjustments as concerns export production. We need briefly to consider some of these matters, for, as we shall see, they have important implications concerning the development impact of plantations.

Reference was made earlier to the importance of the food-supplying function of agriculture to sustain the growth process. But it is not simply a matter of providing increased food supplies. The *kind* of food supplied is critical. As consumer incomes increase, their expenditures on different kinds of food change in certain well-observed ways. Expenditures on starchy foods as a group decline relative to other foods and even among the former there are shifts in demand which favor cereals and disfavor starchy fruits and roots. On the other hand, the demand for meat, dairy products, fresh fruits, and vegetables rises substantially with increasing incomes, while that for sugar, and oils and fats may be indifferent to income changes. The appropriate output requirements of the agricultural sector must therefore be such as to provide for adjustments of the output mix in line with differential rates of change in demand for different types of food. Otherwise, agriculture will keep supplying products that consumers do not want. In the general case, we find on the supply side that, in the early stages of development, agricultural output consists largely of starchy foods because at low levels of income, as characterized by subsistence production, starchy foods are the cheapest source of calories and are therefore in heavy demand. If supply is to be continuously adjusted subsequent to changes in demand, resources must be flexibly deployed away from production of starchy foods toward that of livestock, fruit, and vegetables. If the flexibility of adjustment of resource use is insufficient to bring this about, the result is that increases in demand for these high-income elasticity products will have to be met by imports, resulting in wasteful use of export earnings and/or balance-of-payment pressures.

The question of linkages between agriculture and industry is of crucial importance in the development process. All primary production requires some kind of product elaboration before reaching the consumer. So foodstuffs on leaving the farm have to be graded, sorted, processed, packaged, stored, and transported for final consumption. This gives rise to the development of off-farm activities associated with food production. This effect is accentuated by the development process. For as consumers' incomes increase they demand more and more services packaged with the food they buy. Expenditures on processed foods increase dramatically and more marketing services have to be performed to satisfy increasing demand for convenience—for example, placing foodstuffs in more convenient places, and making the form of the product better to suit consumers. As this demand for services increases, intermediate institutions specializing in their provision emerge and many activities previously performed on farms are transferred to non-farm enterprises. With development, the demand for services associated with food rises at a much faster rate than the demand for food itself. Consequently, any given increase in food output at the farm level induces a far greater increase in off-farm activities associated with food. This means that even small increments in agricultural production can stimulate development spread effects which are some multiple of the change in farm output. Most of the services associated with food are relatively labor intensive so that the employment effects induced by a rise in food output are quite substantial.

In like manner the commercialization of agriculture involves an increasing demand for supplies of farm inputs. At early stages of development many of these inputs are supplied on the farm itself —manure, for example—but improvements in technology have made it possible to produce many of these inputs in factories: artificial fertilizers, herbicides, pesticides, improved varieties of seed, and all kinds of farm equipment and building materials. As farm incomes increase, the demand for these off-farm inputs rises and stimulates production outside of agriculture, contributing further to the growth of output and incomes. Production of these inputs is, however, less labor intensive than in the case of services associated with farm output, so the employment effect here is normally not as great. Another kind of linkage to be noted is the final demand linkage. Here we recognize that the bulk of the population in underdeveloped countries is to be found in the agricultural sector. Thus the major market for non-agricultural production is among farm families. Increases in incomes in the farm sector re-

sulting from a rise in agricultural output and productivity, therefore, induce an expansion of demand for goods and services produced by the non-agricultural sector and lead to increased output
and incomes.

Some of the literature on agriculture and economic development
has emphasized factor transfers, particularly labor and capital,
from agriculture as an important element in the growth of other
sectors of the economy. Two aspects of this matter have been
largely ignored. The first concerns the skill content of labor in agriculture compared to the requirements of the non-agricultural sector. And the second concerns rigidities or leakages in the potential
flow of capital from the agricultural sector. On the first, it is to be
noted that some types of agriculture are more skill-intensive than
others; for example, commercial family farming involves the family not just in supplying relatively skilled labor but the performance of managerial functions as well; while, as we have seen,
labor employed in plantation agriculture has a very low skill content. The ease with which labor can be adapted to new non-agricultural activities varies substantially between these two types. It
should be noted, however, that one factor which gives plantation
labor an advantage over commercial farm family labor in this
connection is that the former will be more amenable to factory
routine and discipline having been accustomed to following orders
on the plantation. On the question of capital transfers, two points
are to be noted. In some agricultural situations social considerations result in continuous reinvestment in land, and the economic
effect of surplus funds seeking profitable investment opportunities
outside of agriculture is materially dampened as a result. The second point is that foreign ownership of agricultural units results in
a leakage of the agricultural surplus. These two considerations reduce the scope for capital transfers from agriculture of a kind that
could promote expansion of the non-agricultural sector.

One more generally neglected question is the terms of trade
problem. The importance of agriculture as an earner of foreign
exchange in underdeveloped countries is frequently emphasized.
However, the importance of this is modified quite considerably by
adjustments in the terms of trade. Arthur Lewis recently reopened
this matter in terms relevant to the underdeveloped countries. In

his 1969 Wicksell Lectures he pointed out that the extent to which these countries benefit from improvements in productivity in export production depends on the relationship of export production to food production in the underdeveloped countries on the one hand, and on the relationship between production of manufactures and food in the advanced countries on the other.[5] To trace the net effects we can take some examples. If productivity in food and manufactures in the advanced countries remain constant and if the only change in underdeveloped countries is an increase in productivity in export production, then the relative price of exports will fall, which would be beneficial to the advanced countries. If the underdeveloped countries rely on imports of manufactures from the advanced countries, then the underdeveloped countries will secure favorable terms of trade effects only when productivity in manufactures in the advanced countries rises faster than that in food production in those countries and export and food production in the underdeveloped countries. It would seem, from the limited data provided by Lewis, that this has hardly been the case in the past. So that the export performance of underdeveloped countries has not had as dramatic effect on their development as is usually suggested by the literature on agriculture and economic development.

Finally, we wish to consider the general factors that contribute to the development of agriculture itself, as distinct from those related to the interaction of agriculture and over-all economic development. We have seen that the development process requires an expansion of agricultural output at the same time that labor must be transferred from agriculture to facilitate the expansion of other sectors, assuming that labor is already fully employed. This means that the productivity of the labor force remaining in agriculture must increase substantially. Technological change is crucial in this regard. For this, research plays an important role since it serves to increase knowledge of new inputs and of possibilities for raising the productivity of old inputs. Capital accumulation is also essential to the process as the increased competition for labor resulting

5. W. Arthur Lewis, *Aspects of Tropical Trade, 1883–1965* (Wicksell Lectures, Stockholm, 1969), pp. 17–27.

from the growth of other sectors increases the need for more capital-intensive techniques of production in agriculture. The dynamic effects of technological change and capital accumulation can come into play only if certain preconditions for agricultural development exist. Among these are a highly motivated population to provide the basic human resources (managerial and technical skills, and adaptable labor power), adequate supplies of complementary resources—land and capital, and appropriate institutional arrangements for uniting all the available resources in the productive effort.

Economists have frequently noted these general preconditions, but of the three mentioned above, least consideration has been given to the need for appropriate institutional arrangements. Next to the need for a highly motivated population, we consider this neglected area to be of greatest importance. Shortage of land and capital is generally of much lesser significance. This ordering is based on our view of the development experience and performance in the underdeveloped world as a whole. The primary importance we attach to a highly motivated population—the human element—is based largely on the achievements of Israel where in spite of severe natural limitations in regard to land a viable agriculture has emerged. As concerns the importance we attach to institutional arrangements, it is to be noted that, in spite of abundant supplies of land and capital throughout Latin America, agricultural development in those countries has been extremely slow, primarily because structural factors have inhibited the unity of available resources.

Both the human element and the institutional arrangements in any situation are largely influenced by the pattern of social organization. It is the social environment that determines whether the population of a country is highly motivated in the service of the development effort or not. This motivation is intensified in societies where there is normative consensus with social and cultural homogeneity, but it becomes severely retarded in societies where dissensus prevails along with social and cultural plurality. The institutional arrangements determine whether or not large-scale units of collective action can be organized; and, as Brewster has emphasized, this largely determines whether the opportunities for agricultural development can be seized.[6] The particular institutional arrangements that exist in any situation are determined by social structure and organization, tradition, values, beliefs, and attitudes —all of which derive their flavor from the particular dominant rural institution existing in a country. Thus we should expect to find differences between agricultural systems, such as plantation, peasant, feudal, and state-controlled systems. It is the particular system which determines the nature of the social institutions and, therefore, the kind of institutional arrangements that exist for uniting resources in the productive effort and for promoting agricultural development.

For agricultural development to proceed at a satisfactory rate it is necessary for available resources continuously to be made available to those people in the society best able to transform resource services into products for consumption. And we have seen earlier that there is need for flexibility in resource use in order to bring about adjustments necessitated by changing income opportunities. To achieve these, the required social institutions must be such as to facilitate the greatest possible degree of resource mobility— particularly in respect of access to land and capital by the more capable farmers, and the flexibility that exists for adjustments in patterns of land use over time. In addition, the social and economic institutions must be capable of ensuring a continuous extension of technical knowledge relating to agricultural production, adequate means of supplying farmers with new inputs and providing marketing and credit services, incentive for effort, progress-oriented values, and good government. Different social systems have different inherent capacities for providing all these prerequisites for agricultural development.

It is clear from this that we need to analyze seriously the social dimensions of any particular situation. We shall attempt to do this for the plantation system later in this chapter. What relevance all

6. See John M. Brewster, "Traditional Social Structures as Barriers to Change," H. M. Southworth and B. F. Johnston (eds.), *Agricultural Development and Economic Growth* (Ithaca, New York, 1967), pp. 66–98. This article by Brewster is one of the very few contributions which give sufficient primacy to the structural factors influencing agricultural development. It deals specifically with the peasant case.

the other foregoing considerations have for the development problem in plantation economy is the next subject for consideration.

3. Structural factors and the economics of underdevelopment

We are now in a position to continue our review of the development impact of plantations against the background of the dynamic forces identified in the general case just considered. The analysis suggests that structural factors inherent in the plantation system retard the process of development and structural transformation and induce a dynamic process of underdevelopment.[7] The approach adopted here is to see what elements in the plantation system contribute to the failure to meet the dynamic requirements of development, as we have identified them. In other words, we are interested in explaining the persistence, not simply the existence, of underdevelopment in plantation economies. In our view, economists have been too much concerned with trying to explain the process of development without first trying to understand the nature of underdevelopment.

We have seen that agriculture must provide increasing supplies of particular types of foodstuffs as an economy develops. Plantation agriculture is certainly not geared to supplying the food requirements of plantation economy but it influences this supply by diverting resources away from domestic-oriented production. Two considerations are of importance here: the extent to which this resource diversion retards the growth of domestic food supplies and the extent to which export earnings of plantations can compensate for this diversion by paying for food imports. Domestic food supplies in all plantation economies come largely from the independent efforts of peasants. Our earlier analysis of the peasant-plantation conflict in Chapter 1 indicated that typically resource competition is intense and that plantations always have the advantage in these situations. It follows, therefore, that normally we can expect plantations to inhibit the expansion of domestic food supplies in plantation economy. This is particularly so in countries

---

7. Recall here our earlier proposition in the Introduction that underdevelopment is a process rather than a stage or condition.

where land is in relatively short supply and will eventually be so in every case since the natural history of plantations is marked by a transition from a situation of open resources to one of closed resources.

The retarding effect on domestic food supplies need not impede the development process if plantation export earnings increase at a sufficiently rapid rate to allow imported food supplies to satisfy the expanding demand. In general, this is unlikely to happen. The reason for this is that plantation output consists of primary products with relatively low income elasticities of demand while the incremental food demand will be heavily weighted toward high income elasticity kinds of foodstuffs. If the prices of exports and food imports remain constant then any given increase in consumer incomes in both plantation economy and the metropolis will induce a greater increase in the demand for food imports in plantation economy than for plantation exports in the metropolis. This means that the volume of plantation exports will have to rise at a much faster rate than the growth in demand for food so as to earn the amounts of foreign exchange required to pay for food imports. Alternatively, the price of plantation export output must rise continuously, relative to food import prices. In other words, over time the commodity terms of trade between plantation exports and food imports must move consistently in favor of plantation exports. Historically, the general pattern has been the reverse. So that the export earnings of plantations have failed in the past to meet the food import requirements of plantation economy. And this has served to retard the development of these economies. We shall return later to further discussion of general terms of trade effects.

As concerns adjustments in the product mix as an economy develops, it is to be noted that most of the high-income elasticity foodstuffs (for which demand is expanding most rapidly) are derived from livestock—meat and all kinds of dairy products. Now livestock production requires extensive tracts of land but plantations have a virtual monopoly of the land, and, for one reason or another (as indicated in Chapter 6), their owners are not interested in livestock production. This distortion in resource use impedes the adjustment to potential high-income agricultural production in plantation economy. We should also note in this

connection that of all agricultural possibilities, livestock production has the greatest potential for creating linkages in an economy.
In the forward direction, there are meat processing of all kinds;
milk and cream processing; butter, cheese, bone meal for fertilizers; hides for tanning and leather and for the associated footwear
production; and transportation and distribution services for all
these products. And in the backward direction, there is the farm
demand for feedstuffs, building materials, and dairy equipment. In
all, these linkages add up to a significant volume of output, income, and employment. Particularly in the forward direction many
of the induced activities are relatively labor-intensive, at least in
comparison to most manufacturing activity. Given the high levels
of unemployment typically found in plantation economies, the failure to seize these opportunities is especially important.

The underdevelopment bias resulting from foregone linkages
and spread effects associated with livestock production would not
be very great if plantation export production itself generated com-
pensating linkages. This is not the case, however. Actually, plantation export agriculture has the potential for linkages which have
a high income-generating effect but relatively low employment effect. These are in the areas of shipping, product elaboration, and
metropolitan distribution in the forward direction, and factory
equipment, building supplies, and fertilizers in the backward
direction. However, as we saw in Chapter 5, these linkages have
been canalized within the complex of metropolitan plantation enterprise and thus have largely served to generate incomes in metropolitan, not plantation, economy. The question naturally arises
as to why these linked activities are located in the metropolis and
not in plantation economy. There are many reasons for this, but
perhaps the most important is that metropolitan enterprise minimizes risks by locating these activities in the surer political environment of home base.

In a study of the rationality of metropolitan location of product
elaboration of "colonial raw materials," Leubuscher advanced a
number of explanatory factors.[8] These can be summarized as fol-

8. Charlotte Leubuscher, *The Processing of Colonial Raw Materials*
(London, HMSO, 1951), pp. 172–74. These generalizations are based
on special studies of cocoa, oilseeds, sisal, and sugar.

lows: (1) where processing involves splitting the raw material into two or more commodities (for example, cocoa and oilseeds), shipping the undivided raw material is more advantageous except where there is a large domestic market in the exporting country for at least one of the products; (2) processing at the market base increases the flexibility of the outturn of two or more products in line with changes in demand; (3) processing nearly always involves the use of auxiliary materials (especially chemicals) which are not available in the Third World countries; (4) manufacture may involve mixing two or more raw materials, one of which may not be available in the exporting country (cocoa and sugar for chocolate manufacture, for example); (5) with processing nearer to the market, there is greater flexibility in end use for the finished product (for example, palm oil can be used either as crude or as refined if destined for use in soap or tin-plating); (6) in many Third World countries, output of the particular raw material may be insufficient to feed a processing plant of economic size—furthermore, regularity of supply and continuity of operation may be important for lowering costs and a single supply source would therefore be risky; (7) sometimes there is a need to blend several varieties of the same material to get a high-grade final product; (8) interchangeability between different raw materials (for example, vegetable oils) makes it necessary to give manufacturers a choice, as determined by relative prices; (9) the existing organization of industry and trade carries much weight—in most cases, overseas buyers prefer unprocessed to fully processed material because later stages of processing are financially and technically interlocked with the manufacture of finished goods; (10) the wide variety of consumer demand can best be met by locating later stages of processing closer to the market; and (11) fiscal measures—high import duties, import quotas, and embargoes in metropolitan countries on processed materials with relatively free entry of unprocessed materials.

This list of reasons for the present absence of processing linkages from export production within plantation economy is long and it would be worthwhile to identify those which are most serious. On closer examination we find that items 3, 4, 6, and 7 apply as much to metropolitan economy as to plantation economy. Many of the other items are associated with market constraints within plantation economy and proposals to deal with these will be offered in the next chapter. The two most formidable and intractable reasons listed are 9 and 11—the bias induced by the existing organization of industry and trade, and trade restraints imposed by metropolitan governments. Again we shall have occasion, in the next chapter, to consider ways in which governments in the Third World countries can overcome these obstacles. For the time being, we will simply conclude that plantation export agriculture does not now confer sufficient linkages on plantation economy to compensate for the foregone linkages associated with, say, livestock production. Consequently, the spread effects from plantation activity are weak; and this, in part, explains the persistent tendency toward underdevelopment in plantation economy.

Two other factors, from previous general discussion of the dynamics of development, which further contribute to the persistence of underdevelopment are rigidities and leakages in regard to factor transfers from agriculture, and the terms of trade problem. In the plantation setting the tendency for excess investment in land for unproductive reasons and the conspicuous consumption of metropolitan goods and services (overseas travel and metropolitan schooling for children are examples) among family plantations considerably reduces the scope for capital transfers from plantation agriculture for expansion of other sectors. And in the case of company plantations which are subsidiaries of metropolitan enterprise, interest and dividend payments abroad are important leakages. The capital transfer contribution of plantations to the development of plantation economy is much less than can be inferred from "development models" dealing with this issue.

In the past, adjustments in the terms of trade between plantation economy and metropolitan economy have been such as to transfer the benefits of productivity improvements in export production to metropolitan economy. To revert to the Lewis model, this has resulted from the fact that productivity in plantation exports has increased at a faster rate than that of food production in both plantation and metropolitan economy. We have already seen that low productivity among peasants growing food for the home market is a direct consequence of the plantation presence. The dynamic effect of this is that so long as peasant productivity remains low, productivity improvements in plantation production are of little or no benefit to plantation economy. Indeed, Lewis detected this more than fifteen years ago when he wrote:

> So long as the peasant farmers have low productivity, the temperate world can get the services of tropical labour for a very low price. Moreover when productivity rises in the crops produced for export there is no need to share the increase with labour, and practically the whole benefit goes in reducing the price to industrial consumers. Sugar is an excellent case in point. *Cane sugar is an industry in which productivity is extremely high by any biological standard. It is also an industry in which output per acre has about trebled over the past seventy years, a rate of growth unparallelled by any other major agricultural industry in the world—certainly not by the wheat industry. Nevertheless, workers in the cane sugar industry continue to walk barefooted, and to live in shacks, while workers in wheat enjoy among the highest living standards in the world.* However vastly productive the sugar industry may become, the benefit accrues chiefly to consumers.[9]

In the circumstances underdevelopment persists even though plantation productivity increases. Plantation economy is thereby caught in a stagnant "backwash" from terms of trade adjustments.[10] This is clearly a structural condition that perpetuates underdevelopment.

We may note, in passing, that in more recent decades productivity improvements have brought more benefit to plantation economy than in the past. This has resulted from trade-union activity which has managed to cream off some of the benefits in the form of higher money wages for plantation labor. However, rising

9. W. Arthur Lewis, *Theory of Economic Growth* (London, 1955), p. 281. Emphasis added.
10. Much of the debate about the direction of secular trends in the terms of trade between industrial and underdeveloped countries is irrelevant in this context. As Lewis points out, it is not a matter of the relative prices of exports and imports of industrial goods but rather the double accounting between prices of food in both sets of countries, exports, and industrial goods. And historically changes in the double factoral terms of trade have been to the benefit of the metropolis, not of plantation economy.

prices have eroded some of these money benefits and against this must be balanced the consideration that improvements in productivity on plantations have invariably involved the oft-neglected cost of increased unemployment. Another consideration is that, despite deteriorating terms of trade, export agricultural output has continued to increase quite spectacularly. The reason for this is that the terms of trade have no significance to private foreign plantation owners. Terms of trade is a social concept which has little or no relevance to the private accounting of plantations. Put differently, the terms of trade of the firm may be altogether different from the terms of trade of the society.[11]

There are a few more structural characteristics of the plantation system which create underdevelopment biases other than those already considered. One is that the low skill content involved in plantation work does not generate over time a diffusion of skills among the population. Related to this is the very unequal distribution of income in plantation society as a whole. This pattern of income distribution retards development because the low aggregate effective demand limits the size of the market, thereby ruling out establishment of industries with significant scale economies, and because the low incomes of the bulk of the population restricts household savings and the scope for domestic investment.[12] Another factor is that where company plantations are important, the multinational character of metropolitan plantation activity results in the possible leakage of funds which are earmarked for reinvestment in plantations. In other words, surpluses generated in one country may be reinvested in any other country where the firm owns plantations or in new countries where it is advantageous for the firm to become established. So that quite apart from the normal leakage for interest and dividend payments, there is this further potential drain from particular plantation economies.

Yet another factor is the inflexibility of resource adjustment

11. I am grateful to Havelock Brewster for bringing the two points in this paragraph to my attention.
12. This last consideration would not necessarily obtain if the small high-income group had a much higher propensity to save than the low-income group. However, this is hardly the case in plantation society where, as we have noted, the propensity to consume of the high-income class is very high because of social considerations.

that derives from the vertically integrated structure of company plantations and from distortions in the structure of output prices for the full range of agricultural products that can be produced in plantation economy. We have noted that resource misallocation results from these characteristics. Now we can add that because of the high degree of specificity of plantation enterprise investment and the distorted structure of output prices, and because foreign investors have little or no interest in production for the domestic market, opportunities for agricultural development deriving from changing patterns of consumer demand tend not to be taken up.

The combined weight of all the underdevelopment biases we have uncovered in the foregoing analysis is very substantial. But that is only half the story, for up to now we have considered only the economic variables. Sociological considerations must be taken into account since the human element and the institutional environment ultimately determine what economic arrangements are to exist.

4. The social economy of underdevelopment

For economic development to proceed with certainty in any country, a social environment favorable to it is absolutely necessary. This study has argued that economic development requires a highly motivated population with progress-oriented values directed to the development effort and with social institutions that provide the necessary incentives and rewards. In addition, development requires a high degree of factor mobility, good government to organize the collective will of the society, and social stability to engender confidence in the future. The list of concrete social requirements of development includes an educational system designed to promote national consciousness, to improve the quality of labor, and to provide the basis of a fuller life for the individual —with this education accessible to everyone in the society; health and recreational services contributing to greater labor productivity and the well-being of the population; scientific research to extend the boundaries of human knowledge, thereby to expand production possibilities; well-defined strong local communities to associate the efforts of smaller groups with the needs of their imme-

diate environment; and every individual in the society having
something at stake in the future of his country. The discussion that
follows indicates that plantation society fails, in many important
ways, to fulfill these basic social requirements of development.

We begin with the observation that social organization in plantation economy is such that the bulk of the population is denied
access to the means of production, especially land. The effect of
this is to inhibit the fullest possible utilization of the economy's
human resources and to deny the majority a stake in the country.
Furthermore, the rigid pattern of social stratification that is characteristic of plantation society is an obstacle to social mobility and
materially dampens incentives among lower status groups who see
no possibility of deriving benefits from increased effort. In general
this also inhibits factor mobility—which is necessary for structural transformation. We recall, from our analysis in Chapter 3,
that the particular type of social stratification is based on race,
color, and other ascriptive characteristics. The development potential is therefore limited by the fact that individuals with ascriptive
characteristics associated with low status are denied opportunities
for advancement in line with their true potential. So that these individuals cannot contribute as much to the development process as
they otherwise would be able to. Since such individuals normally
make up the bulk of the population in plantation society the extent of this underutilization of human resources is very substantial
indeed.

Our earlier analysis also indicated that race, class, and caste in
plantation society create a plural social order characterized by dissensus and "pregnant with conflict," to use M. G. Smith's term.
As a conflict society, there is continuous social instability resulting
from underlying social tension and recurrent explosion and crisis.
In the circumstances, the population has a limited and constrained
confidence in the future. Investment is limited largely to assets
that can survive in the situation—land among the privileged and
education of children among the underprivileged, for example.
And as social explosions occur, substantial resources are used up
just to replace fixed assets destroyed in the process. The unre-
solved conflict and the relatively slow rate of development that has
persisted in Guyana since 1953 is perhaps the clearest example of

the retarding influence of social instability. But the underlying social tension, aggravated by racial divisions, in all plantation societies is certainly a factor that contributes to the persistence of underdevelopment.

Again, our analysis in Chapter 3 indicated that plantation society is socially integrated mainly in the areas of economic production and achievement motivation. But in both these areas the associated social ethos is a strong individualism which is entirely divorced from meaningful co-operation. Individuals are forced to compete with each other in a manner that serves less to promote greater production and productivity than it does to induce a clash of interests. Thus we find considerable interpersonal rivalry to secure land and jobs and to win favor with plantation owners for individual mobility within plantation community.[13] This particular kind of individualism makes co-operative action difficult to mobilize and retards the execution of many community projects that could enhance the well-being of people in individual localities. Social aspirations of all groups in plantation society are in the direction of the life style of the planter class. And the demonstration effect of this metropolitan-oriented group with its characteristic conspicuous consumption, high propensity to consume imported (metropolitan) goods and services, and to overinvest in land sets the stage, in the society as a whole, for patterns of consumption and investment which are inimical to economic development. Costly woolen suits and hats, and parties that have a distinct "great house" flavor (for example, expensive scotch whiskey), are quite common among the poorest people in plantation society.[14]

We also noted that plantation community is loosely organized with very weak social cohesion and that this is one factor contributing to the absence of local government authorities in the administration of government. Absence of local government means that many opportunities for development at the local or regional level are missed. For one thing, central government is not likely to be

13. The business of house servants and other favorite slaves reporting on other slaves still persists in all plantation societies today.
14. The dresses, suits, and hats that are worn by poor people in plantation villages on a Sunday afternoon belie their low levels of living. Any visitor to the scene not knowing the situation would be impressed by the obvious signs of opulence.

as aware of local needs as local government is. But, more important, the opportunity of raising local taxes for expenditure on local
projects cannot be seized. People are more willing to pay taxes to
a local authority because they can see and feel the immediate benefits of the subsequent expenditure. Central government is too far
removed and their expenditures spread too thinly in a geographic
sense for people to identify their tax payments with subsequent
benefits. Consequently, in the absence of local government many
development projects which could be undertaken by mobilizing
local resources never come into being.

Within plantation community, interpersonal relations reflect the
authority structure of the plantation itself. In every aspect of life a
strong authoritarian tradition can be observed. Any one with the
slightest degree of power over others exercises this power in a
characteristic exploitive authoritarian manner, and attitudes toward work clearly reflect the plantation influence. Overseer types
never do manual work which is degrading to their social dignity,
and laborers consistently devise ways and means of getting pay
without actually doing the work—it is simply a case of always
trying to beat the system. On the whole the plantation has a de-
moralizing influence on the community. It destroys or discourages
the institution of the family and so undermines the entire social
fabric. It engenders an ethos of dependence and patronage and so
deprives people of dignity, security, and self-respect. And it
impedes the material, social, and spiritual advance of the majority
of people. In the circumstances we could hardly expect to find a
highly motivated population displaying the kinds of characteristics
that development demands. The energies of most people are spent
in trying to beat the system in one way or another.

Within plantation society, the tradition, values, beliefs, and attitudes which have become established as a result of long periods of
plantation influence are, for the most part, inimical to development. Paternalism, anti-technologism on family plantations, and
general attitudes toward life and work contribute to the persistence of underdevelopment. Hutchinson concludes his study of
value orientations in the Brazilian Northeast with the observation
that there are indications that the values of the bulk of the population coincide with those of the planter class and that

the sum of these value orientations in the Northeast plantation context does not add up in a way which promises modernization. . . . Starting with a rejection of nature as a viable partner, the rejection of innovation, the rejection of cooperation and a rejection of long range planning, they add up to continued tradition and to a continued cycling of crises.[15]

Even where company plantations have replaced the planter, these traditions have remained in the community so that the observation applies to plantation society elsewhere in the New World and parts of Asia as well. However, it must be pointed out that company plantations have contributed much to scientific research and have been responsible for introducing the elements of a scientific tradition in these countries, thereby eroding the anti-technologism bias.

In the field of education too the plantation system induces underdevelopment biases. Restrictions on the availability of education and its limited technical content contribute to an underutilization of the human resource potential of plantation society. Within the system, knowledge which is acquired and disseminated is generally directly related to the requirements of plantation production. Thus a considerable fund of technical knowledge relating to *the* particular crop is accumulated in plantation economy while very little is known of technical possibilities relating to other crops. In consequence, resources cannot really be deployed in an optimal fashion. More generally, education is rationed among groups within plantation society. Initially, slave plantation society provided no education for slaves; the children of plantation owners and managers were (and still are, for the most part) schooled in the metropolis. Subsequently, the educational system that developed was some variant of that existing in the metropolis; and a limited kind of education became available, chiefly for the half-castes in plantation society. Free primary schooling for everyone has never been realized, although in recent years governments have attempted to move in this direction. Secondary schooling is selective; for the most part students are admitted on the basis of

15. H. W. Hutchinson, "Value Orientations and Northeast Brazilian Agro-Industrial Modernization," *Inter-American Economic Affairs,* Spring 1968, p. 88.

social status. And university education was, until quite recently, nonexistent.

For the most part, what education became available was irrelevant to the environment and to the needs of a dynamic society. Geared as it is to the immediate needs of the plantation system, the content of education is heavily weighted to the supply of administrative (clerical) skills with little or no emphasis on technical and managerial skills. Since management decisions are made in the metropolis, there is really little need to have qualified managers in plantation economy; and since allied engineering activity is located in the metropolis there is little or no demand for highly skilled technicians. In the circumstances, the system produces an army of clerks from among those fortunate enough to secure an education. Medicine and law are the only two professions that win favor in the process, for everyone places a high premium on physical survival and numerous legal issues arise in a conflict-centered society with a high premium on land ownership. On the whole, the educational system of plantation society is technologically backward and contributes to the persistence of underdevelopment.

Our observations on the social economy of underdevelopment in plantation society are substantiated by Nicholls's study of the United States South. In an interesting book entitled *Southern Tradition and Regional Progress,* Nicholls argues that "tradition" has been the chief barrier to progress in the plantation South. His analysis of the development experience in the region deals with the elements in "Southern traditions which have seriously impeded its economic progress" and is summarized in the following way:

1. *Dominant agrarian values that are a legacy of the slave plantation* have impeded balanced and broadly based regional progress because the particular philosophy of agrarianism created a land-oriented scale of social prestige, thus minimizing non-agricultural development; it insulated the large planter from competing economic forces; it discouraged mobility; and it made a tradition of leisure which discouraged enterprise.

2. The South's *rigid social structure* has been unfavorable to development because the aristocratic ideal of the planter class was based on white supremacy; the spirit of extreme individualism discouraged social responsibility; the abnormal subordination of the

rural middle class prevented this group from participating fully in economic progress; the upper classes came to accept as normal and inevitable the system which kept the majority of people in a low-income position; and the rigid rural social substructure gave little ground to the development of cities.

3. *The undemocratic political structure,* "based on the overriding end of maintaining white supremacy whatever the cost," has impeded progress because it embodied a blind sectionalism that promoted coercive federalism; it utilized the states' rights doctrine to deny low-income groups access to federal grants-in-aid; the restrictions on the suffrage of black people and poor whites created a narrow electorate with low voter-participation rates attributable to a one-party system; it gave disproportionate political influence to the tradition-bound planter class; and it "perpetuated political control by a coalition of economic conservatives and racial extremists who continue to use racial antagonism as a means of maintaining the status quo against the liberalizing influences of the new social forces abroad in the South."

4. The *weakness of social responsibility* in the Southern tradition has resulted in inadequate support for public school education. Nicholls describes this as a "formidable barrier to regional economic progress" because it kept the majority of people in relative ignorance; it led "responsible" political leaders to propose abolition of public schools as a solution to the school-integration controversy; it encouraged a continued belief that the low-income groups in the society are poor because they are innately inferior, thus preventing action toward improvement of the social and economic organization; and it contributed to the outmigration of black people, thus depleting the potential industrial labor force.

5. *Conformity of thought and behavior* in the Southern tradition has created a general intolerance of intellectualism, encouraged "an acceptance of violence as an ultimate weapon against nonconformity and dissent," and corrupted higher education by repudiating innovation and novelty in thought and behavior. In consequence, technological and social innovation was slow; the best minds migrated to other regions; violence was generally accepted and sanctioned, whereas industrialization thrives only in

an atmosphere of law and order; and academic freedom and the public school basis which are necessary for development were threatened.[16]

These five major elements in the plantation tradition of the United States South go a far way toward explaining the backwardness of that region relative to the progress of the rest of that country. They are also to be found in varying degrees of importance in all plantation societies of the world and help to explain why plantation economies have lagged behind the advanced countries of the North Atlantic in the process of modernization that began with the Industrial Revolution. A study of the social economy of underdevelopment is likely to be far more revealing than narrow studies (and models) of the economics of development with their emphasis on analysis of the proximate economic variables.

5. The dynamics of underdevelopment

Our discussion in the foregoing sections can now be briefly summarized. Initially plantations have an important development impact for several reasons: they create an infrastructure of social capital, they bring previously unused land into production thereby increasing output and income, they provide former subsistence farmers with the wherewithal to produce for markets and so to bring about a transformation of "primitive" subsistence economy to money and exchange economy, and, in many countries, they have been responsible for the introduction of scientific farming. These developments have been hindered somewhat by the frequent foreign ownership of plantations, the high import content of plantation investment, and the relatively high import propensity of consumption in plantation society. Nevertheless, the net development impact is large enough to bring about a transformation from a condition of undevelopment to one of underdevelopment. Plantation economy never gets beyond the stage of underdevelopment. For within the system itself there are structural factors which impede further economic progress for plantation society as a

16. W. H. Nicholls, *Southern Tradition and Regional Progress* (Chapel Hill, North Carolina, 1960), pp. 157–63.

whole. In both economic and socio-political terms, the system influences the human element in ways that seriously retard development and transformation and the institutional arrangements that exist contribute to perpetuation of a continued state of underdevelopment. The factors operating in this direction are numerous and have considerable weights which when aggregated explain why plantation economy has been left behind in the backwash created by metropolitan economic and social advances.

The question that remains to be explored is how the system perpetuates itself. To put it more elegantly, we need to understand the dynamic equilibrium of underdevelopment. The simplest general answer to this question is that every system has the capacity for self-perpetuation and at the same time carries within it the seeds of its own destruction. Whether these seeds germinate or not depends largely on forces external to the system since within the system factors contributing to self-perpetuation always carry a greater weight than those working in the direction of self-destruction. Let us now consider the plantation system more specifically against the background of this general proposition. In plantation society economic, social, and political power resides firmly with the small planter class; the obverse of this is that the majority of people have limited access to the wherewithal for material advance and are culturally and psychologically dependent. The institutional arrangements of the plantation system are such as to contribute to its self-perpetuation. To take one example in the economic sphere, the way in which financial intermediation is organized prevents the dispossessed majority from making significant material advances. Allen's description of the credit system in the United States South is illustrative of this general phenomenon.

The credit system as it functions in the South not only continually pumps new blood into the survivals of slavery but is a powerful factor retarding the technical and rational development of agriculture in the South. . . . In the cotton belt the credit institutions accept only cotton as collateral security and will extend credit only to those whose major crop is cotton. . . .

They therefore discourage production of other crops. In addition, the raising of foodstuffs has been particularly discouraged since it frees the farmer from the necessity of obtaining food on credit, and thus deprives the merchant and plantation owner . . . of a lucrative business.[17]

Elsewhere in the plantation world, the organization of the banking system—with its characteristic metropolitan branch banking facilities—has similar effects.

Numerous other examples can be derived from our previous analysis of the economics of underdevelopment to verify that the institutional organization in every aspect of plantation economy contributes to a perpetuation of the system. Likewise, sociological, political, and psychological factors contribute further to the realization of a dynamic equilibrium. Basically, the dominant class of decision makers in plantation society have their self-interest at heart and control the system so as to ensure continuously this self-interest. On the other hand, the dispossessed majority of people do not like their condition and are a *potential* threat to the destruction of the system. However, it is difficult for this threat to be transformed into action because the system itself has engendered divisions within the dispossessed groups. The weak social cohesion of plantation community was considered earlier and the manipulation of race by the planter class effectively sets one group of dispossessed against another, thus avoiding total confrontation of the dispossessed against the system itself. This is evident everywhere —Tamils vs. Sinhalese in Ceylon, Indians vs. Negroes in Guyana, and black people vs. poor whites in the U.S. South are some of the more notable examples of this.

A further consideration is that the future which the system offers the majority of people leads to substantial out-migration from plantation society. In the process, the society is deprived of some of the best minds who could assist in the mobilization of the dispossessed elements for a confrontation with the system. The conclusion is that forces inherent in the system and which could contribute to its destruction are weak relative to those enhancing self-perpetuation. Nonetheless, on occasion the forces of destruction have gained an ascendancy and revolution, rebellion and revolt have resulted. Examples are Haiti toward the end of the eigh-

17. James S. Allen, *The Negro Question in the United States* (New York, 1936), pp. 98–99.

teenth century; Cuba, 1959; the West Indies in the late 1930's, Indonesia after World War II; and Black Power in the New World at present. In most instances, the social explosions accompanying the threatening action of the dispossessed people have resulted in modifications of the system rather than in its total destruction. These modifications have improved somewhat the material lot of people in plantation society but have hardly changed their basic psychological and cultural dispossession. Our conclusion, therefore, is that the plantation system generates its own self-perpetuation by effectively containing internal threats to its destruction. Consequently, a dynamic equilibrium of underdevelopment is endemic in plantation economy.

6. A note on the balance of social costs and benefits

Our conclusion in Chapter 6 was that the true social costs of plantations are quite substantial, while the analysis in the present chapter indicates that although the initial economic development impact of plantations is considerable, subsequent dynamic forces contribute to a secular persistence of underdevelopment. If we consider the natural history of plantations as consisting of two phases—*establishment and consolidation,* then *maturity*—we can then say that in the first phase economic benefits (from the opening up effect) are greater than social costs but that the situation is reversed in the second phase. However, we dare not ignore the inhumanities usually associated with the establishment of plantations (decimation of the Indians, slavery, etc.). So that even during establishment the social costs often exceed the economic benefits. The conclusion is inescapable that the sum of social costs always tends to outweigh the sum of social benefits by a significant margin.

This conclusion has not entirely escaped the notice of other scholars who have undertaken studies of particular plantation economies. Indeed, several of these studies provide comforting empirical support for the conclusions drawn from the analysis in the present book. These studies also indicate that regardless of the type of plantation that predominates in any given situation, the result is always the same—a persistent tendency toward underdevelopment. Some outstanding examples of such studies are: Guerra's study of the economic history of Cuban agriculture, Nicholl's study of underdevelopment in the United States South, the Inter-American Committee for Agricultural Development (CIDA) report on land-tenure conditions and socio-economic development in Brazil, Snodgrass's recent book on economic development in Ceylon, Geertz's study of the process of ecological change in Indonesia, and an article by Watters dealing with sugar and culture change in Fiji.[18]

These six studies cover a representative sample of the plantation economies and sub-economies of the world and they consider the development impact of a variety of plantation types and situations. Their conclusions are all the same as those derived in this more catholic study. We may also note that Jacoby has previously arrived at some of our conclusions regarding the balance of social costs and benefits on the basis of his extensive knowledge and study of Southeast Asia.[19]

18. The specific references are as follows: R. Guerra y Sanchez, *Sugar and Society in the Caribbean* (New Haven and London, 1964); W. H. Nicholls, *op. cit.*; CIDA, *Land Tenure Conditions and Socioeconomic Development of the Agricultural Sector—Brazil* (Pan American Union, Washington, D.C., 1966); D. R. Snodgrass, *Ceylon—an Export Economy in Transition* (Homewood, Illinois, 1966); Clifford Geertz, *Agricultural Involution—the Process of Ecological Change in Indonesia* (Berkeley and Los Angeles, 1963); and R. F. Watters, "Sugar Production and Culture Change in Fiji—A Comparison Between Peasant and Plantation Agriculture," *Pacific Viewpoint*, March 1963.

19. See E. H. Jacoby, *Agrarian Unrest in Southeast Asia* (New York, 1961) and "Types of Tenure and Economic Development," *The Malayan Economic Review*, April 1959.

8

Possibilities for change and transformation

The persistence of underdevelopment in plantation economies derives basically from the nature of the plantation system itself. It would appear then that the process of transformation to a development path that would ensure benefits to everyone in plantation society must involve radical change in the institutional structure—particularly the economic, social, and political arrangements. This is bound to be painful. But development is always a painful process—sacrifices have to be made in the short and the medium terms as an investment for benefits that can accrue only in the long run.

There are several reasons why the plantation system creates persistent underdevelopment, as we saw in the last chapter. In our view, the most important of these are: (1) the plantation system denies the majority of the people of plantation society a real stake in their country; (2) the system creates a legacy of dependence because the locus of decision making concerning fundamental economic issues resides outside of plantation society, so that a chronic dependency syndrome is characteristic of the whole population; and (3) the majority of people are not sufficiently motivated toward the development effort because of the first two considerations. No meaningful social change can take place without measures to correct these three basic deficiencies.

To put the matter rather bluntly, the plantation system must be destroyed if the people of plantation society are to secure economic, social, political, and psychological advancement.

1. The major development obstacles and previous attempts at change

The plantation system is itself the major obstacle to development in plantation economy. The structure of the system is such that many of the proximate economic, social, and political variables that contribute to development do not come into effective play. The major economic obstacles that derive from the plantation influence are the following:

1. a fracturing of resource supply and demand;
2. inequality in the distribution of wealth and income;
3. foreign ownership of producing units that drains the supply of investible funds from the income stream;
4. the export orientation of plantation production that results in a cumulation of backwash effects from terms of trade adjustments;
5. the low skill content of plantation work that inhibits the diffusion of skills and improvement in the quality of labor inputs;
6. resource-use distortions that prevent the flexible deployment of resource services to high-income producing activities;
7. the canalization of linkages and associated development potential by metropolitan plantation enterprise;
8. the multinational character of investment allocation by metropolitan enterprise that further reduces the flow of investible funds;
9. limited technical knowledge of production possibilities apart from the particular plantation crop which results from the excessive concentration of research by company plantations and which prevents a rational pattern of agricultural development.

The major social and political obstacles to development that are directly attributable to the plantation influence include:

1. weak community structure and loose family organization that prevent the emergence of viable local and regional units of administration and control, thereby making it difficult to raise local taxes and to execute local development projects;
2. a rigid social structure that inhibits factor mobility;
3. the strong correlation between race and class that creates a caste system and generates social tension and instability;

4. a general absence of social responsibility that results in poorly developed educational systems;

5. strong central government administration with a generally undemocratic political structure that discourages effective popular participation in the development process;

6. excessive power of the planter and associated classes that is exercised more in the interest of the small dominant class than in that of the society as a whole;

7. the low incidence of progress-oriented values among all the people of plantation society which derives from the strong element of tradition among the planter class and the general hostility to intellectualism which is essential for innovation and change;

8. a strong individualism that contributes more to clashes of interest in interpersonal relations than to co-operative activity;

9. an exploitive authoritarian tradition that prevents co-operative decision making and associative productive effort;

10. pervasive value orientations that reflect aspirations to a "great house" life style with characteristic high propensities to consume imported luxuries and to invest in nonproductive assets.

For the most part, the obstacles to development listed above have not been recognized sufficiently by policy makers in plantation society. The only two which have received significant attention to date are the foreign-ownership problem and the associated drain of investible funds, and the unequal distribution of land in plantation economy. Several countries have, in the past, introduced measures to deal with these two obstacles but these efforts have not paid much dividend in terms of induced development. In at least one country, Cuba, the development obstacles were so pronounced that the resulting social injustices sparked a revolutionary change directed at changing the whole institutional structure of plantation society. As concerns past attempts at change and transformation in plantation economy, we can identify two general categories: adjustments on the margin by the introduction of legislation to regulate plantation activity in one way or another, and structural adjustments to change the system entirely. Ceylon represents the first category and Cuba the second. The experiences in these two countries are now very briefly considered.

Since independence all government administrations in Ceylon

have introduced measures to regulate plantation activity to bring it more in line with national interests. Policy measures have included rigorous taxation of the tea plantation industry to finance national development, restraints on the export of capital, efforts to build up the importance of the Colombo auctions, measures to secure employment of Ceylonese management and staff, encouragement of smallholder tea production beginning with state plantations, and attempts to solve the problem of Indian Tamil labor which has been a bone of contention in the high unemployment atmosphere of Ceylon. Ceylon has perhaps done more than any other country in the direction of regulating plantation activity. For example, fiscal charges on tea exports are higher than they are anywhere else in the world, representing "something like 23 per cent of the average export price." And legislation has been designed "to make it impossible for sterling companies to sell their estates and repatriate the proceeds, and in general to restrict the export of wealth of all kinds, whether corporate or personal." [1] In general, public accountability of plantations was to be effected through the Tea Control Act. In spite of all these efforts, Ceylon appears to be still in the underdeveloped equilibrium trap created by the plantation structure.[2] Elsewhere the position is much the same, as plantations have successfully managed to circumvent any measures governments have introduced to regulate them.[3]

Cuba is a different case entirely. There the forces of destruction inherent in the plantation structure exploded violently, and the plantation sugar industry was nationalized by a revolutionary government that came to power in 1959. Attempts to establish a cooperative-based industry failed and state plantations are now the

1. D. M. Forrest, *A Hundred Years of Ceylon Tea* (London, 1967), pp. 238–47.
2. This is clearly demonstrated by the recent study by Donald Snodgrass, *Ceylon—An Export Economy in Transition* (Homewood, Illinois, 1966). Although Snodgrass attempts to show that things are changing (as the title of his book implies) the data and analysis do not support his thesis. For a discussion of some of the ways in which plantations have circumvented government measures, see N. Ramachandran, *Foreign Plantation Investment in Ceylon, 1889–1958* (Colombo, Central Bank of Ceylon, 1963).
3. See, for example, W. Gorter, "Adaptable Capitalists: The Dutch in Indonesia," *Social and Economic Studies,* September 1964.

order of the day. Much has been achieved there in the social adjustment of the plantation system—rural unemployment is said not to exist; color, class, and caste are said to be of lesser significance; education is now universal and is directed more to the needs of the country; rural health has improved considerably with the establishment of widely dispersed medical facilities; and the population is highly motivated toward national development and defense.[4] However, the underdevelopment legacy of the plantation can still be observed at several important levels. Perhaps the most important is the dependency syndrome which affects relations with the rest of the world. This has resulted in the introduction of economic policies which are likely to contribute to persistent underdevelopment, and the adoption of an alien ideology which might not be adequate to heal the social fractures of plantation society.

In connection with the first, the emphasis given to sugar production and the related integration of the Cuban economy with metropolitan Soviet economy seem likely to encourage continuing predominance of primary production and to inhibit structural transformation. It is understandable that dependence on a large metropolitan sugar importer was inevitable because Cuba produces such a high share of world export output of this commodity. However, the possibility exists that economic policy makers in Cuba may still be suffering from intellectual colonialism and that this may account for a policy which reflects a neo-classical conceptualization of international trade with its notions of commodity specialization deriving from static comparative advantage.[5] In

4. Documentation to support the statements made here is to be found in Dudley Seers et al., Cuba—The Economic and Social Revolution (Chapel Hill, North Carolina, 1964), and United Nations, Economic Commission for Latin America, Economic Bulletin for Latin America, July 1964, Chapter III, "The Cuban Economy."
5. The evidence and the argument in support of this possibility are presented in G. L. Beckford, "A Note on Agricultural Organization and Planning in Cuba," Caribbean Studies, October 1966, pp. 5–7. It must be noted, however, that heavy reliance on sugar is inevitable in the medium term since diversification can be achieved only in the long run. More information on post-revolution planning and policy problems associated with foreign trade policy is provided by Edward Boorstein, The Economic Transformation of Cuba (New York and London, 1968). The question of the relative effects on underdeveloped countries of trade relations between them and metropolitan "capital-

connection with the second, we observe that the Communist ideology that the Cubans have embraced originally developed from the
feudal-capitalist historical sequence of Europe which left a legacy
of social organization and structure appreciably different from
that of plantation society. Consequently, the social dynamics created by this ideology may not be adequate for the development
needs of plantation economy. As shall be argued later in this
chapter, the ideal development path for plantation economy and
society will demand, among other things, economic integration
with similarly placed economies, and a political ideology derived
from the specific plantation heritage.

We need, however, to be somewhat equivocal in our conclusions about the future development of Cuba because the ten-year
experience of change in that country is much too short for percep-
tive analysis and because we do not have sufficient information on
what has gone on so far, or of what is being planned for the long
term. Future and continuing study of the Cuban experience must
be a priority for everyone interested in the problem of transformation and development in plantation economies.

Our tentative conclusion from the consideration of attempts at
change in Ceylon and Cuba is that so far there is no evidence of
successful measures to eliminate the major underdevelopment
biases of the plantation system. It is necessary, therefore, to indicate what possibilities are suggested by the analysis provided in
this book.

2. Overcoming the obstacles to development: theoretical possibilities and issues

Perhaps the most significant historical experience of change in all
the plantation economies of the world was that of the forced adjustments induced by World War II. During the period of hostili-
ties when ocean lanes for merchant shipping were partially closed,
imported goods were hard to secure and everywhere plantation

ist" vs. "socialist" economy is explored by Edwin Charle, "The Con-
cept of Neo-Colonialism and Its Relation to Rival Economic Systems,"
Social and Economic Studies, December 1966, and by Jay R. Mandle,
"Neo-Imperialism: An Essay in Definition," *Social and Economic
Studies,* September 1967.

economy achieved a measure of diversification. Light manufacturing developed, particularly in processed foods like edible oils and margarine, building materials like cement, and relatively labor-intensive industries like matches and footwear. And agricultural production was diversified to provide supplies of foodstuffs, like vegetables, root crops, and livestock products, all of which were previously imported in one form or another. Much of the actual economic growth and development which these countries have achieved has come in recent decades and has been based essentially on the foundations laid during the war. The cynic would conclude that what these countries need is another war. That may well be so, and it may come down to this. But for now we conclude that the war experience provides us with a major clue about possibilities for change and transformation. It is that plantation economy is far too open for development to take place, and measures to bring about some degree of closure must be included in the bag of policy instruments. This is one of the obvious omissions in the Cuban case. The Cuban economy is still much too open for induced development. The degree of openness is, we suspect, not unrelated to the adoption of alien ideology. It is of some interest to note in passing that all the materially advanced countries in the world have passed through periods in which the foundations for development were laid, either by closure (for example, United States and Japan) or by expansion of territory (for example, Britain and France). The underdevelopment biases deriving from openness have been studied by several economists.[6]

However, openness is not the only obstacle to development of plantation economy. There are many other economic problems that must be dealt with: securing the linkages from plantation activity, land reform, income redistribution, resource use adjustments, technological change, and appropriate restructuring of economic institutions. These are all now very briefly considered. The intention in this final chapter is simply to outline ideas for

6. See in particular Dudley Seers, "The Mechanism of an Open Petroleum Economy," *Social and Economic Studies,* June 1964; and Havelock Brewster, "Exports, Employment and Wages: Trinidad-Tobago and Mr. Seers's Model of the Open Economy." *Research Papers* (Central Statistical Office, Trinidad, April 1968).

change that are suggested by the analysis. The aim here is not to provide final solutions. All the people of plantation society acting together will have to find the final solutions. It is hoped that the ideas coming out of this book eventually will contribute to that process.

In our analysis in Chapter 7, we reviewed the arguments of Leubuscher in connection with metropolitan location of processing plantation raw materials. We concluded there that the critical factors at present are metropolitan ownership and control of plantation production and limitations deriving from the size of the market in the plantation economies. In addition, technical knowledge and process innovation currently favor metropolitan location of processing. Furthermore, as we saw in Chapter 5, many other linkages associated with plantation activity are now being secured by the multinational enterprises. These include shipping, engineering industry, and product diversification, all of which provide a basis for potential development of plantation economies. If the plantation economies are to secure these linkages for themselves, they will need to do several things. First, they need to wrest all (or some) control of plantation activity from metropolitan enterprise to set the stage for a reversal of the present big-company small-country arrangement. This implies *national ownership of land and capital assets* of metropolitan plantation enterprise, and it opens up the whole question of retaliation and the incipient Third World-metropolitan conflict. It implies as well a high degree of co-ordination among the Third World countries to make it difficult for companies to play off one country against the other. There are at least two alternative paths that Third World countries can follow in this matter. One is to take complete control away from metropolitan enterprise. This will pay the highest development dividends in the long run but is a more painful and conflict-pregnant path. The other involves negotiation with metropolitan enterprise to secure all the linkages that will arise in the future from *incremental* demand. The dividends here are naturally lower and so is the probability of international conflict and violence.

The second major change necessary to secure plantation linkages for plantation economy is regional economic integration. This will increase the size of the market in plantation economy and make it economically feasible to establish industry allied to plantation production—processing, shipping, engineering, and chemical industries in particular. We should also note that regional economic integration will contribute much more to development because this will open up other production possibilities in plantation economy as a result of opportunities for resource combination and export substitution. An example of resource combination is the location of aluminum smelting and manufacture in the Caribbean by·smelting alumina from Jamaica, where power supplies are inadequate, in Guyana where the power potential is great. Export substitution opportunities arise from the trading of a share of the metropolitan market for plantation output in return for a guarantee of the regional market for some other agricultural product (or products). Again an example of this is provided by Jamaica's agreeing to cede the *incremental* demand for bananas in the United Kingdom to the Windward Islands in return for a guaranteed Windward market for Jamaican potatoes or livestock products.[7]

The third major change that is necessary is integration of research and knowledge relating to plantation-associated industry among the plantation economies. This will serve to increase knowledge of production possibilities and to develop new uses of the products and new techniques of processing. We noted in Chapter 5 that the current trend of industrial innovation by plantation enterprise is strongly influenced by the nature of existing investments.[8] So too, the interests of plantation economy will dictate the trend of industrial innovation if industrial research programs are integrated. No single plantation economy can afford the necessary

7. The argument about these concrete possibilities for resource combination and export substitution is made in Norman Girvan, *The Caribbean Bauxite Industry* (I.S.E.R., University of the West Indies, Jamaica, 1967); and G. L. Beckford, *The West Indian Banana Industry* (University of the West Indies, Jamaica, 1967).

8. An example of this is the Tate & Lyle innovation of "The use of spirally welded stainless steel piping for chemical storage, which is resistant to most liquids, does not rust or pit, and is easily cleaned. Products as diverse as gasoline, methanol, benzene and alkylates can be pumped through the same line." It was the company's existing investments in molasses storage facilities that led to this particular innovation. See *Tate & Lyle Times International,* July 1969, pp. 6–7.

investment involved in this research; and industrial research involves significant scale economies. Hence the need for regional economic integration is further strengthened.[9]

The regional groupings may have to include Third World countries other than the plantation economies. To take a concrete example, if Ghana and Nigeria are to capture from metropolitan enterprise the value-added in manufacture of chocolate products they will need to work out an arrangement with Caribbean countries for supplies of sugar. Leubuscher argued that one of the reasons why manufacture of chocolate products could not take place in Ghana was that Ghana did not have the necessary sugar. We are arguing here that Britain grew neither cocoa nor enough sugar. Yet Britain managed to integrate West Indian sugar production with West African cocoa production to secure the lion's share of value-added in both cases for its own economic development. Third World countries will have to do the same thing to secure the development linkages and benefits for themselves.

Land reform and income redistribution are absolutely essential for development in plantation economy. Again, our analysis in this book indicates that the real dynamic for development resides in the peasant sector, not in the plantation sector. In addition, we indicated that the low incomes of the bulk of people in plantation society limit the size of the market (therefore the potential for some industry) and restricts domestic savings and investment. Consequently, a program involving a redistribution of land and income should contribute immensely to the process of transformation. It must be noted, however, that land reform must include appropriate rural economic institutions to provide credit, technical knowledge, and so forth, and, to be effective, it must be part of a process of radical social change to create an ethos in which attitudes to land ownership will change in a way that contributes to effective use of the land. Most of the attempts at land reform in

9. Third World economists, particularly those in the Caribbean and Latin America, have already extended our knowledge of the theoretical gains from regional economic integration in the structuralist terms outlined here. An important example of these contributions is Havelock Brewster and Clive Y. Thomas, *The Dynamics of West Indian Economic Integration* (I.S.E.R., University of the West Indies, Jamaica, 1967).

plantation economy have failed to induce the required development because these have been carried out in a piecemeal fashion,
without supporting institutional changes and with no change in the
social ethos surrounding attitudes to land ownership.[10] In addition
we should note that the land to be made available to peasants
must be the best quality plantation land and not just the marginal,
rocky, and infertile hillside estates and the like, as has been the
case with most "land settlement" schemes previously implemented
in several of the plantation economies.[11]

Income redistribution will place a very heavy strain on available food supplies in plantation economy because increased supplies take time before they can be available and because the redistribution will immediately increase the demand for many
foodstuffs. The chief bottleneck in this connection will be in the
area of livestock products. For animals cannot be grown overnight
and the poor people of plantation society have a heavy backlog of
pent-up desires for animal protein. In this context, food rationing
will be necessary in the short term and medium term in order that
available supplies are spread in some reasonable way and so that
price inflation can be contained. Cuba has experienced this phenomenon since the redistribution of income and land in that country during the early 1960's, and food rationing is still necessary
there.[12]

In order to secure the resource-use adjustments that are neces-

10. The literature on land reform in plantation economy reveals considerable confusion about analyzing the effects of land reform and the
social costs and benefits of land reform programs. See, for example,
Ungku Aziz, *Subdivision of Estates in Malaya, 1951–1960,* 3 volumes (University of Malaya, Department of Economics, Kuala Lumpur, 1962); Garyl Ness, "Subdivision of Estates in Malaya, 1951–
1960—A Methodological Critique," *Malayan Economic Review,*
April 1964, pp. 55–62; G. David Quirin, "Estate Subdivision and
Economic Development—A Review Article," *Malayan Economic
Review,* April 1964; and Ungku Aziz, "Subdivision of Estates in Malaya, 1951–1960—Author's Reply," *Malayan Economic Review,*
October 1966.
11. See our discussion of this in Chapter 1 above.
12. The Cuban experience in this matter is examined at greater length
in George L. Beckford, "A Caribbean View of Cuba," *New World
Quarterly,* Croptime 1966, and in several of the references given earlier in this chapter.

sary for development (for example, switching land use from sugar to livestock production), measures to deal with present distortions in the structure of output prices will be necessary. The analysis in Chapter 6 indicated that the price structure is currently distorted to encourage incremental flow of resources into plantation export production. This has to be corrected by lowering the price of exports and raising prices received by farmers for things like livestock products. Guaranteed prices for these products are not enough. Measures must be taken to ensure that adequate marketing facilities become available, and agricultural credit schemes should favor production oriented to the domestic market over that for export. The present tendency of policy makers in plantation economy is to rationalize the present patterns of land use by the consideration that the value of output per acre of land is higher in plantation export output than in alternative products for the domestic market.[13] That argument is irrelevant for at least two reasons: the divergence of private and social returns and the fact that many of the alternative products have the potential for generating more spread effects in the long run than plantation export production. Another fallacy of the policy makers is that metropolitan preferences on plantation products are a subsidy by the metropolitan treasury. In point of fact, plantation economy provides, in return, a guaranteed market for metropolitan manufactures; the result is that the people of plantation society have to pay more for goods like textiles and footwear when imported from the metropole than when imported from third countries (like Japan and Italy). We find, therefore, that the subsidy for plantation export production is really borne by the people of plantation society and weighs heavily on the poorest sections of the society.

In the area of agricultural research as well, measures are needed to reorient expenditure and effort from the present concentration on export crops and toward the needs of production for the domestic and regional markets. This reorientation is likely to bring higher returns to investment in agricultural knowledge than

13. An example of this kind of theorizing can be found in a recent metropolitan-authored study of the Jamaican sugar industry. See *Report of the Commission of Enquiry into the Jamaican Sugar Industry* (Government Printer, Kingston, 1968).

now obtain with the excess concentration on export crops. Much of the present agricultural research in plantation economy is financed by the plantations themselves. So that when national ownership is secured, it would not be difficult to tax the export production to provide the funds necessary for research into problems related to production for the home markets. Associated with the research question is the problem of agricultural extension to take the new knowledge out to farmers. Again, for this to succeed we need appropriate institutional arrangements and a hospitable social ethos.

The necessary restructuring of economic institutions to promote economic development is very elaborate and only sketches can be provided now. The foreign-owned commercial banks need to be nationalized so as to make the savings of people in plantation economy available for investment there. Informal credit institutions, like partner or sou-sou, need to be legitimized and expanded so as to make small lot savings available for investment in development projects. Regional development banks must be set up in order to provide financing for regional projects, such as industrial and agricultural research. Marketing organizations will be necessary to stimulate the flow of products and to manipulate the price structure to advantage, also to regulate the continuing export trade. Shipping councils will be needed to acquire ships, regulate the export and regional trade, and develop the fishing industry, which has significant potential spread effects. Research institutes are needed to undertake both agricultural and industrial research. Publicly owned communications media will be necessary to keep people continuously informed of developments in the society, the region, and the world, so as to foster and maintain a high level of development motivation and involvement; to transport produce within the nation and the region; and to influence the daily lives of people in important ways. An educational system directed to every individual in plantation society is essential, and the content of education must be such as to expand the creative horizons of people in order to promote greater use of the resource endowment of plantation economy. These are only a sample of the kind of institutional adjustments that will be necessary. There are many more which may be of equal importance but what we have listed is sufficient to provide general indication of the magnitude of the adjustment problem.

It is very clear, from the ideas outlined above, that the process of transformation envisaged here will be very painful (food rationing and international violence are only two of the obvious areas of pain). It will also demand great sacrifices by the people of plantation society in the short term and the medium term. As well, it will require a new social ethos to bring this kind of change about. And it is obvious that a considerable degree of government intervention is necessary. We can respond to these observations only by noting that without these changes plantation economy can never achieve the kind of economic development that metropolitan economy has achieved. That economic development is a painful business, regardless of the development path, because development involves change and social change is never without pain. That the majority of people in plantation society for a long time have been on the receiving end of international violence—slavery was the greatest manifestation of this and dispossession after Emancipation was only a milder form. That the majority of people in plantation society, throughout their history, have been making great sacrifices for which the benefits have accrued to white planters, metropolitan enterprise, and metropolitan economy; consequently, they are accustomed to sacrifice and ought to be willing now to make it on their own behalf.[14] And, finally, we note that government intervention is nothing new to plantation economy; always this has been a feature of the system, but the intervention up to now has been chiefly by metropolitan government on their own behalf, while what is involved here is intervention by governments of plantation society on behalf of the people living there.[15]

Economic change alone is not sufficient. Indeed, as we have argued above, many of the economic changes can succeed only if there is a favorable social ethos. We need, therefore, to give some

14. The major new sacrifice will have to be made by the small minority of people in the planter-associated classes. But it is full time that these people make a contribution to their country.
15. Examples of metropolitan government intervention in plantation economy are imperial preference, navigational acts to force shipping in only metropolitan-owned bottoms, and so forth.

consideration to how the social environment of plantation society can be adjusted in a manner that will facilitate the kinds of economic change envisaged above.

3. The politics and social dynamics of transformation and change

Since the state has a major role to play in plantation economies overcoming the major development obstacles, we need to consider the politics of transformation. Our analysis in Chapter 3 indicated that with the present pattern of social organization and distribution of power, political leaders in plantation society have not been able to manipulate state power sufficiently on behalf of the majority of people. It follows, therefore, that what is required is a fundamental change in social organization and new political leaders emerging from the rank and file of the dispossessed groups. We should note that the redistribution of land and income will alter the structure of power. The power of the state, and of the previously dispossessed, increases while that of the previous plantation owners declines. Plantation owners are therefore unlikely to take kindly to this kind of change. Presumably many will leave, as happened in Cuba, and those who remain will no doubt attempt to undermine attempts to make the change effective with respect to development but they can be contained by the majority and some will doubtless adjust to the new situation as time goes on.

The social reorganization that is required by the kind of economic change we have outlined must be such as to heal the fractures inherent in the plantation system—fractures that appear covertly in the supply of and demand for resources, particularly land, and fractures that show up more starkly in social relationships between groups in the society. The healing of these fractures will serve to integrate plantation society and to make the social and political obstacles to development less formidable. This process of social integration can best be institutionalized by linking it with the single institution that now binds all segments of the society together—that is, the plantation itself. The inference we draw from this is that ownership, control, and production of the plantations must be shared equally among all the pluralities that make up the particular plantation society. Each plurality has an allegiance with the plantation as a result of the historical legacy. And now each must be given an opportunity to share the benefits equally. This will provide the basis for meaningful social integration, for developing social consciousness and responsibility—thereby creating a favorable social ethos—and for integrating resource supply and demand.

This kind of social reorganization must involve several things if it is to heal permanently the social fractures left by the plantation system. Among these things, the more important are equality between the races and equality of educational opportunities. For the process of social reorganization to begin, it will be necessary of course to mobilize the society for change. Because of the existing weakness of social cohesion and loose community organization, the problem is immense. The process can begin only with a new style of politics based on a sequencing that, first, mobilizes national consciousness about what is wrong with the present system of social and economic organization and what can be done to correct the resulting injustices; second, to heighten this consciousness and win commitment for making the change; and third, to translate the commitment won into action. This is, of course, all easier said than done.

Given the existing situation, the question naturally arises as to how such a new style of politics can emerge. The answer is that it is in process of emerging already. Two developments have contributed to this. One is that the social and economic injustices of the plantation system have become aggravated in recent years and therefore the forces of self-destruction are gaining an ascendancy through an increasing consciousness among people of the state of chronic dispossession. And the other is that Third World analysts have been producing fresh insights into the structural limitations of the colonial system. Fanon is perhaps the best known of these analysts and he represents a whole army of Third World writers who have made important advances in our understanding of the persistence of material and cultural dispossession among Third World peoples.[16] This understanding has provided the infrastruc-

16. It is not a coincidence that the analysts of plantation society have contributed a disproportionately high share of Third World output of

ture for much of the publicist activities of individuals and groups throughout the Third World which has served to broaden and heighten consciousness, and to sow the seeds of commitment among small groups of people everywhere. Black power is only one example—perhaps the best known—of what is going on already. All that is now required is further analysis to feed the furnaces that already have been lit by previous analysis.

The importance of analysis cannot be overemphasized. Part of the reason why present and past political leaders in plantation society have failed to bring about the necessary social and economic transformation is related to the fact that they have been largely guided by policy advisers whose understanding of the development problems is based on economic models which were developed out of the metropolitan experience and reality and which do not fit the properties of plantation economy. We are impressed by the statement of John Maynard Keynes that

the ideas of economists and political philosophers, both when they are right and when they are wrong, are more powerful than is commonly understood. Indeed the world is ruled by little else. Practical men, who believe themselves to be quite exempt from any intellectual influences, are usually the slaves of some defunct economist.[17]

Keynes was quite correct in this observation. What is being suggested here is that policy advisers in plantation societies today do not realize that Keynes himself is now the "defunct economist" and that they have badly advised political leaders as a result.[18] We do not wish to make the case that these leaders would indeed accept advice for radical economic change because our analysis in Chapter 3 suggests

scholarship. In addition to Fanon, there is an impressive list of names of outstanding writers born and raised in plantation society —Furtado, Césaire, Garvey, Carmichael, and James are only a small sample of this large class of men. The reason is that in plantation society the injustices are more marked than, say, peasant colonial society.

17. J. M. Keynes, *The General Theory of Employment Interest and Money* (London, 1957), p. 383.

18. This is not quite fair to Keynes, for he never addressed himself to the problems of underdevelopment in Third World countries. Keynes was concerned with economic adjustment problems in advanced industrial (metropolitan) economies. His work has in fact been misused by development economists.

quite the opposite. The case being made here is simply that analysis is a necessary, though *not* sufficient, condition for the change envisaged.

Another matter related to the dynamics of social change is the political ideology that is needed to mobilize action eventually. All we can say in this connection is that the appropriate ideology will emerge out of the dynamics of change. We can state, in a negative fashion, that the existing political ideologies in the world at large were not derived from the plantation experience. Capitalism, socialism, communism, and all the other known "isms" developed out of the feudal-capitalist systems of Europe, the settler-homestead-capitalist systems of North America and elsewhere, and the feudal-semi-capitalist systems of Asia and elsewhere. All those various systems of social and economic organization have very different social structures and class systems than plantation society. It might well be, therefore, that political ideologies that relate to those experiences are not adequate for the social and political realities of plantation society. We cannot be entirely sure of this. But it is of some interest to note that in spite of the very high level of material advancement for the nation as a whole, the United States has not managed to solve its own plantation problem. In fact, the plantation South of that country has profoundly influenced the social order of the national society by exporting its plantation-based pattern of social organization to other regions. The persistent state of black dispossession, material and social, in that country is the stark manifestation of this fact.

We conclude, therefore, that a new political ideology will be necessary to stimulate social change and action in plantation society. Exactly what this ideology will be like we do not know. What is certain is that it will develop out of the process of change that has already begun; on that account it will be *the* appropriate ideology for servicing the needs of the new society eventually conceived out of the process.

9

A concluding note on
the strategy of transformation
and the general third world scene

The reader who is a cynic is likely to respond to the ideas outlined in the preceding chapter with the question: "But man, where
do we begin"? After all, we have said that this or that is needed
but that some other precondition is necessary for this or that to
happen. The traditional reaction is that we are caught in the trap
of the chicken-and-the-egg. We submit that the precondition of all
preconditions for change and transformation is a structuring of the
minds of people to accommodate the change. Once this is accom-
plished all other things will develop. Because of the historical legacy, all the people of plantation society see themselves as inferior
and incapable of carrying out major schemes. That black people in
the New World generally regard their own people—themselves,
that is—as ugly, lazy, and irresponsible is only one example of
the phenomenon.[1] The point is that change must begin in the
minds of people, relating to the concept they have of themselves.
(Black power has made an important contribution in this connection by the emphasis it places on black beauty and black dignity.)
For whatever a people contemplate to do is determined, in the

1. Black people themselves regard Negro hair as "bad" and Negro features as "ugly," just to take two well-known examples of the general
   self-contempt.

final analysis, by what they think they can do. In short, thought services action.[2]

There is no chicken-and-egg problem at all. We begin by changing the view that the people of plantation society have of themselves. This creates self-confidence and sets the stage for a head-on confrontation with the plantation system to destroy it and to create a new social order, of the general nature we have outlined. In the ensuing process, the social dynamics of the situation create successive rounds of preconditions for the rounds still to come and the whole process becomes self-determinate in much the same way as there is self-determinacy (for underdevelopment) within the existing framework of social and economic organization. That we have been able to demonstrate past self-determinacy by analysis is possible only because we have the historical empiricism to support us. We do not, of course, have that kind of support in looking at the future new development path. So the certainty of the analysis is considerably reduced. One thing is certain; it is that an important part of the process of changing the minds of people is the understanding that analysis provides. That is the spirit in which this book is offered to the people of plantation society.

Let us restate here the basic dilemmas of the people of plantation society. First, the system denies the majority of people a real stake in their country. Second, a chronic dependency syndrome is characteristic of the whole population. And, third, people are not sufficiently motivated to make sacrifices and to expend effort. These are direct legacies of the plantation system. Only by destroying the system can they be overcome. Destroying the system involves revolutionary change in the institutional structure—that is, the economic, social, and political arrangements. It is possible to release the creative energies of people once they have a stake and have confidence in themselves.

We begin, therefore, by recognizing that the present dependency syndrome in our psychological makeup is a legacy of the system

2. On this score, see the very stimulating article by Lloyd Best, "Independent Thought and Caribbean Freedom," *New World Quarterly,* Cropover, 1967. Best further developed the ideas in that article in subsequent issues of the *Quarterly* and has written more on this particular topic in relation to the plantation setting than any other scholar.

we are destroying. This provides the basis for becoming genuinely independent. It sets the stage for mobilizing the human resources of plantation society to take full control of our resources and to use these resources to the fullest advantage of all segments of the population. This, in turn, gives people a real stake in the affairs of state and creates an environment that induces people to become highly motivated behind efforts to promote the welfare of the society as a whole. After that, institutional arrangements to ensure popular participation in decision making will have to be introduced in order to maintain the social dynamic. Once genuine independence is seen to be a real possibility, people gain confidence in themselves and in their fellow man. Once confidence is gained and the society has control of its resources, all things are possible.

Our conclusion is that the development problems of plantation economy and society are not intractable in any physical or technical sense. The most intractable problem is the colonized condition of the minds of the people. Until we decolonize the mind, there is little hope that genuine independence can be achieved. Genuine independence is the ultimate objective of the process of decolonization which today characterizes the struggles of all colonial peoples.

We need further to recognize that among the people of plantation society the most colonized minds are to be found within the higher ranks of the social order. Social mobility within the plantation system is based on the acquisition of ascriptive characteristics and culture traits of the North Atlantic (white) colonizers. Education has played an important role in this connection because the perspectives provided and the knowledge imparted are fundamentally North Atlantic. So we find that by and large the intellectual classes have the most colonized minds. Partly for the same reason, the least colonized minds are to be found among the lowest ranks of the social order. Therein lies the greatest potential for a revolutionary break with the existing system. And that is why the political leadership for decolonization must come from "below." The intellectual classes cannot lead in the struggle; they need first to decolonize their own minds and to develop genuinely independent scholarship in the process. That will place them in better stead to service the technical needs of the new societies.

Finally, we wish to make some observations on the implications of the present study of plantation economy for other Third World countries which seem as well to be trapped in an equilibrium of underdevelopment but whose underdevelopment cannot be associated with the plantation influence. Where the plantation has not been the dominant institution in Third World countries, the main rural social systems are either some kind of peasant system, as in Africa, or a variant of the feudal system, as in parts of Latin America. The inference we draw from our own study of plantation economy is that social scientists in these countries should begin seriously to analyze the structural properties of these economies and societies to determine whether or not these properties contribute to the persistence of underdevelopment. When we know this, it will be far easier to understand the changes that are necessary to promote development in those countries. Meanwhile, there are certain aspects of plantation economy which apply as well to other Third World economies. For example, the colonial heritage resulted in the peasant-based export economies becoming as open and dependent on metropolitan economy as is the case with plantation economy. And the banking systems, the cannibalizing of linkages by metropolitan enterprise, and to some extent the view that people of these societies have of themselves, are all similar to the plantation case. To that extent, the analysis in this book is applicable in some ways to many other Third World countries. But the full dimensions of the development problem and the social dynamics for change in those societies can be understood only by specific study of their institutional environment.

If this book stimulates that work, it would have made a greater contribution to the Third World movement than we at first contemplated. Meanwhile, the present study suggests that there are numerous areas in which collaboration between all Third World countries, regardless of the pattern of internal organization, will secure greater development benefits for them. This derives from their common relationships with metropolitan economy. Collaboration is required to break the stranglehold of metropolitan enterprise over all Third World economies; to promote programs of agricultural and industrial research; to arrange shipping and air transport among Third World countries and between these and the North Atlantic. And for a host of other things—not the least of which, perhaps, is the military defense of Third World independence when this is finally won.

I

Plantations in underdeveloped countries and regions

There is no single source of information on the relative importance of plantations in Third World economies. Reference must be made to data relating to individual countries in order to get such information. We have attempted to do this on a somewhat preliminary basis and that general information is summarized in the second section of this Appendix. Recently the International Labor Organization (ILO) carried out a survey to ascertain the importance of plantations in a number of countries. The information provided by that survey is summarized below.

1. Summary of a recent ILO survey

The information presented here is derived from a report on an International Labor Organization (ILO) survey carried out in the period 1962–64.[1] The survey involved field studies by a team of "experts" and covered twelve countries as follows:

Latin America—Colombia, Costa Rica, Ecuador, and Peru
Asia—Ceylon, India, Indonesia, and Malaya
Africa—Cameroon, Ivory Coast, Mauritius, and Tanzania
Consideration is also given to Brazil in the ILO report.

1. International Labor Organization (ILO), *Plantation Workers* (Geneva, 1966), especially pp. 9–10, 12–13, and 55–57.

For the thirteen countries considered in the survey, the land area occupied by plantations varied from 24 million hectares in the four Asian countries to about 14 million in the five Latin American countries and to 2 million in the four African countries. The plantations of India and Brazil alone account for some three-quarters of the total plantation area of the thirteen countries. The land area occupied by plantations in comparison with that of total cultivated land varies substantially among the countries surveyed. The ratio of plantation land to cultivated area is very high (more than half) in Mauritius, Malaya, Ceylon, Ivory Coast, and Brazil and in the first three countries the cultivated area represents a very high percentage of total land area. In the four Latin American countries surveyed, cultivated area is a small percentage of the national territory (less than 10 per cent) and plantations occupy between 25 and just over 40 per cent of the cultivated areas. In Cameroon and Tanzania plantations cover only 5 per cent of the cultivated area whereas in India and Indonesia they account for between 10 and 20 per cent.[2]

The importance of plantation exports in the total exports of individual countries is significant in almost all the countries surveyed. Apart from Peru and India, the value of plantation exports generally exceeds one-half the total value of national exports. In five cases—Mauritius, Costa Rica, Ecuador, Ceylon, and Colombia—the share of plantation exports is said to exceed 80 per cent. In four others—Brazil, the Ivory Coast, Cameroon, and Tanzania—it is said to be between 60 and 75 per cent, whereas in Malaya and Indonesia the share is just over 50 per cent. For the two exceptions noted above, Peru and India, plantation exports are between one-third and one-quarter of national exports so that even in these cases the proportion is not insignificant. We find as well that in most of these cases (again, Peru and India being the exceptions) national exports are highly concentrated, not more than two "plantation products" providing the bulk of total export earnings. Coffee in Brazil and Colombia, bananas in Ecuador, tea in Ceylon, rubber in Malaya and Indonesia, and (most extremely) sugar in Mauritius are cases where a single commodity accounts

2. *Ibid.*, pp. 9–10.

for a high percentage of total exports. Coffee and bananas in Costa Rica, and coffee and cocoa in the Ivory Coast and Cameroon are two-commodity cases. And, lastly, three products—sisal, cotton, and coffee—account for 60 per cent of Tanganyika's exports.[3]

The importance of plantations as a source of employment can be partially ascertained for only six of the countries surveyed by the ILO team—Mauritius, Colombia, and the four countries in Asia. In Malaya and Mauritius, plantation employment is said to be a source of income for almost all of the agricultural labor force in these countries—92 and 100 per cent, respectively. Indeed in Mauritius, plantations in 1962 employed 60 per cent of the country's total labor force. And in Tanganyika, plantation employment as reported by the Sisal Growers' Association for September 1962 represented "approximately 59 per cent of the country's active agricultural population." [4] In India and Indonesia, although the absolute numbers of plantation workers are reported to be substantial (over 1 million in India and 600,000 in Indonesia), the plantation share of the agricultural labor force is small in each case (less than 1 per cent in India and 3 per cent in Indonesia).[5] The table below summarizes the picture presented in the ILO survey in respect of the occupation of active agricultural population (in thousands) and the role of plantations in providing employment: [6]

	Total active population	Total active agricultural population	Plantation workers
Ceylon	2,993.3	1,584.1	645.4
Colombia	3,775.6	2,260.0	737.8
India	188,675.5	137,545.9	1,214.6
Indonesia	32,708.6	23,516.2	618.0
Malaya	2,164.9	1,244.8	1,150.1
Mauritius	187.4	69.5	69.3

3. The information in the ILO survey relates to Tanganyika, which is only part of the national territory of Tanzania encompassing Tanganyika and Zanzibar.
4. International Labor Organization, *op. cit.,* p. 57.
5. *Ibid.,* pp. 55–56.
6. These data relate to a time during the period 1960–1963, except for Malaya, which is 1957. The figures for Ceylon on total active and

These data show clearly that plantations are important in providing employment in several countries. There is a substantially larger number of countries similar to those listed above which were covered in the survey. These will be considered in the next section. What we wish to note here is simply that even in those countries which do not meet the criteria by which we differentiate "plantation economies" (see Chapter 1), plantations still employ large numbers of people. India is an outstanding example of this.

This survey of a relatively small number of countries in which the plantation system is found indicates that whatever index is used (land area, employment, or export earnings), plantations are of considerable economic importance in several national economies in the Third World today.[7] This importance varies significantly as between countries. Among the thirteen countries considered in the ILO survey, Mauritius is the most dominated by plantations and India and Peru the least. Summary information on other Third World countries from a variety of sources is provided next.

_____

2. A descriptive survey of the major plantation regions

The chief plantation regions of the world are the Caribbean, Southeast Asia (including Ceylon), and the islands of the Indian and Pacific oceans. In Chapter 1 we noted as well that plantations dominate the social and political economies of Northeast Brazil, and the United States South, and the Caribbean lowlands of Central America. These areas and the Caribbean islands constitute

active agricultural population are for 1953 and those for total active population of Colombia are for 1951. The figures given in the tabulation for total active agricultural population and plantation workers for Mauritius refer to a period during the sugarcane harvest (September). Corresponding figures for an out-of-season period (March) are given as 60.2 and 60.1, respectively. See ILO, *op. cit.*, Appendix III.

7. It is apparent that some of the data presented by the ILO survey team need to be treated with circumspection. Apparently most of the data are official estimates provided by the governments of the countries visited. As with all economic data of this type, there are normally wide margins of error. Nevertheless they provide at least some indication of general orders of magnitude of a kind that is quite satisfactory for our purpose.

Plantation America. The following is a summary discussion of the
relative importance of plantations in these major regions.

I. PLANTATION AMERICA

Almost all the Caribbean islands satisfy our criteria for plantation
economies (see Chapter 1). The old plantation structure of *Cuba*
has been radically transformed since the Castro government came
to power in 1959. The formerly foreign-owned plantations have
now all become a part of the public sector. Since 1964 the balance
of public and private ownership of agricultural land has remained
basically unaltered. State plantations occupy roughly 65 per cent
of all farm land while the remaining 35 per cent is occupied by
200,000 private farmers who are organized under the National
Association of Small Farmers (ANAP), which channels government services to these farmers and which is the basis for central
control of their production. The private sector of Cuban agriculture is most important in the production of vegetables, coffee, tobacco, and livestock. The state-owned plantation sector is responsible for Cuba's sugar production.[8] Sugar is of course the very life
blood of the Cuban economy, accounting for very high shares of
income, employment, foreign-exchange earnings, and land area in
cultivation. However, the non-economic influences of the plantation are not very marked as a socialist pattern of social and political organization is gradually replacing the traditional plantation
system which existed prior to the revolution.

In *Jamaica* plantations occupy about 56 per cent of the farm
land. In 1960, 300 estates of over 500 acres occupied 40 per cent
of the agricultural land. The main plantation crop here is also
sugar. Roughly half of the sugarcane is grown on the sugar estates
owned by companies which process the whole crop. And the remaining half is grown by "cane farmers," among whom those with
larger farms (mainly family plantations) account for the bulk of
cane farmers' supplies. During the period 1964–66, sugar accounted for about 23 per cent of total exports; the value of sugar
production and its by-products was roughly 42 per cent of the

8. George L. Beckford, "A Note on Agricultural Organization and·Plan-
ning in Cuba," *Caribbean Studies,* October 1966, pp. 4–5.

gross domestic product of the agricultural sector as a whole. Sugar occupies most of the best arable land, is the largest single employer of labor in the economy, and contributes substantially to government revenue.

In *Haiti* plantation agriculture is said to be insignificant because the production structure is dominated by the peasantry. However, it is estimated that there are probably 1,000 estates owned by local urban elite and most of these are exploited through rental and sharecropping arrangements. Coffee which is the main export crop is based almost exclusively on peasant production. However, in addition to the locally owned estates there are important foreign-owned plantations which account for the second and third most important exports—sugar and sisal. The United States-owned Haitian American Sugar Company, for example, owns 27,000 acres of cane lands and accounts for 80 per cent of total sugar production; and the chief sisal producer is the U.S.-owned Daphere holding of 10,000 acres in the Northeast. The plantations in Haiti all occupy the best cultivable areas and since less than one-third of the country's land area is considered capable of raising crops, it would appear that plantation control of good agricultural land is substantial. And it is claimed that "the sugar industry normally furnishes employment for a substantial part of those counted in the labor force." [9] In addition, all the non-economic characteristics of the plantation system seem to apply.

The cornerstone of the economy of the *Dominican Republic* is sugar which accounts for more than half of the country's exports. This sugar is a plantation-based industry and there are banana plantations as well as others. Up until recently there was enough land room for both plantations and peasants but reportedly today the increase in population and the expansion of production through larger landholdings is rapidly forcing the Dominican peasants (and population) into the mountainous areas.[10] The plantation

9. W. F. Buck, *Haiti's Agriculture and Trade* (U.S. Department of Agriculture, ERS-Foreign 283, Washington, D. C., 1969), p. 7. Other information on Haiti provided in this paragraph was obtained from this source and from R. C. West and J. P. Augelli, *Middle America—Its Lands and Peoples* (Englewood Cliffs, New Jersey, 1966), pp. 154–57.

10. R. C. West and J. P. Augelli, *op. cit.,* pp. 145 ff. A good deal of the information on the rest of the Caribbean is also derived from this source.

hegemony of land and the importance of sugar in the economy places this country squarely in the category of plantation economies.

In *Puerto Rico* sugarcane occupies almost a half (the better half) of all cultivated land. Cane has traditionally dominated the coastal plains and interior valleys and is said to be now pushing back into the lower mountain slopes. The sugar plantation industry is the most important single employer of labor and it contributes substantially to income, export receipts, and government revenue.

Antigua is clearly a monocrop plantation economy, based on sugar production. Sugarcane occupies the best land in the central plains and valley bottoms; sugar accounts for 80 per cent of total exports; and the industry employs the bulk of the labor force. *St. Kitts* is an even more extreme case; it is really just a large sugar plantation. Almost all of the cultivable land is under cane and of this all but a few hundred acres are estate-owned. It is claimed that "there are practically no small landowners on the island" and St. Kitts has been described as "one of the few remaining examples of the almost pure estate economy of the 19th century." [11]

In *Guadeloupe* and *Martinique,* the pattern is much the same, though less marked than St. Kitts and Antigua. According to West and Augelli, "the economy of the French Antilles differs only in degree from that of a century ago. It is still dominated by plantations controlled by local planters and absentee stockholders." Sugar and its by-products and bananas account for over 90 per cent of total exports with absolute dependence on the protected French market. In Guadeloupe, the sugar plantations own over half of the sugar lands and the less desirable parts of the sugar plantation lands are divided into small plots and worked on a sharecropping basis by *colons*.[12]

In *Dominica, St. Lucia, St. Vincent* and *Grenada* the plantation pattern of production is not as evident. However, we do find that

11. H. J. Finkel, "Patterns of Land Tenure in the Leeward and Windward Islands and Their Relevance to Problems of Agricultural Development in the West Indies," *Economic Geography,* April 1964, pp. 165–66.
12. R. C. West and J. P. Augelli, *op. cit.,* pp. 209–14.

in Dominica most of the productive coastal land is owned by approximately eighty-five estates and in Grenada about half the land is in estates, most of which are run by managers for absentee owners. In these four islands, exports are highly concentrated on bananas. Even if the plantation pattern of production is not very marked, the fact that non-economic aspects of life reflect the plantation legacy bring these territories within our constituency.

Barbados is a clear case of a monocrop plantation economy, as it has been for the past 300 years. Sugarcane takes up 90 per cent of the cultivable land and sugar and its by-products account for 95 per cent of exports. Basically, everybody in that country is tied to sugar in one way or another; 240 estates hold four-fifths of the country's land.

In *Trinidad* although estates are less than 1 per cent of all farms they nevertheless control 40 per cent of the country's farm land. Sugar is the main plantation product but coconuts and cocoa are also involved. In terms of national income and output sugar is far outdone by petroleum but is the next industry in importance to the economy. Sugar's contribution to employment is, however, far greater than petroleum and the industry is the single most important source of employment. Production of sugarcane represents 60 per cent of the value of agricultural output. And sugar and its by-products substantially contribute to export earnings and government revenue. Non-economic aspects of life clearly reflect the plantation influence.

Moving across to the continent, we find the plantation influence again very pronounced in the Guianas—Guyana, Surinam, and Cayene. For *Guyana* Wilfred David recently provided certain basic information which reveals the economic importance of the sugar plantation industry. According to David, "sugar is the major single support of the economy of Guyana" and he concludes an analysis of the growth experience during the period 1953–64 with the statement: "The governing dynamic of the economy was the foreign-owned export sector comprised of sugar and bauxite." [13] Sugar and its by-products accounted for an average of 50 per cent

13. Wilfred David, *The Economic Development of Guyana, 1953–1964* (London, 1969), p. 374. The rest of the information in this paragraph is derived from this same source.

of the total value of exports over the period 1954–64; its contribution to G.N.P. was of the order of 17 to 20 per cent and in 1965 sugar accounted for 20 per cent of total fixed private investment. As labor displacement in the industry proceeded in recent years, its share of the labor force has fallen from 20 per cent in 1956 to about 15 per cent by 1960; however, the industry still remains the single most important employer of labor. And in recent years income and excise duties on sugar and its by-products contributed roughly 20 per cent of total government revenue; in addition the industry pays additional sums from time to time in indirect taxes of one kind or another. As concerns sugarcane production peasant cane farming is insignificant as foreign-owned plantations account for about 98 per cent of total cane production. One plantation company, Booker McConnell Limited, dominates the scene.

In *Brazil,* the traditional plantation area is the Northeast where the earliest slave plantations in the New World were established. However, plantations are important in other regions of that country as well. According to Manuel Diégues, "The basic types of Brazilian plantations are: sugar cane plantations in the Northeast; vast rubber plantations in the Amazon Valley; coffee plantations in the state of São Paulo and in Northern Paranà; cacao fazendas of Southern Bahia; banana plantations along the coast of São Paulo and Rio de Janeiro; and the *yerba mate* plantations of southern Mato Grosso." [14] From this, it appears that plantations are very widely dispersed throughout this vast country. According to the evidence presented by the Inter-American Committee for Agricultural Development (CIDA) study of land tenure in Brazil, the plantation influence is dominant throughout the entire agricultural sector of Brazil. But it still remains true that the Northeast best fits the criteria of plantation economy and society as used in the present study.

On the Caribbean lowlands of Central America the plantation influence on national economy is strongest for *British Honduras.* Up until the 1950's the dominant company there was "the Belize

14. Manuel Diégues, Jr., "Land Tenure and Use in the Brazilian Plantation System," in Pan American Union, *Plantation Systems of the New World* (Social Science Monographs, VII, Washington, D. C., 1959), p. 104.

Estate and Produce Co. Ltd., whose headquarters are in London. . . . Of the total six million acres of land in the colony, the Belize Estate and Produce Co. owns one million acres comprising forests and some of the most fertile land in the territory." [15] And since the 1950's the establishment and development of the sugar industry has extended the plantation influence. Foreign-owned plantations produce all the sugar which accounts for more than 30 per cent of exports and a considerable amount of employment. Elsewhere in Central America the plantation influence is limited to the coastal valleys of the Caribbean. In Honduras, Guatemala, Costa Rica, and Panama, large-scale foreign-owned banana plantations provide virtually the only source of income and employment for people living in the Caribbean lowlands. In addition, plantation banana exports are a high percentage of total national exports in Honduras and Panama—44 and 48 per cent, respectively. The share of bananas in total exports is 24 per cent in Costa Rica but only 7 per cent in Guatemala.

For the *United States South* there are no adequate data which can be used to describe the plantation profile. The agricultural censuses of that country in recent decades have generally ignored information relevant to the plantation system.[16] What qualitative evidence there is suggests that the plantation influence is strongest in the region described variously as the "Southeast" or the "Old South" or the "Black Belt." This region consists chiefly of the following nine states: Virginia, North Carolina, South Carolina, Georgia, Alabama, Mississippi, Louisiana, Arkansas, and Tennessee. The plantation influence extends beyond these nine states but the long history of its presence in the states named gives it a prominence that is not as marked elsewhere in the South.

II. PLANTATION ASIA

The geographical region of Asia where the plantation influence is greatest at the level of national economy and society is the more

---

15. Kathleen M. Stahl, *The Metropolitan Organization of British Colonial Trade* (London, 1951), p. 31.
16. For a discussion of this problem, see Merle Prunty, Jr., "The Census on Multiple-Units and Plantations," *The Professional Geographer,* September 1956.

southern part of what is generally described as Southeast Asia. Malaya, Indonesia, and the Philippines are the chief countries. And together with Ceylon, these constitute Plantation Asia.

In *Ceylon* the plantation influence is paramount. According to Forrest, "It is a commonplace to say that tea is the lifeblood of Ceylon; it provides two-thirds of the country's export revenue, while the wages it pays, its countless minor offshoots and the services which feed it, represent a further massive slice of her internally circulating wealth." [17] In tea production, plantations account for about three-quarters of total acreage and over 55 per cent of the total is under corporate ownership. In the case of rubber, another important part of the economy, plantations account for less than half of total acreage and company estates only a quarter of the total. It is also claimed that the plantation sector, with its associated activities, influences all levels of the economy—banking and credit being cited as examples. [18]

Malaya depends heavily on its rubber industry. According to McHale writing in the *Malayan Economic Review,*

. . . The rubber industry has been the single most important source of Malaysian national income generation for over half a century. . . . the industry has contributed somewhere between a fifth and a fourth of the gross domestic product of the Malaya-Singapore area in recent years. . . .

. . . Approximately one-fourth of the gainfully employed labour force are directly employed in the rubber industry. . . .

On a gross basis, the industry has probably contributed, directly and indirectly, between 30 and 40 per cent of total government revenue since the end of World War II. . . .

In the last decade, rubber accounted for over 70 per cent of the net exports of Malaya and Singapore. . . . In the agricultural sector of the economy, rubber trees accounted for about two-thirds of the total cul-

17. D. M. Forrest, *A Hundred Years of Ceylon Tea* (London, 1967), p. 19.
18. United Nations, *Economic Survey of Asia and the Far East, 1968* (Bangkok, 1969), pp. 37–41. See also Donald Snodgrass, *Ceylon—An Export Economy in Transition* (Homewood, Illinois, 1966) for more information on the nature of the Ceylonese economy.

tivated acreage and over nine-tenths of the long-term asset value of "improvements." At current market values, capital in the form of rubber trees represents . . . roughly five times the total investment in industrial plants in Malaysia.[19]

Of course not all rubber production activity is attributable to plantations; smallholders have become increasingly important in the industry. Nevertheless, estate production still accounted for about 40 per cent of total rubber production in 1967 and the remaining 60 per cent grown by smallholders depends in large measure on services provided by the plantations. Oil palm cultivation in Malaya is entirely a plantation industry under foreign ownership, as is the rubber industry. The dominance of plantations in economic spheres is therefore unquestionable and indications are that this is so socially and politically as well.

In *Indonesia,* of roughly 16 million acres of farm land under cultivation in 1958, "about 1,500 estates were reported to cover an area of 5.4 million acres, of which 1 million was planted with rubber, 247,000 with oilpalm, and 208,000 with tea." In Java alone "42 per cent of the total planted area is under estate crops." [20] The northeast Sumatran estates produce more than half of all estate rubber in Indonesia, 90 per cent of the palm oil and palm kernels, and most of the quality cigar tobacco and other minor export crops. One-third of all estate land is located in Java where all the sugar is produced. The former Dutch-owned plantations were taken over by government at the end of the 1950's but are now in the process of being returned. The plantation sector produces the bulk of export receipts and substantially dominates other national economic aggregates.

In the *Philippines* the system of large landholdings (*haciendas*) originated in the *encomienda* system of Spanish colonization and the pattern still exists. In 1902 the United States Congress passed legislation placing a legal limit on the size of landholdings to a maximum of 1024 hectares. But this has never really been operative. Sugar has been the leading export commodity in the Philip-

19. Thomas R. McHale, "Natural Rubber and Malaysian Economic Development," *Malayan Economic Review,* April 1965, pp. 16–18.
20. E. H. Jacoby, *Agrarian Unrest in Southeast Asia* (New York, 1961), p. 71.

pines for a long time. And although in recent years it has been matched (and often surpassed) by the smallholder-based coconuts, sugar is still the foundation of the economy. As elsewhere, it is a plantation-based industry with unique features of crop sharing between mills and *colono* cane farmers which supplements directly estate produced cane.

III. ISLANDS OF THE INDIAN AND PACIFIC OCEANS

In the Indian Ocean, we find that the plantation system dominates all aspects of life in *Mauritius, Réunion* and the *Comoro Islands.* Mauritius is, like Barbados, a monocrop plantation economy par excellence. The growing and manufacture of sugar accounts for about 35 per cent of the G.N.P. and moreover the output of many other industries, such as transportation and construction, is part of the sugar industry's activities. Meade *et al.* have indicated that if account is taken of direct and indirect contributions, the sugar industry's output is "certainly well over a half of Mauritius' output." [21] Sugar alone occupies 90 per cent of the arable land, equivalent to 43 per cent of the total island area. The industry employs two-thirds of the total labor force and normally contributes about a third of total gross capital formation. Seventy per cent of the sugarcane area is owned by twenty-five large sugar estates which crush and mill all the cane produced in the country. Sugar and its by-products are 95 per cent of total exports. Sugar is also the foundation of the economy of Réunion where it accounts for 80 per cent of exports and monopolizes the land area of the coastal plains. In the Comoro Islands, planters and plantation companies own 35 per cent of total land area and are the major source of export production of a mixed bag of essential oils, vanilla, cinnamon, cloves, sisal, and copra. [22]

In the Pacific *Fiji* and *Hawaii* are two clearly identifiable plantation economies. Sugar is the cornerstone of the Fiji economy.

21. J. E. Meade *et al., The Economic and Social Structure of Mauritius* (London, 1961), p. 44. The rest of the information on Mauritius is also derived from this source.
22. Information on Réunion and the Comoro Islands is from R. J. Harrison Church *et al., Africa and the Islands* (New York, 1965), pp. 463–65.

Over the last decade or so it has contributed between 36 and 58 per cent of total exports, with coconut products accounting for another 20 to 25 per cent. The foreign-owned Colonial Sugar Refining Company is said to be "the largest single land owner" but it produces only an insignificant amount of cane. Its cane-producing activities are actually carried out by tenant farmers under long-term leases which bind the tenant to cultivation practices approved by the company. The company reserves the right to remove a tenant for neglect or misuse and this together with advances to tenants for supplies and the provision of technical advice ensure the company of its cane supplies. The company is the only buyer of cane for its mills. According to Gerard Ward, because sugar has been the mainstay of the economy for well over half a century, the Colonial Sugar Refining Company "has, with reason, been referred to as 'the other government.' " [23] The plantation influence is equally strong in Hawaii where sugar plantations for a long time have been a major source of income and employment, and more recently the pattern has been reinforced by pineapple and other company plantations. Most of the island residents have been for long dependent on the sugar and pineapple plantation industries for income and employment. And together sugar and pineapples are the leading generators of income. Since Hawaii is constitutionally part of the United States we give it the status of a "sub-economy."

23. R. Gerard Ward, *Land Use and Population in Fiji* (London, 1965), pp. 37 and 124.

APPENDIX

II

Economic organization of plantations

An understanding of how plantations are organized and what factors influence decision making is important background knowledge for analyzing resource use and development problems in plantation economy and society.

1. Types of plantations in third world economy

In looking at the current Third World scene, it seems sufficient to concentrate our attention on four types of plantations: company, tenant, family, and state. These four types cover the field adequately, as the following review indicates.

Company plantations generally dominate the plantation export industry of the world. They account for the bulk of world trade in sugar, tea, rubber, oil palm products, bananas, and sisal. And they are the most important type found in most of the Caribbean, the Guianas, Central America, plantation Asia, and the Pacific. In many instances, these company plantations are foreign owned. In the sugar dominated Caribbean region, both British and American plantation companies are of importance. Subsidiaries of the British refining firm, Tate & Lyle, produce the bulk of sugar exported from Jamaica, Trinidad, and British Honduras; and another British firm—Booker McConnell Limited—accounts for nearly 90 per cent of Guyana's sugar output. United States companies produce most of the sugar from Puerto Rico, Dominican Republic, and

Haiti. Two American companies produce three-quarters of the Dominican Republic's crop; and one American sugar company owns and controls some 400,000 acres in both the Dominican Republic and Puerto Rico. All the sugar produced in Haiti comes from two United States-owned companies. Company plantations also account for all of Hawaii's sugar output and that of Mauritius and the Philippines, although the degree of foreign ownership is much less marked than is the case for the Caribbean.[1] In most of these sugar producing countries, some of the cane which is transformed into sugar by the companies is actually grown by peasants but this does not alter the fact that the companies dominate the picture. Without the companies to provide milling capacity, peasants would be unable to produce the cane.

One rather unique company-type sugar industry is the one in Fiji where the milling company grows an insignificant amount of the cane ground by it. The Colonial Sugar Refining Company had a virtual monopoly in Fiji sugar production by 1920. But with the termination of Indian indenture and the resulting difficulty of securing labor, the company resorted to leasing land to tenant farmers *to produce its cane.* Long-term leases running for ten years and renewable, agreement to buy cane at fixed prices, advances to tenants, purchases of fertilizers, and supervision of the tenants by company overseers make up the package arrangement.[2] In this particular case the superficial impression is that of a tenant situation, but because of the very tight supervision of tenants by the company and the fact that decision making really resides with the company and not with the tenant suggests that this case ought to be included with the class of company plantations.

Company plantations are also important in the sugar producing Northeast of Brazil and in Louisiana and Florida in the United States South. However, in these cases the companies are not foreign owned. In Brazil the usual pattern found is that of a family corporation which has the characteristics of a private company. Since the family members with shares in the company are not nor-

1. William Morgan, *Economic Survey of the Sugar Plantation Industry* (International Federation of Plantation, Agricultural and Allied Workers, Geneva, 1962), p. 10.
2. See P. P. Courtenay, *Plantation Agriculture* (London, 1965), p. 93.

mally resident on the plantations, the internal structure of these is very much akin to the company plantations existing elsewhere— that is, plantation operations are supervised by a resident manager who runs the plantation on behalf of absentee owners. In the U.S. South the pattern is more generally that of a large corporation with widely dispersed share ownership.

Central American banana production is almost exclusively a foreign-owned company affair with two United States companies accounting for almost the whole of export production. In 1966 United Fruit Company controlled 100 per cent of export banana acreage in Guatemala, 70 per cent in Costa Rica and Panama, and 56 per cent in Honduras. The balance of export banana acreage in Honduras and Costa Rica is controlled by the Standard Fruit and Steamship Company. In recent years these companies have introduced "associate producer" programs which provide contracts with farmers in the countries mentioned for the production of bananas on behalf of the company. The arrangements in these cases are generally similar to the situation described for sugar production in Fiji. But up to the present time the output of associate producers is only a small percentage of the export bananas produced in these countries.[3]

The Asian tea industry is also primarily a company plantation business. "The ownership of Ceylon's 600,000 acres of tea land is divided on a more or less tripartite basis" between sterling companies with 32 per cent, rupee companies with 26 per cent, and individual Ceylonese ownership with 22 per cent, the remainder being mostly smallholdings. Through a process of amalgamation, groups of estates have come under the control of single entities and "on the largest groups one man may be personally responsible for the growing and processing of up to 3 million lb. of tea a year— enough to keep one of the smaller European countries supplied." [4] Foreign capital therefore owns at least one-third of the industry and is said to be much more important than that in the marketing and export of tea. "Most of the foreign firms in marketing are sub-

3. H. B. Arthur, J. P. Houck, and G. L. Beckford, *Tropical Agribusiness Structures and Adjustments—Bananas* (Boston, 1968), Chapter 4.
4. D. M. Forrest, *A Hundred Years of Ceylon Tea* (London, 1967), pp. 21–23.

sidiaries of larger organizations in the main consumer markets." [5]
In all, at least 60 per cent of Ceylon's tea output comes from company plantations. The tea plantations in Indonesia were formerly company-owned units but several are now under government control though there is evidence that they may be soon transformed to their former status.

Company plantations are also of considerable importance in rubber and oil palm production. In Ceylon company estates occupy a quarter öf the country's total rubber acreage but only 14 per cent of the acreage is said to be owned by foreigners. While in Malaysia, "fully three-fourths of total planted acreage in rubber estates was European-owned in 1950; by 1958 it had fallen to 63 per cent and by 1966 to 55 per cent. Nevertheless, production from European-owned estates still accounted for two-thirds of estate rubber output in the latter year." [6] In Indonesia, subsidiaries of foreign companies still account for a significant share of rubber production though there is still the transitional difficulty posed by government intervention. Rubber production in Liberia is chiefly by foreign-owned companies and one company, Firestone, dominates the scene. The companies encourage production by Liberian farmers who contribute a small share of output from their individually owned plantations. Companies also control most of the oil palm areas of Malaya and Indonesia as well as coconut production in the Solomon Islands. The chief company involved is the Anglo-Dutch owned Unilever. Finally, world sisal production comes mainly from company plantations in Tanzania.

Tenant plantations are of particular importance in three places: the United States cotton plantation belt, some areas of Brazil, and in the Philippines. This category includes various types of tenancy arrangements but concern here is only with those tenancy situations which largely leave decision making in the hands of the plantation owner; and thus maintain the central authority and control which is characteristic of plantations as we have defined them.

5. United Nations, *Economic Survey of Asia and the Far East, 1968* (Bangkok, 1969), p. 37.
6. *Ibid.*, pp. 37 and 49. These data relate to estate or plantation output of rubber. Peasants produce half or more of total rubber ouput in Malaya.

Fiji sugar production, already described, fits the category. In other places, the two main sub-types are sharecropper and share-renter tenancies. The first involves tenant supply of labor power in return for a share, usually half, of the crop. The second involves tenant supply of labor power in addition to certain other inputs (animal or tractor power, implements and working capital; or a part of these) in return for a share, usually two-thirds, of the crop. In both cases, the plantation owner (or landlord) retains control over production decisions and the tenant simply carries out those decisions. These arrangements are described in greater detail in Section 3 below. Here we wish simply to identify what we mean by tenant plantations. This type of plantation varies somewhat from the others identified for study in that the plantation owner may be either an individual or family, or a company, or even the state in rare cases (the Gezira cotton scheme is an example of the latter). It thus cuts across other types but in a way that makes it quite distinct; and, as we shall see, the particular tenancy arrangements have important implications for resource use and the welfare of the tenant-workers.

The existence of these tenant-type plantations in the United States South is difficult to determine precisely because census data are not presented in a form that permits this. Merle Prunty has indicated that up to the 1940's about 60 per cent of plantations in the U.S. cotton belt were organized on a sharecropper basis and perhaps another 20 to 30 per cent were on a share-rent basis.[7] And Frank Welch informs us that before the advent of the AAA program, 95 per cent of plantations in the Yazoo-Mississippi Delta were operated by croppers and tenants.[8] However, indications are that with the acceleration of mechanization in the postwar period, sharecropping and share-tenancy arrangements have

7. Merle Prunty, Jr., "The Renaissance of the Southern Plantation," *The Geographical Review*, October 1955, pp. 463, 467, and 475. On the problem posed by the census data, see Merle Prunty, Jr., "The Census on Multiple-Units and Plantations," *The Professional Geographer*, September 1956.
8. Frank J. Welch, *The Plantation Land Tenure System in Mississippi* (Mississippi State College, Agricultural Experiment Station Bulletin No. 385, June 1943), p. 15. This area at the time produced half of the Mississippi cotton crop and half of the total U.S. long staple output.

declined rapidly in the U.S. South as a whole and have been replaced by quasi-share and wage labor. The quasi-share arrangement is a combined wage-and-sharecrop system in which "The quasi-share laborer receives remuneration in two ways: wages for day labor for the landlord, and in addition either a share of the crop on a small patch, or else the full crop on a patch one-half the size." [9]

Sharecropping and share tenancy are said to be important on Philippine plantations, especially in sugarcane production. Two types of arrangements seem to exist. One is the *colono* arrangement where tenant farmers produce cane under contract to a factory to supply it with cane from a specified acreage. The mills furnish transportation and share the crop with the tenant by keeping between 30 and 40 per cent of the sugar. Another arrangement is the *kasama* or share tenancy where the plantation owners supply seed and working capital while the tenant supplies labor and, often, working animals and receives in return half of the crop less half of the expenses of cultivation.[10] In Brazil, sharecroppers (*parceiros*) and share tenants (*rendeiros*) are said to be important in the sugarcane areas of Pernambuco and Alagoas. These arrangements are also said to be common in the coffee region and to a much lesser extent in the cocoa areas. On the coffee plantations the predominant share type is the *meiacao* where the tenant (*meeiro*) receives a piece of land to cultivate and is obliged to plant, cultivate and harvest the crop; the plantation owner provides seed and tools and sometimes gives money advances to the cropper. The *meeiro* provides labor (and sometimes seeds and implements) and receives a half of the crop less expenses in return. On the whole, sharecropping exists on about 14 per cent of Brazilian plantations.[11]

9. Paul S. Taylor, "Plantation Agriculture in the United States: Seventeenth to Twentieth Centuries," *Land Economics,* May 1954, p. 144.
10. See United Nations, *op. cit.,* p. 59, and E. H. Jacoby, *Agrarian Unrest in Southeast Asia* (New York, 1961), p. 207. The other kind of tenancy found in the Philippines is the *inquilinato,* a straight cash tenancy which does not qualify for consideration here.
11. See Manuel Diégues, Jr., "Land Tenure and Use in the Brazilian Plantation System," Pan American Union, *Plantation Systems of the New World* (Social Science Monographs, VII, Washington, D. C., 1959), pp. 110–15.

Although there are no doubt very large numbers of individual and *family plantations* still in existence in the world today, they do not constitute a very important type of plantation in the overall Third World economy. Historically, this type has been of declining importance on account of certain factors which made it difficult for them to adjust to certain modern developments. Nevertheless, the family plantation is still of sufficient importance to merit special consideration although there is a shortage of information and data regarding this type. From what we can ascertain, this type is perhaps most important in the sugar industries of Barbados and Mauritius and in coffee and cocoa production in Brazil. Family plantations can perhaps be found almost everywhere but they do not seem to be of great importance in other places. In Brazil the family owning unit is usually an extended family and frequently the formal plantation organization is a family corporation. Family plantations may involve residence on the plantation in some cases but frequently absentee ownership is involved.

State plantations also exist in many parts of the world and are sometimes development projects or research plantations. However, so far as commercial production is concerned this type is important in very few places. Among these are Cuba and Indonesia. The government-owned plantations in Indonesia were acquired between 1957 and 1959 from former foreign companies but since the overthrow of Sukarno many of these have been returned to their former owners. Cuba is therefore the only outstanding example of this type, the sugar industry there being a state plantation enterprise. The organization of state agriculture in Cuba is based on fifty-eight regional "enterprises" established in 1965, each of which is an administrative unit of production. State planning and the implementation of production decisions are carried out through these enterprises.[12] Lack of information prevents further detailed consideration of this particular type.

One more type of plantation which deserves mention is the plantation co-operative. This type is important in the export production of bananas, cocoa, and coffee in Cameroon; and in banana

12. See G. L. Beckford, "A Note on Agricultural Organization and Planning in Cuba," *Caribbean Studies,* October 1966, for further details on this.

production in the Ivory Coast and Colombia. However, there is not enough information on these to say much more; nor to allow at this time an attempt at studying their political economy.

On balance, it seems that the two most important types of plantations in the world in terms of value of output and exports today are company plantations and tenant plantations. State plantations and family plantations are of decidedly lesser importance. Consequently, the first two types are our main focus of attention.

To conclude this consideration of types of plantations, some general remarks on plantation organization and how this is likely to vary by type seem to be in order. We should note, to begin with, that all plantations have one thing in common—that is, a high degree of central control and co-ordination. This requires appropriate administrative structures for exercise of the management function which are likely to vary according to the nature of the plantation. In addition, there are a number of differences related to the forms of capital and their relative importance in different situations; in the use of labor varying with the nature of the labor supply; and in occupancy patterns on the land. As concerns capital and the distribution of investment, it is important to note that whereas land normally represents the bulk of investments on tenant plantations (and family plantations too), the bulk of investments on company plantations tend to be concentrated in plant and equipment. Whereas land represents anywhere from three-quarters to nine-tenths of total investment on tenant plantations in the U.S. South, factories, machinery, equipment, and social overhead capital may represent those same amounts on company plantations. This naturally affects the organization of the plantation and decisions relating to production as well. The nature of management also varies by type. On resident family plantations, ownership and management reside in the same person; on company plantations the owners are represented by a paid resident manager. When the owner resides on a large tenant plantation he may employ a tenant supervisor to oversee the tenants. And large mechanized family plantations may have the owner residing on them in addition to having a paid plantation manager. In these instances the lines of communication between worker and owner are broken.

The organization of labor depends on the extent to which the labor force is resident on the plantation, lives in nearby villages, or is migratory; also on the terms and conditions of work. Labor cost is usually a high percentage of total cost of production on plantations and requires considerable organization in order to optimize its use. Sharecroppers need supervision and this may be provided by the owner on family tenant plantations whereas on company plantations a paid supervisor is usually involved. On wage labor plantations different payment systems are used. Three main types can be identified: payment by task, by piecework, and by hourly rate. Supervision requirements vary with the particular system of payment. Finally, the type of labor and cultivating power in use influences the land occupancy patterns.[13] On the company plantation utilizing resident labor, workers live in a nuclear area centering on the factory area whereas on the tenant cropper and share plantations units of residence are more widely dispersed. And these differences in occupancy patterns influence the character of infrastructure of roads and other amenities.

2. Organization of company plantations

There are several sub-types of company plantations varying from small private plantations (some of which may be family corporations) to large plantation organizations or enterprises engaged in several activities associated with plantation production, and in which the plantation company itself is a subsidiary of a larger complex. Small plantation companies may exist side by side with larger companies and in many of these instances, the smaller company may rely on the larger one for a number of services. Looking at the world scene as a whole we find that, in general, small plantation companies tend to be locally owned and the large companies are normally foreign owned. In terms of output the large foreign-owned plantation company is the dominant type in world agriculture. These companies have come about largely because individual planters in the past were unable to cope with the organi-

13. Merle Prunty, Jr., has analyzed these influences on occupancy patterns for a group of plantations in the U.S. South in her article, "The Renaissance of the Southern Plantation," *op. cit.*

zational and financial requirements of a changing world economic order. The companies that filled the breach were usually established by firms which were already involved in some aspect of economic activity related to plantations. Thus we find that merchants who had been involved in the export marketing of plantation products and with the imports of plantation inputs and provisions were important in the formation of these new enterprises. This was particularly so in the West Indian sugar industry, in the Asian countries of Ceylon, Malaya, and Indonesia, and in the cotton industry of the U.S. South. At a later stage, we found that metropolitan processors of plantation raw materials provided the basis for new plantation companies. In the case of tea, several cases are recorded of retail merchants dealing in the plantation product organizing plantation enterprises. And there are many instances of firms initially engaged in the transportation of plantation produce eventually establishing plantation companies.

There are several reasons why firms already in the general line of business were important in the formation of these companies. Some have been advanced in Chapters 4 and 5 of the text. Here we may note that one general consideration was the economies which these firms could secure because of their strategic location. The merchants, retailers, transporters, and processors in the metropolitan market had already created an infrastructure for the distribution of plantation produce and the additional output from their plantation subsidiaries could be fitted in at virtually zero marginal cost. Again, merchant firms which had previously supplied planters with inputs and provisions were already securing imported machinery and equipment, working capital, and provisions in sufficiently large consignments that any additional supplies for the firm's plantations could be secured at close to zero marginal cost. Another consideration is that these firms already had access to financial capital in metropolitan capital markets and could therefore easily find the capital resources necessary for plantation activities.

In some cases, engagement in plantation production was a necessity for the profitability of an existing enterprise. One example of this is the Empian Group which built railways from the upper Congo to the African Great Lakes and then found it necessary to establish plantation and trading companies to provide freight. The most outstanding example of this case is found in the history of the United Fruit Company. In the late nineteenth century an American engineer, who had originally contracted with the government of Costa Rica to establish a railroad to the Atlantic coast, found that he needed to establish banana plantations to provide sufficient freight for his railroad to make his company a profitable investment. And this laid the foundation for the present giant banana plantation enterprise that is United Fruit Company. In like manner, metropolitan traders and processing firms dealing with plantation raw materials found it necessary to become involved in production in order to have assured supplies.

The upshot of these considerations is that most of the larger plantation companies in the world at present began as, and continue to be, part of wider organizational complexes involved in productive and service activities directly related in some way to the plantation itself. The plantation company in these instances is a subsidiary of a parent organization located in a metropolitan country and decisions relating to its operation are directed from that center. Organization of activities on the plantation is therefore designed to ensure that decisions taken at the center by the parent company are implemented in the best possible manner. Because of the distance of the plantation from the center of decision making not all decisions can be left to the center. Certain decisions have to be made on the plantation itself. By and large, the situation is as follows: decisions relating to the long-term organization of the plantation are made by the parent company. These include investment decisions affecting the adjustment of capacity, and fixed capital commitments in general. Management on the plantation itself is therefore more generally concerned with the day-to-day operations of the company with a view to implementing the long-term decisions of the parent body and to achieving the objectives set by it. The way in which these companies are organized is illustrated in what follows by reference to one particular case which has been systematically studied and reported. An attempt is subsequently made to generalize that particular situation for other plantation companies on the basis of what information is available.

A COMPANY PLANTATION IN JAMAICA

The case reported here is that of Innswood Estate Limited, a relatively small company plantation producing sugar and by-products in Jamaica. It is used here not because it is representative of most company plantations in the world but simply because information on its organizational structure is available from a recent study done by Foster and Creyke.[14] This particular company plantation covers an area of roughly 8000 acres in an area bordered by a sizable town and several villages. The plantation occupies a median position in the hierarchy of Jamaican sugar plantations. It produces sugarcane and manufactures raw sugar, rum and other spirits, and molasses. And it is a subsidiary company of a British-owned sugar complex, Booker McConnell Limited. (The total operations of this enterprise are described in Chapter 5 along with those of similar enterprises.) Innswood Estate Limited comes under the management portfolio of Bookers Agricultural Holdings Limited, another subsidiary of the parent company, which controls the operations of all Booker plantations wherever these are located.

The estate company is generally supervised by a board of directors which is responsible to the parent company in the United Kingdom. Most of the members of the Board of Directors reside in Jamaica but not on the estate itself. General co-ordination at the policy level is provided by an executive committee of the board which meets formally every month although its members are in close communication at all times. Day-to-day management of the estate is in the hands of a general manager, a resident of the estate who bears the responsibility of ensuring that the decisions

14. Phillips Foster and Peter Creyke, *The Structure of Plantation Agriculture in Jamaica* (University of Maryland, Agricultural Economics Experiment Station, Miscellaneous Publication 623, College Park, Maryland, May 1968). That study was carried out at a time when the company was in a stage of transition, having been only recently acquired by the parent company, Booker McConnell Limited. Certain aspects of the company's organization reported in that study are modified in the presentation here to allow for these transitory features. These modifications are based on our own knowledge of the situation.

of the executive committee and board of directors are implemented in the most satisfactory manner. Implementation of decisions from above and responsibility for making on-the-spot decisions consistent with those larger policy decisions rest with an
estate managerial staff working under the general manager. At the
highest level, this staff consists of the secretary to the estate who
is mainly responsible for the financial end of the business and acts
as financial co-ordinator, assisted by a cost accountant and an officer manager; a personnel manager concerned with all estate workers; a field manager, assisted by a deputy field manager, and responsible for all field operations on the plantation; a factory
manager in charge of processing operations in the factory; and a
distillery manager in charge of the distillery plant.

The largest department in the administrative structure is the
Field Department which employs up to 1350 workers during the
crop—80 per cent of the plantation labor force during this period. Even during the non-harvest season, this department is still
the largest, employing then about 60 per cent of the labor force.
Field operations are organized and managed on a functional basis
with specialization by activity.[15] Three assistant field managers
work under the field manager and deputy field manager, each with
specific responsibilities: one for irrigation, drainage and fertilizer
operations; another for land preparation, planting and weeding;
and the third for harvesting. The over-all organization of the field
department is summarized on the following page in Chart II.1.
During crop time of 1966, the breakdown of the plantation's labor
force in various areas was as follows: cultivation, 386; reaping
966; factory, 275; transport, 52; apprentices 11; for a total of
1690. Harvesting was therefore easily the most important area of
employment. Part of the field manager's responsibility, as is the
case of other departmental heads, is preparation of an annual budget which presents cost estimates for the next year's work. And in

15. Prior to the change in ownership the plantation field operations had
    been organized on an area basis which involved subdivision of the
    estate into three units, each under the control of an overseer respon-
    sible for the work done in his unit area. But this is said to have pro-
    duced diseconomies in the use of labor and capital as co-ordination
    of "area" activity proved unwieldy. *Ibid.*, p. 30.

Chart II.1. The formal power structure of the field department at Innswood Estate, Jamaica, August 1, 1966

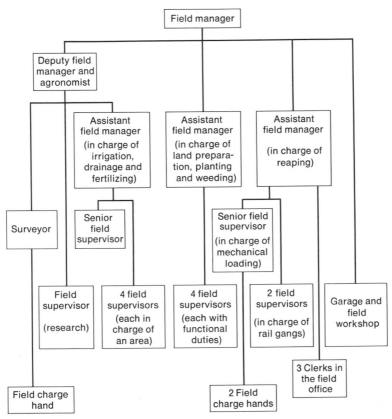

Source: Phillips Foster and Peter Creyke, *The Structure of Plantation Agriculture in Jamaica* (University of Maryland, Agricultural Economics Experiment Station, Miscellaneous Publication 623, College Park, Maryland, May 1968), p. 31.

this exercise, he needs to consult with each of his assistant field managers.

Operations on the plantation as a whole are co-ordinated by a management committee meeting weekly to consider work progress, undertake routine planning, and review departmental budgets.

This committee consists of the five department heads, the general manager, and the secretary. Once a month, the committee considers matters of policy; recommendations which emerge from these discussions have to be submitted for ratification by the board of directors if financial matters or important policy changes are involved. Other minor or non-financial recommendations require only the general manager's approval. In summary, then, the structure of decision making is as follows: decisions relating to the over-all objectives of the plantation and to long-term commitments are made by the parent company, Booker McConnell Limited, in London; medium-term (crop to crop) decisions relating to the operation of the plantation company are made by the board of directors; short-term (within the crop) decisions on the plantation itself are the responsibility of the general manager; and day-to-day decisions consistent with those higher up are left to department heads on the estate. All important long-term decisions are therefore taken in a metropolitan center far removed from the plantation itself and from the people who must implement them.

According to the report of Foster and Creyke, the long-term objective of this plantation company is to maximize profits, subject to constraints imposed by the need to exist in the Jamaican environment. These constraints derive largely from government policy and from trade union activity. On the estate itself, alternatives are evaluated in terms of cost relative to output. It appears from this report that maximization of profit is further constrained by the company's choice of what to produce. The company is concerned only with the production of sugar because production of this commodity better fits the pattern of the parent company's over-all operations. This is illustrated by the fact that when Bookers acquired the estate in 1960, Innswood had been producing, in addition to sugar, high quality citrus; supported two commercial cattle herds of over 1000 head in all; and bred mules and racehorses for sale. "Bookers' policy was to specialize in sugar production only. The cattle and horses were sold off and the citrus orchards allowed to deteriorate." [16] It is clear from this that the objective of the com-

16. *Ibid.*, p. 41.

pany is not really maximization of profits but simply maximization of profits *from sugar production.*

Once this objective became operative, the rest of production decisions followed logically. In order to increase factory efficiency, modernization was necessary and this involved an expansion of capacity. And since factory efficiency requires the fullest possible utilization of capacity it was necessary to expand sugarcane acreage. The policy laid down by the board of directors was therefore that cane should be grown on all suitable land and "the staff was charged to produce as much cane as possible, as efficiently as possible, so long as the cost of producing an additional ton of sugar was less than the estimated revenue it would bring when sold." [17] Resolutions of basic production decisions on what, how much, and how to produce can be seen in this instance to follow directly from the basic parent company objective of maximizing profits from sugar production. Consequently, very little real initiative is left to those people who live and work on the plantation; nor for that matter to any of the company personnel who live in the plantation economy. This factor is of considerable importance in understanding how, over time, the psychology of dependence becomes rooted in plantation societies. This structural situation also affects the efficiency of resource use in the plantation economy, a matter which we considered in Chapter 6.

There are other aspects of the organization of this company plantation which are important to note here. These include the capital structure, the input-output relations of the plantation to other subsidiary companies in the group, the physical layout of residences of staff and workers, and the general social organization. Data provided by Foster and Creyke indicate that at the end of 1965, the book value of capital employed on Innswood Estate was of the order of £1.5 million. Factory plant and machinery was valued at £586,455, land at £397,811, and buildings at £203,380. It is not clear where the value of the factory building is included. However, we can state that factory capital represents upward of one-third of total estate capital. It is easy to understand, therefore,

17. *Ibid.,* p. 43.

why utilization of factory capacity is such an important factor influencing production decisions. Commercial bank loans and overdraft facilities account for 45 per cent of the estate's capital financing.

The parent company of this plantation is involved in several activities related to sugar and, as far as is economically feasible, the plantation secures inputs from within the corporate family and disposes of output in the same manner. All the major machinery in the factory and distillery is reported to have been made by member companies of the Booker group and we are told that when pumps were needed for wells on the plantation, "Bookers . . . put pressure to use pumps manufactured by one of the Booker Group of companies, but they could not compete with the American pumps in terms of efficiency or delivery dates." [18] On the output side the parent company does not buy raw sugar so there is no tie-up there; but by-products are sold to member companies. Both rum and alcohol made by the plantation company are sold to member companies.

Finally, let us consider physical layout and general social organization. The factory is the nucleus of the plantation. Around it are found all administrative offices, equipment sheds, general manager's house, other senior staff housing close by, clinic, canteen, shop, and some workers' dormitories. The plantation owns (and runs or used to run) a shop and canteen, a school, a church, and a postal agency. It is a more or less self-contained community in terms of social amenities; and the social and authority structure in the community are very much related to occupational status on the plantation. The general manager is at the top of the social hierarchy and his executive staff of department heads, and categories close to them, constitute a social grouping which remains quite separate from the intermediate group of other staff and from the lower social grouping of estate workers. Income and housing help to accentuate these social distinctions. However, it should also be pointed out that proximity of the plantation to a large urban center and to smaller nearby communities serves to dampen the over-all effect of the plantation's social structure on individu-

18. *Ibid.*, p. 89.

als working there, many of whom have social outlets outside of the immediate plantation community.

GENERAL NATURE OF COMPANY PLANTATIONS

The situation described for this particular company plantation in Jamaica does not fit in every detail that which obtains on all company plantations in the world. However, the basic pattern or outline describes a type of organization which is characteristic of many corporate enterprises. Mollett, in a recent study of sugar plantations in Hawaii, describes management and labor organization for two companies. One of these was somewhat larger than Innswood with 10,515 acres of cane and 39,227 tons of sugar production. The other was nearly four times the size of the Jamaican plantation with 28,482 acres and 164,058 tons of sugar. The organizational scheme of the smaller of the two Hawaii plantations described by Mollett is more or less identical to that outlined above for Jamaica; and the larger Hawaii plantation "naturally requires a larger administrative staff but the basic pattern of authority, responsibility, and function is similar." [19] The Jamaican example used above seems, therefore, to be generally representative of certain company plantations—at least those of somewhat comparable size.

The functional organization noted in these examples does not seem to be the pattern for some of the larger company plantations in the world. For example, the United Fruit Company's banana plantations in Central America are differently organized. There production activities are organized by "divisions" which range in size from 10,000 to 30,000 acres. Each division seems to correspond in size to the sugar plantations in Jamaica and Hawaii described above. In the case of banana companies:

Each division is divided into unit farms of from 500 to 1,000 acres, each of which is operated as a separate unit with its own operating fa-

19. J. A. Mollett, *The Sugar Plantation in Hawaii: A Study of Changing Patterns of Management and Labor Organization* (University of Hawaii, Agricultural Experiment Station, Agricultural Economics Bulletin 22, Honolulu, July 1965), p. 29; see also pp. 12–39 for the detailed description of plantation organization in the two cases mentioned.

cilities (for irrigation and disease control) and labor force. Transport and communication systems connect each farm with the division headquarters, described by some as small cities because of the wide range of facilities provided for linking the various farms to each other as well as to the outside world.[20]

Some indication of the scale and nature of the operations of a division in banana-company production is given by the following example:

In a recent year, Standard Fruit Company's Honduras Division of about 12,500 acres employed approximately 6,000 workers; operated on an annual budget of $15 million; had some 300 miles of railroad track with over 900 rail cars and 20 diesel locomotives; applied fertilizer and irrigation water to all its farms; controlled sigatoka by aerial spraying on all farms; . . . fulfilled the legal requirements of providing free housing for workers, elementary schooling for workers' children (2,346 students enrolled in company schools) and medical care for workers and their families (i.e., company hospitals and preventive medicine); manufactured corrugated boxes for shipping the fruit; operated a power plant supplying La Ceiba; and ran the port from which the bananas were shipped.[21]

The pattern of divisional (or aereal) organization of plantation activity applies as well to the Firestone rubber plantations in Liberia. Wayne Taylor describes that situation as follows:

The plantation is made up of divisions of from about 1,500 to 2,500 acres, depending upon natural boundaries and the needs of efficient supervision. . . . Each division has a central headquarters consisting of an office, a warehouse for supplies and equipment, and a collection station . . . Nearby are the villages in which the tappers live and the divisional store, carpentry and repair shop, health center, and school. The divisional superintendent—either an American or European— also usually has his house near the headquarters. His staff . . . consists of several overseers, a clerk, a male nurse or a dresser, and a

20. H. B. Arthur, J. P. Houck, and G. L. Beckford, *op. cit.,* p. 53. See also Stacy May and Galo Plaza, *The United Fruit Company in Latin America* (National Planning Association Study of U.S. Business Performance Abroad, Washington, D. C., 1958).
21. H. B. Arthur *et al., op. cit.,* pp. 53–54.

number of skilled and semiskilled workers at the collection station and the carpentry and repair shop.[22]

In these cases, the divisional superintendent is roughly the equivalent of the general manager of the sugar plantations considered earlier. His responsibility is the day-to-day operation of the company plantation. And his authority and control over the livelihood and lives of people within the divisional boundary is more or less absolute. However, like the general manager, he has little control over long-term policy affecting the plantations. That level of decision making is the responsibility of a board of directors at the metropolitan center where the parent company is located. And the co-ordination of activities on all divisions of a company is usually effected by means of a management committee or board of directors of the "plantation group." Plantation managers take their orders from people outside the area in which the plantations are located and see to it that these orders are executed by those who make up the plantation community.

Within the community itself, a need exists for an organizational structure in which clear lines of authority are established. If decisions which are transmitted are to be executed efficiently, internal authority and control are paramount. The company holds the general manager or divisional superintendent fully accountable for activities on a plantation or in a division. So that within the community that individual has absolute authority. Because of his personal responsibility to the company, the general manager or divisional superintendent is unlikely to delegate too much authority and control to others in the community. But because he is neither omnipresent nor omnipotent he needs to delegate some responsibility to others. So the general has his field lieutenants—department heads —who in turn delegate some authority to field supervisors who move step by step with the workers in the campaign. The internal delegation of authority does not, however, carry with it a responsibility of those delegated to the ultimate decision makers. That responsibility resides purely with the general. Consequently the stage is set for an authority structure which is exploitive—which

22. W. C. Taylor, *The Firestone Operations in Liberia* (National Planning Associatin, Washington, D. C., 1956), pp. 61–62.

generates harsh penalties on those who do not follow orders to the letter.

In general, organizational systems of management can be classified into four broad categories which reflect differences in the structure and nature of authority. These categories are described by Likert as "exploitive authoritative," "benevolent authoritative," "consultative," and "participative group." [23] The terms are really self-explanatory and describe situations ranging from the extreme of authority concentration in a group or individual at the top to one in which the group engaged in production arrive at decisions through some device in which popular participation is exercised —in elementary political terms, as commonly used, from a situation of dictatorship to one of democracy with full local government. By and large, the pattern of plantation organization to date has been exploitive authoritative. There is, however, a trend in more recent times for plantations to adjust toward less extreme forms of authority structure. The main factors contributing to this trend are the increasing scientific basis of plantation production and the unionization of plantation workers. At the management level, the staff of modern company plantations at present is likely to be made up of agricultural scientists who have command over areas of knowledge which may be alien to that possessed by the general manager or division superintendent. This requires therefore that the division superintendent's authority be tempered by a good deal more consultation, if not benevolence, than traditionally has been the case. At the other end of the spectrum, trade-union organization of plantation workers over the last few decades and the concomitant increasing government involvement have reduced the degree to which plantation host environments are willing to tolerate traditional "exploitive authoritative" systems of management organization. In general, the monopoly position of plantations has been weakened by these trends and, in some instances, by increasing nonplantation employment opportunities. Exploitation is normally associated with monopoly.

Mollett has noted this shift in the pattern of plantation manage-

23. Rensio Likert, *New Patterns of Management* (New York, 1961), p. 279, as cited by J. A. Mollett, *op. cit.*, p. 40.

ment for the Hawaii sugar plantations which he studied. He concludes his analysis with the observation: "Operating characteristics are indicated to be mostly typical of the 'consultative authoritative' and the 'participative' groups. Within the last two decades, a marked shift has occurred from the 'exploitive' or 'benevolent' authoritative pattern of management . . . to the new pattern." [24] Hawaii is perhaps more advanced in this direction than most other plantation areas of the world because both the scientific basis of production and worker organization have reached a high level of development there, and because alternative employment opportunities and easy migration possibilities have weakened the monopoly position of plantations in the labor market. Elsewhere in the world, the pattern that obtains in any particular case will depend on the stage of development of these other factors. The stronger the monopoly position of plantations, the more we are likely to find management systems approximating the "exploitive authoritative" pattern.

A characteristic of the company plantation which is worthy of our notice at this point is the general self-sufficiency of the organization. The company provides not just a place of work but a place of living for those involved. It runs dormitories, schools, hospitals, clinics, canteens, stores, and even churches. Consequently, the people who make up the plantation community have to depend on the company to an overwhelming degree for most of the basic amenities of life. Their housing is provided by the company; and their food and clothing are purchased out of the company wages they earn in the company store which imports these from elsewhere. Dependence on the company is normally extreme and this fashions the structure of social relationships within the plantation community. Because plantations normally cover wide geographic areas, there are usually only tenuous links between the plantation community and other communities of people. And even these links come within the orbit of the plantation's control. Communication with communities outside the plantation is provided by the company on company roads, in company vehicles, and with com-

24. J. A. Mollett, op. cit., p. 41. See pp. 40–51 for the analysis and patterns observed.

pany telegraph and radio facilities. The plantation is a total economic and social institution with the company in complete control
of the lives of people who live and work on it.

The company, of course, is an impersonal element. Within the
plantation community it is personified by the general manager or
division superintendent. It is important to note in this connection
that on almost all company plantations the division superintendent
is usually white, of European stock. On the other hand, the unskilled plantation workers are always of non-European stock—
that is, black people of one kind or another and, in a few instances, yellow people of Chinese stock. The authority structure
inherent in the economic organization is accentuated by race,
color, and culture of those who make up the system. It is therefore
not surprising to find that the social structure of a plantation community is characterized by patterns of stratification that are associated with differences in race and color. The control and authority of the white general manager over a large work force of
non-white people of a different cultural background demand a social structure which consists of intermediaries who can straddle
the gulf between the two cultures and facilitate effective communication. The tendency, therefore, is for higher levels of plantation
management personnel to be from a similar cultural background
as the general manager; and for descending levels in the authority
structure to be closer to that of the work force. Consequently, the
general manager's chief lieutenants are usually white or near white
in some respect and the plantation personnel become less white
moving down the hierarchical scale.[25] This sets the stage for the
particular type of social and political organization that characterizes plantation societies (see Chapter 3).

3. A note on family plantations

The category of family plantations covers those which are owned
and run by an individual or family residing on the plantation it-

25. The term "white" is being used here in a social sense rather than in
the narrow sense of physical race. It includes non-whites who have
assimilated white culture and who exhibit this in their behavior patterns.

self, in the country within which the plantation is located, or outside of the country. In Brazil where this category is important, absentee ownership is common; plantation owners reside in the larger cities and urban centers and visit the plantation from time to time. Elsewhere, we find cases of family plantations with owners residing in another country—usually a metropolitan country. And plantations with resident owners are to be found in most places. In all these instances, the pattern of plantation organization is much simpler than that described for company plantations. There are two classes of family plantations so far as economic organization is concerned. In the one case, ownership is divorced from plantation management whenever the owner employs a paid manager or supervisor responsible for day-to-day operations. In the other, they are fused with the resident owner managing the enterprise himself. However, not all cases of resident ownership involve this fusion. There are many instances of resident owners who employ a manager or overseer; and when this occurs there is likely to be a kind of hybrid of the two classes in which the owner manages in consultation with his overseer.

The organizational structure of the family plantation is relatively simple. Where a resident owner does his own management, he is in more or less direct contact with his plantation workers; and, beside making all production decisions himself, gives the orders to workers and personally supervises the execution of these orders with the immediate assistance of a foreman to do the necessary leg work. This is the normal pattern on relatively small family plantations. On larger ones, the organizational structure is likely to be somewhat more complex. Harry Hutchinson describes such a case in his study of two Northeast Brazil plantations. In a hierarchical diagram of what he describes as a private plantation (to distinguish it from the other, a corporate family plantation), Hutchinson depicts a situation in which the owner is in direct contact with three persons—a cowboy, an overseer, and a contractor. The contractor has control over migrant workers; and the overseer, with the assistance of a foreman, is in control of the resident workers.[26] The degree of direct contact between owner and worker

26. H. W. Hutchinson, *Village and Plantation Life in Northeastern Brazil* (Seattle, Washington, 1957), p. 70.

varies from plantation to plantation but even where there are intermediaries between the owner and workers, a good deal of personal contact exists. Workers are often able to take up matters directly with the plantation owner and there are numerous instances where owners set aside a particular time for such communication. Matters discussed on such occasions cover a wide area and any aspect of the worker's life is likely to be considered. His personal troubles and problems with other workers can be, and usually are, raised at this level. The individual plantation owner is, therefore, in a position to arbitrate on all matters affecting the lives of workers and normally is expected to do so. In this way, the owner's control extends beyond the work to be done to the lives of all those residing on the plantation. A strong tradition of paternalism is characteristic of this type of plantation.

The literature is full of examples of paternalism on family plantations. Dependence of workers on plantation owners is even more acute where the plantation owner operates a store and sells food and clothing to workers. This is not unusual for family plantations although more recent trends are toward fewer family plantation stores with the growth of villages and towns near to the plantations. Because family plantations do not normally cover extremely wide areas, workers in these situations are able to make easy contact with outside communities which they may visit weekly to purchase supplies and socialize. Indeed, at both ends of the scale the family plantation community needs to be more open than that of the company plantation. The authority system on the family plantation creates a small community in which the social structure is completely polarized. The owner may participate in the social activities of workers but when he attends at such social occasions as baptisms, he does so in his capacity as the patron and must behave in a manner which will maintain his authority status within the system. So to fulfill his own social needs, the owner must find social peers outside the boundaries of his plantation, usually among other plantation owners and professional or administrative groups of people meeting occasionally in a nearby town or city.

The process of decision making on the family plantation is likely to be somewhat more complex than that on a company plantation. The owner decides, but his decisions have to be tempered by the general social situation. He may not try simply to maximize profits for a number of reasons. At one level, family considerations influence his decisions. This may involve foregoing production opportunities which could increase profit in the short run if these pose a threat to long-run family security. For example, he may not wish to make use of available credit if this involves mortgaging property which he hopes to leave as a legacy for his children. Again, if land ownership is an important basis of defining the social status of the planter and his family, as is normally the case, he is likely continuously to invest in land instead of more productive capital improvements to land already owned. And so on. At another level, the owner needs to make production decisions which will ensure that his workers are sufficiently satisfied with their lot to remain loyal to him. This could involve the setting aside of part of the plantation land for workers to produce what they like for their own subsistence or to market themselves. Such an arrangement may be permanent and cannot, without risk of losing workers, be withdrawn to expand acreage of the plantation crop when market prices become favorable. At yet another level, we find that knowledge of the individual owner is likely to be much less perfect than that of those at the head of company plantations. This includes both technical knowledge regarding production of the crop and knowledge about markets and prices. So that even if profit maximization were the sole objective, the individual planter could not be expected to make adjustments on the margin as efficiently as company plantations. The general objectives of owners of family plantations are therefore likely to be some complex combination of profit maximization and family security, subject to constraints of plantation community needs and limited knowledge.

For all family plantations the owner decides. Even when a manager, overseer, or other administrator is involved, basic decisions are made by the owner; and the manager or whoever has responsibility for seeing that the work force carries out what needs to be done following from the owner's decision. The authority structure is likely to be either "exploitive authoritative" or "benevolent authoritative" because in most cases the administrator is chosen for his ability to supervise the work of the people; although knowledge of production techniques may be an important qualification in some cases, it is unusual to find knowledge of management principles in a modern business sense among such people. The paid administrator on the family plantation, like those working under him, simply carries out the orders of the owner. It is not unlikely that the authority structure on family plantations may be moving away from the "exploitive authoritative" toward the "benevolent authoritative." The nature of these paternalistic, semi-feudal communities is such that the owner must impart a good deal of benevolence to maintain the status quo. And as development occurs elsewhere within the possible reach of plantation workers, their level of tolerance of exploitive situations is reduced. It is not farfetched, therefore, to speculate that family plantations would normally exhibit a management pattern which fits the benevolent authoritative case.

The family plantation is not one that permits the emergence of participative group authority. Its very nature prevents this. Basically the typical power structure is autocratic. A recent CIDA study on Brazil provides a good summary picture of the pattern that obtains in these cases. In the following, *latifundismo* is basically synonymous with our category of family plantation. According to that study,

> Latifundismo is a system of power. A *latifundio* is always a highly autocratic enterprise, regardless of the number of people working on it or whether the owner lives on it, nearby or far away . . . the final decisions on important issues, such as what and how much to plan [t], or what, when and where to sell, or even on any minor issues if necessary, rests with him. These minor matters may be those regarding the life and welfare of his workers. . . . What makes this power distinctive is its near absoluteness and vastness. An estate owner's decisions are orders.[27]

The CIDA study goes on to point out that even where the plantation owner delegates some power to subordinates, the power is

27. Inter-American Committee for Agricultural Development, *Land Tenure Conditions and Socio-Economic Development of the Agricultural Sector—Brazil* (Pan American Union, Washington, D. C., 1966), pp. 136–37.

always limited and is qualified by the owner's right to intervene; and any minor decisions made by these subordinates are always subject to explicit or implicit sanctions by the owner. The socio-economic structure of these plantations is said to be rigid, "with a chain of command which is rigid and undisputed." Even on small- and medium-sized plantations the organizational structure is said to be as autocratic as on the large family plantations. When the owner is absentee, the administrator exercises autocratic control on his behalf.[28] Those lower down the organizational hierarchy are hardly allowed the freedom to act on their own initiative. The wage worker at the bottom of the ladder

has no right whatever to make decisions on the work he performs. He is *assigned* work. Normally he is furnished the tools to do it. On large farms where foremen supervise the tasks it is usual for a worker to be assigned a very small footage of land to cultivate, and when the task is done he either just waits until he is assigned another area or asks where to work next. He is not allowed to move on his own. He is a work animal, once he is hired.[29]

In the Brazilian family plantation community the plantation owner is in many instances "the highest, and often the only, authority—he is the judge, the police, the storekeeper—he remains for the worker the only source of the facilities which society offers urban people." [30] The social structure on the individual plantation is roughly three-tiered with the owner and his family at the top, foremen and skilled workers in the middle, and unskilled workers at the bottom. In Brazil, these three groups are more than likely to be respectively of white European extraction, *mestizos* (people of mixed parentage), and black people, Indians and mestizos. The element of race and color enters the picture in much the

28. *Ibid.*, pp. 139–40. According to the evidence in this study some of the Brazilian plantations seem to be more exploitive-authoritative than benevolent. Cases are described for the Northeast where plantation owners are reported to be "like slaveholders and the worker has no right to claim anything" and in the case of one powerful family it is said that "they think of their relationship with the farm workers only in terms of violence and dismissal" (p. 143).
29. *Ibid.*, p. 144.
30. *Ibid.*, p. 148.

same way as on the company plantation; though in the family
plantation case the owners are likely to be of the same national
origin as the workers and others in the community.

4. The nature of tenant plantations

Tenant plantations may be owned by either a family (or individual) or by a company. What distinguishes this category from the
other two is the particular way in which labor needs of the plantation are met and the corresponding organizational pattern. As
mentioned earlier this type is most important in Brazil, the United
States, and the Philippines. Much more information is available
for the United States than for the other two places; though the
U.S. information is somewhat dated. For the Philippines, Lasker
informs us that the *kasama* (sharecropping) system existed before
Spanish conquest and that the Spanish utilized the system to secure the labor services of the indigenous people on the large estates they had assigned to themselves. He describes the *kasama* as
"a peon who works the land of the owner and keeps part of the
crop. That part rarely suffices, and debt ties him to the
cacique." [31] This pattern has been carried on up to the present
time when

> Modern enterprise often is carried on by companies that rent sections
> of . . . estates, and *since the local people have no other means of live-*
> *lihood* than acceptance of a share contract on such terms as the com-
> pany is willing to grant, they may be properly described as peons: they
> go with the land, not as a matter of law but as one of economic neces-
> sity.[32]

It appears that the pattern of tenancy in the Philippines and Brazil
is very much similar to that for the U.S. South which we now turn
to consider.

   In the United States South, three main classes of tenancy are to
be found on plantations: "renters" who hire land for a fixed rental
which is paid either in cash or crop values; "share tenants" who
furnish their own farm equipment and work animals and obtain

---

31. Bruno Lasker, *Human Bondage in Southeast Asia* (Chapel Hill,
    North Carolina, 1950), p. 85.
32. *Ibid.,* p. 86. Emphasis added.

the use of land by agreeing to pay a fixed proportion of the cash crop (usually a quarter to a third); and "sharecroppers" who are furnished with everything by the plantation owner and provide labor in return for a share (usually half) of the crop. In the last two instances, the worker's share of the crop is net of deductions made by the landlord to cover inputs supplied by him and any advances he made to the worker. The basic characteristics of these three systems of tenure are summarized in Table II.1.

Table II.1   Systems of tenure on plantations in the U.S. South

Method of renting

	Share-cropping (croppers)	Share renting (share tenants)	Cash renting (cash or standing tenants)
Landlord furnishes	Land House or cabin Fuel Tools Work stock Seed One-half fertilizer Feed for work stock	Land House or cabin Fuel One-fourth or one-third of fertilizer	Land House or cabin Fuel
Tenant furnishes	Labor One-half fertilizer	Labor Work stock Feed for stock Tools Seed Three-fourths or two-thirds of fertilizer	Labor Work stock Feed for stock Tools Seed Fertilizer
Landlord receives	One-half of crop	One-fourth or one-third of crop	Fixed amount in cash or lint cotton
Tenant receives	One-half of crop	Three-fourths or two-thirds of crop	Entire crop less fixed amount

Source: Reproduced from E. A. Boeger and E. A. Goldenweiser, *A Study of the Tenant Systems of Farming in the Yazoo-Mississippi Delta* (U.S. Dept. of Agriculture, Bulletin 337, Washington, D. C., 1916), pp. 6–7.

The number of people in each of the three categories varies from place to place in the plantation South and over time in any one place. Over time the tendency has been for an increase in sharecropping during periods of low plantation output prices and for a decrease during periods of high prices. But on the whole, "renters" have not been an important category at any time and most of the workers involved have been usually croppers and/or share tenants. At least four distinct variations of sharecropping are reported to have developed in the U.S. South. One variant is *hoe-cropping,* usually practiced by families which "lost the main breadwinner. The widow and children, as hoe-croppers, receive only one-fourth of the crop, because they do not provide the labor to work with teams that sharecroppers usually perform." Another variant is *patch-cropping* where the laborer in addition to working on a share basis on a patch of the plantation also works for wages on the landlord's own crop. The wages are paid in kind as the worker gets the full output of his labor on the patch (that is, the landlord's share is given to him in lieu of wages). Working *"through and through"* under contract is yet another variant. In this instance, "croppers on the plantation work together in gangs without regard to any individual's crop, instead of each confining his labors to his own allotted field." Finally the *quasi-share laborer* who receives wages for day work for the plantation owner and a crop share on a small patch (or full share on one-half the size).[33]

More recently, wage labor has become an important category in the U.S. plantation South. But in an earlier period (during the late 1930's) Blalock noted that on the typical plantation there was "little fundamental difference between wage hands, croppers and share tenants regarding their characteristics, living conditions and opportunities except in the method of compensation." [34] At that time, wage workers were resident on the plantation and were provided with housing and some facilities like firewood, transportation and occasional use of teams and implements for cultivating

33. Paul S. Taylor, *op. cit.,* p. 144; see especially note 19.
34. H. W. Blalock, *Plantation Operations of Landlords and Tenants in Arkansas* (Arkansas Agricultural Experiment Station Bulletin No. 339, Fayetteville, Arkansas, May 1937), p. 7.

patches. Of the several methods of securing labor for plantation work the type adopted by plantation owners depended on the amount of supervision they wished to give to plantation operations. The least amount of supervision occurs where land is rented to cash or share tenants while the greatest degree of supervision is needed for wage workers. Where the plantation owner utilizes both wage labor and croppers or share tenants, he usually makes little distinction in the supervision given to each. Where the owner is absentee he would have a preference for renting the land on a cash basis.

Plantation tenants have little or no choice in the selection of what to plant, methods of cultivation, harvesting and marketing of the crop. In addition they rely on the plantation store or commissary for their basic consumption requirements. The plantation owner or operator (where a company or absentee owner is involved) makes all the basic production decisions and must organize the work force in the most profitable manner. Many rapid changes are said to have occurred in the organization of tenant plantations in the U.S. South over the past two decades or so. Mechanization has increased appreciably and with that the relative importance of tenant labor has declined while that of skilled machine wage labor increased. The organizational structure of any tenant-type plantation will vary according to the size of the unit and the system of labor which is used. Chart II.2, illustrates the case for two cotton plantations in the U.S. South during the 1950's: one (B) a small unmechanized plantation and the other (A) a larger mechanized one.

Pedersen and Raper describe (A) as "tractor plantation" and (B) as "mule plantation." On the latter, most of the cotton is produced by sharecroppers under the usual half and half arrangement while on tractor plantation most is produced by wage labor paid on a weekly basis. Most of the wage laborers on tractor plantations are resident on the plantation and in several cases the wives of these workers have sharecropping arrangements for working small plots. Tractor plantations still depended on sharecroppers for hoeing and certain hand labor; and it is claimed that "the decision to retain a sharecropper arrangement on a portion of the plantation is made not so much in terms of the economies of the

284

Chart II.2. Organizational structure of two tenant cotton plantations

A. Organization Chart for Mechanized Cotton Plantation,
Mississippi, 1951 (5000 acres)

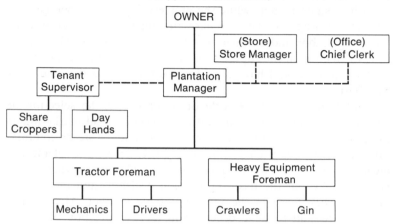

B. Organization Chart for Unmechanized Plantation,
Mississippi, 1951 (3160 acres)

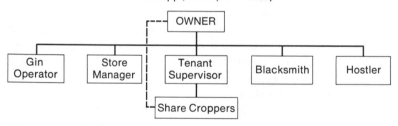

Source: H. A. Pedersen and A. F. Raper, *The Cotton Plantation in Transition* (Mississippi State College, Agricultural Experiment Station Bulletin No. 508, January 1954), p. 13.

operation as it is in terms of the availability of labor." [35] As is clear from the chart, the organizational structure of the larger mechanized plantation is more complex than that of the smaller

35. H. A. Pedersen and A. F. Raper, *The Cotton Plantation in Transition* (Mississippi State College, Agricultural Experiment Station Bulletin No. 508, January 1954), p. 26.

one. In the latter case, the owner is in direct communication with every tenant or worker. Although a tenant supervisor is involved his primary function is to see that the crop is put in and taken care of. He does the basic leg work while the owner still retains a direct link with workers—he personally does the "furnishing" and "settlement"; and tenants go to the owner directly with special problems, personal or otherwise. On the larger tractor plantation, on the other hand, a plantation manager, with prime responsibility for the performance of all machine operations, is employed and the link between owner and workers becomes more tenuous.[36]

An important feature of tenant plantations is the system of furnish and credit that generally characterize the arrangements. In the U.S. South, many of the larger tenant plantations are said to have non-agricultural enterprises as adjuncts to production and marketing of the plantation crop. These include cotton gins, shops, mills, and commissaries. The system whereby plantation owners supply current credit to tenant workers is described as "furnishing." Food and other necessities are advanced to the tenant worker during the crop production period and the owner is paid for these advances out of the tenant's share of the crop at harvest time. When the plantation owner runs a commissary or a store, he does the accounting on behalf of the tenant worker and settles the account by withholding advances plus interest from the worker's share of the crop. Often the worker does not know what he is being charged for items advanced nor the rate of interest he is paying. The plantation owner or operator is in full command and this creates a situation in which the abuse of power tends to be perpetrated. The business of furnishing tenant workers can be an important source of income for the plantation owner. According to Rubin, reporting on a survey in the early 1950's, "the plantation store is still the main shopping center for the tenant; it is a flourishing business for the plantation owner, despite his risks." On one plantation, it was reported that the commissary is "a seven-to-ten-thousand-dollar-a-year net profit enterprise." [37]

The credit system internal to the tenant plantation system in the

---

36. See *ibid.*, pp. 14 ff., for further details of the comparison.
37. Morton Rubin, *Plantation County—Field Studies in the Modern Culture of the South* (Chapel Hill, North Carolina, 1951), pp. 19 and 31.

U.S. South extends outside the individual plantation into the wider economic community. Plantation owners secure short-term loans by giving a first lien on the plantation crop and sometimes additional liens on livestock and implements. Commercial banks were a principal source of these loans though the introduction of government loan programs has lessened this dependence. Merchant loans have generally decreased in importance though credit is advanced for store supplies. In general, interest rates on these short-term loans are high and they set the stage for interest rates charged on the internal advances of owners to tenant workers. The owner takes liens on the crops and such farm implements as tenant workers possess and charge the latter rates of interest two or three times as high as the owners themselves pay for short-term credit. The plantation owner is therefore the link between worker tenants and the wider economic community in every important respect, including access to the very means of survival (food and clothing). He has absolute control over the lives of tenant workers and their families and the economic and social structure of tenant plantation communities reflect this fact.

As with the other two plantation types described earlier, tenant plantation owners are often of different racial and cultural origins from the tenant workers who make up the community. In the United States South a large proportion of these tenant workers traditionally have been black people who had little alternative opportunities to escape the stranglehold of the plantation over their lives after the abolition of slavery. But not only black people are involved; a large number of "poor whites" are included in this category, but even in these cases racial identity with owners does not serve much to temper social relationships because of cultural differences.

Bibliography

Allen, G. C., and A. G. Donnithorne, *Western Enterprise in Indonesia and Malaya—A Study in Economic Development* (London, 1957).

Allen, J. S., *The Negro Question in the United States* (New York, 1936).

Arthur, H. B., J. P. Houck, and G. L. Beckford, *Tropical Agribusiness Structures and Adjustments—Bananas* (Boston, 1968).

Augelli, J. P., "Patterns and Problems of Land Tenure in the Lesser Antilles: Antigua, B.W.I.," *Economic Geography,* October 1953.

Aziz, Ungku, *Subdivision of Estates in Malaya 1951–1960,* 3 volumes (Kuala Lumpur, 1962).

———, "Subdivision of Estates in Malaya, 1951–1960: Author's Reply," *Malayan Economic Review,* October 1966.

Baldwin, R. E., "Patterns of Development in Newly Settled Regions," *The Manchester School of Economic and Social Studies,* May 1956.

———, "Export Technology and Development from Subsistence Level," *Economic Journal,* March 1963.

Beckford, G. L., "A Caribbean View of Cuba," *New World Quarterly,* Croptime 1966.

———, "A Note on Agricultural Organization and Planning in Cuba," *Caribbean Studies,* October 1966.

———, *The West Indian Banana Industry* (Mona, Jamaica, 1967).

———, "Towards Rationalization of West Indian Agriculture." Paper presented at the Regional Conference on Devaluation, Institute of Social and Economic Research, University of the West Indies, 1968.

Benedict, Burton, *Mauritius—Problems of a Plural Society* (New York and London, 1969).

Best, Lloyd, "Independent Thought and Caribbean Freedom," *New World Quarterly,* Cropover 1967.

————, "Outlines of a Model of Pure Plantation Economy," *Social and Economic Studies,* September 1968.

———— and Kari Levitt, *Studies in Caribbean Economy,* Volume I: *Models of Plantation Economy* (forthcoming).

Binns, Sir Bernard O., *Plantations and Other Centrally Operated Estates* (FAO Agricultural Studies, No. 28, Rome, June 1955).

Blake, D. J., "Labour Shortage and Unemployment in Northeast Sumatra," *Malayan Economic Review,* October 1962.

Blalock, H. W., *Plantation Operations of Landlords and Tenants in Arkansas* (Arkansas Agricultural Experiment Station, Bulletin 339, Fayetteville, 1937).

Boeke, J. H., *The Structure of the Netherlands Indian Economy* (Institute of Pacific Relations, New York, 1942).

Boorstein, Edward, *The Economic Transformation of Cuba* (New York and London, 1968).

Braithwaite, Lloyd, "Social Stratification in Trinidad," *Social and Economic Studies,* October 1953.

Brannen, C. O., "Limitations of the Plantation System as a Basis for Progress of the Tenants," *Southwestern Social Science Quarterly,* December 1942.

Brewster, H. R., and C. Y. Thomas, *The Dynamics of West Indian Economic Integration* (Mona, Jamaica, 1967).

Brewster, Havelock, "Exports, Employment and Wages: Trinidad-Tobago and Mr. Seers' Model of the Open Economy," *CSO Research Papers* (Central Statistical Office, Trinidad, April 1968).

————, "The Social Economy of Sugar," *New World Quarterly,* Dead Season/Croptime 1969.

Brewster, J. M., "Traditional Social Structures as Barriers to Change," in H. M. Southworth and B. F. Johnston, eds., *Agricultural Development and Economic Growth* (Ithaca, New York, 1967).

Brookfield, H. C., "Problems of Monoculture and Diversification in a Sugar Island: Mauritius," *Economic Geography,* January 1959.

Buck, W. F., *Haiti's Agriculture and Trade* (U.S. Department of Agriculture, ERS-Foreign 283, 1969).

Chandler, A. D., Jr., *Strategy and Structure: Chapters in the History of Industrial Enterprise* (Cambridge, Massachusetts, 1962).

Charle, Edwin, "The Concept of Neo-Colonialism and Its Relation to Rival Economic Systems," *Social and Economic Studies,* December 1966.

Church, R. J. Harrison, *et al., Africa and the Islands* (London, 1964; New York, 1965).

Courtenay, P. P., *Plantation Agriculture* (London, 1965).

Cumper, G. E., "A Modern Jamaican Sugar Estate," *Social and Economic Studies,* September 1954.

David, W. L., *The Economic Development of Guyana, 1953–1964* (London, 1969).

Diégues Manuel, Júnior, "Land Tenure and Use in the Brazilian Plantation System," in Pan American Union, *Plantation Systems of the New World* (Washington, D. C., 1959).

Edwards, D. T., "An Economic View of Agricultural Research in Jamaica," *Social and Economic Studies,* September 1961.

Eyre, Alan, *Land and Population in the Sugar Belt of Jamaica* (University of the West Indies, Department of Geography, Mona, Jamaica, n.d.), mimeo.

Farmer, B. H., "Peasant and Plantation in Ceylon," *Pacific Viewpoint,* March 1963.

Finkel, H. J., "Patterns of Land Tenure in the Leeward and Windward Islands and Their Relevance to Problems of Agricultural Development in the West Indies," *Economic Geography,* April 1964.

Forrest, D. M., *A Hundred Years of Ceylon Tea, 1867–1967* (London, 1967).

Foster, Phillips, and Peter Creyke, *The Structure of Plantation Agriculture in Jamaica* (University of Maryland, Agricultural Experiment Station Misc. Publication 623, College Park, May 1968).

Fryer, D. W., "Recovery of the Sugar Industry in Indonesia," *Economic Geography,* April 1957.

―――, *World Economic Development* (New York, 1965).

Furnivall, J. S., *Netherlands India—A Study of Plural Economy* (Cambridge, 1944).

―――, *Colonial Policy and Practice* (Cambridge, 1948; New York, 1956).

Gayle, B. C. H., *The Financing of Sugar by Commercial Banks in Jamaica* (University of the West Indies, Dept. of Economics, Mona, Jamaica, 1968), mimeo.

290

Geertz, Clifford, *Agricultural Involution—The Process of Ecological Change in Indonesia* (Berkeley, 1963).

Giacottiño, Jean-Claude, "L'économie trinidadienne," *Les Cahiers d'Outre-Mer*, April–June 1969.

Girvan, Norman, *The Caribbean Bauxite Industry* (Mona, Jamaica, 1967).

———, "Multinational Corporations and Dependent Underdevelopment in Mineral-Export Economies," *Social and Economic Studies*, December 1970.

Gorter, W., "Adaptable Capitalists: The Dutch in Indonesia," *Social and Economic Studies*, September 1964.

Goveia, Elsa, *Slave Society in the British Leeward Islands at the End of the Eighteenth Century* (New Haven, Connecticut, 1965).

Greaves, Ida C., *Modern Production Among Backward Peoples* (London, 1935).

———, "Plantations in World Economy," in Pan American Union, *Plantation Systems of the New World* (Washington, D. C., 1959).

Gregor, H. F., "The Changing Plantation," *Annals—Association of American Geographers*, June 1965.

Guerra y Sanchez, Ramiro, *Sugar and Society in the Caribbean—An Economic History of Cuban Agriculture* (New Haven and London, 1964).

Harris, Marvin, *Patterns of Race in the Americas* (New York, 1964).

Hesseltine, W. B., *A History of the South, 1607–1936* (New York, 1936).

Hutchinson, H. W., *Village and Plantation Life in Northeastern Brazil* (Seattle, Washington, 1957).

———, "Value Orientations and Northeast Brazilian Agro-Industrial Modernization," *Inter-American Economic Affairs*, Spring 1968.

Inter-American Committee for Agricultural Development (CIDA), *Land Tenure Conditions and Socio-economic Development of the Agricultural Sector—Brazil* (Pan American Union, Washington, D. C., 1966).

International Labor Organization (ILO), Committee on Work on Plantations (2nd Session, Havana, 1953), *General Report* (Geneva, 1953).

———, *Plantation Workers—Conditions of Work and Standards of Living* (Geneva, 1966).

International Monetary Fund (IMF), *International Financial Statistics*, quarterly.

Jackson, James, *Planters and Speculators . . . Malaya, 1786–1921* (London, 1968).

Jacoby, E. H., "Types of Tenure and Economic Development," *Malayan Economic Review,* April 1959.

————, *Agrarian Unrest in Southeast Asia* (2nd edition, New York, 1961).

Johnston, B. F., "Agriculture and Structural Transformation in Developing Countries: A Survey of Research," *The Journal of Economic Literature,* June 1970.

Johnson, C. S., E. R. Embree, and W. W. Alexander, *The Collapse of Cotton Tenancy* (Chapel Hill, North Carolina, 1935).

Jones, W. O., "Plantations," in D. L. Sills, ed., *International Encyclopedia of the Social Sciences,* Volume 12 (1968).

Keller, A. G., *Colonization: A Study in the Founding of New Societies* (Boston, 1908).

————, *Societal Evolution: A Study of the Evolutionary Basis of the Science of Society* (rev. ed., New York, 1931).

Kepner, C. D., *Social Aspects of the Banana Industry* (New York, 1936).

———— and J. H. Soothill, *The Banana Empire: A Case Study in Economic Imperialism* (New York, 1935).

Keynes, J. M., *The General Theory of Employment, Interest, and Money* (London, 1957).

LaBarge, R. A., "The Imputation of Values to Intra-Company Exports —The Case of Bananas," *Social and Economic Studies,* June 1961.

Langsford, E. L., and B. H. Thibodeaux, *Plantation Organization and Operation in the Yazoo-Mississippi Delta Area* (U.S. Department of Agriculture Technical Bulletin No. 682, Washington, D. C., 1939).

Lasker, Bruno, *Human Bondage in Southeast Asia* (Chapel Hill, North Carolina, 1950).

Leubuscher, Charlotte, *The Processing of Colonial Raw Materials* (London, 1951).

Levin, J. V., *The Export Economies—Their Pattern of Development in Historical Perspective* (Cambridge, Massachusetts, 1960).

Lewis, W. A., "Economic Development with Unlimited Supplies of Labour," *The Manchester School of Economic and Social Studies,* May 1954.

————, "Unlimited Labour: Further Notes," *The Manchester School of Economic and Social Studies,* January 1958.

————, "The Shifting Fortunes of Agriculture: The General Setting," in *Proceedings of the Tenth International Conference of Agricultural Economists* (London, 1961).

———, *Aspects of Tropical Trade, 1883–1965* (Wicksell Lectures, Stockholm, 1969).

———, *The Theory of Economic Growth* (London, 1955).

Lief, Alfred, *The Firestone Story—A History of the Firestone Tire and Rubber Company* (New York, 1951).

Likert, Rensio, *New Patterns of Management* (New York, 1961).

Luna, T. W., Jr., "Some Aspects of Agricultural Development and Settlement in Basilan Island, Southern Philippines," *Pacific Viewpoint*, March 1963.

McHale, T. R., "Natural Rubber and Malaysian Economic Development," *Malayan Economic Review*, April 1965.

Mandle, J. R., "Neo-Imperialism: An Essay in Definition," *Social and Economic Studies*, September 1967.

Marshall, W. K., "Metayage in the Sugar Industry of the British Windward Islands, 1838–1865," *The Jamaican Historical Review*, May 1965.

———, "Notes on Peasant Development in the West Indies," *Social and Economic Studies*, September 1968.

May, Stacy, and Galo Plaza, *The United Fruit Company in Latin America* (National Planning Association, Washington, D. C., 1958).

Meade, J. E., *et al., The Economic and Social Structure of Mauritius* (London, 1961).

Miller, Errol, "Body Image, Physical Beauty and Colour Among Jamaican Adolescents," *Social and Economic Studies*, March 1969.

Mintz, S. W., "Cañamelar: The Subculture of a Rural Sugar Plantation Proletariat," in J. H. Steward *et al., The People of Puerto Rico* (Urbana, Illinois, 1956).

———, "The Plantation as a Socio-cultural Type," in Pan American Union, *Plantation Systems of the New World* (Washington, D. C., 1959).

———, "Foreword," in R. Guerra y Sanchez, *Sugar and Society in the Caribbean* (New Haven, Connecticut, 1964).

Mollett, J. A., *The Sugar Plantation in Hawaii: A Study of Changing Patterns of Management and Labor Organization* (Hawaii Agricultural Experiment Station, Agricultural Economics Bulletin No. 22, July 1965).

Moore, W. E., and R. M. Williams, "Stratification in the Ante-Bellum South," *American Sociological Review*, June 1942.

Morgan, William, *Economic Survey of the Sugar Plantation Industry* (International Federation of Plantation, Agricultural and Allied Workers, Geneva, 1962).

————, *Economic Survey of the Tea Plantation Industry* (International Federation of Plantation, Agricultural and Allied Workers, Geneva, 1963).

Munroe, Trevor, "The Politics of *Constitutional Decolonization, Jamaica 1944–1962* (Mona, Jamaica, 1971).

Myint, Hla, *The Economics of Developing Countries* (New York, 1965; London, 1964).

Ness, G. D., "Subdivision of Estates in Malaya, 1951–1960—A Methodological Critique," *Malayan Economic Review*, April 1964.

Nicholls, W. H., *Southern Tradition and Regional Progress* (Chapel Hill, North Carolina, 1960).

Nieboer, H. J., *Slavery as an Industrial System* (The Hague, 1900).

North, D. C., "Agriculture and Regional Economic Growth," *Journal of Farm Economics*, December 1959.

————, *The Economic Growth of the United States, 1790–1860* (Englewood Cliffs, New Jersey, 1961).

Norton, A. V., and G. E. Cumper, " 'Peasant,' 'Plantation,' and 'Urban' Communities in Rural Jamaica: A Test of the Validity of the Classification," *Social and Economic Studies*, December 1966.

Patterson, H. O., *The Sociology of Slavery* (London, 1967).

Pedersen, H. A., and A. F. Raper, *The Cotton Plantation in Transition* (Mississippi Agricultural Experiment Station Bulletin, No. 508, State College, 1954).

Pelzer, K. J., "The Agrarian Conflict in East Sumatra," *Pacific Affairs*, June 1957.

Prunty, Merle, "The Renaissance of the Southern Plantation," *The Geographical Review*, October 1955.

————, "The Census on Multiple-Units and Plantations," *The Professional Geographer*, September 1956.

Quirin, G. D., "Estate Subdivision and Economic Development—A Review Article," *Malayan Economic Review*, April 1964.

Ragatz, Lowell, *The Fall of the Planter Class in the British Caribbean, 1763–1863* (New York, 1963).

————, "Absentee Landlordism in the British Caribbean, 1750–1833," *Agricultural History*, January 1931.

Ramachandran, N., *Foreign Plantation Investment in Ceylon, 1889–1958* (Central Bank of Ceylon, Colombo, 1963).

Ranis, Gustav, and J. C. H. Fei, "A Theory of Economic Development," *American Economic Review,* September 1961.

———, *Development of the Labour Surplus Economy: Theory and Policy* (Homewood, Illinois, 1964).

Redwood, Paul, *A Statistical Survey of Land Settlements in Jamaica, 1929–1949* (Ministry of Agriculture, Jamaica, n.d.), mimeo.

Report of the Commission of Enquiry into the Jamaican Sugar Industry (Government Printer, Kingston, Jamaica, 1968).

Robock, S. H., *Brazil's Developing Northeast* (Brookings Institution, Washington, D. C., 1963).

Rubin, Morton, *Plantation County—Field Studies in the Modern Culture of the South* (Chapel Hill, North Carolina, 1951).

Schultz, T. W., *Transforming Traditional Agriculture* (New Haven, Connecticut, 1964).

Scisco, L. D., "The Plantation Type of Colony," *American Historical Review,* January 1903.

Seers, Dudley, "Big Companies and Small Countries—A Practical Proposal," *Kyklos,* Fasc. 4, Vol. XVI, 1963.

———, "The Mechanism of an Open Petroleum Economy," *Social and Economic Studies,* June 1964.

———, *et al., Cuba—The Economic and Social Revolution* (Chapel Hill, North Carolina, 1964).

Shugg, Roger, "Survival of the Plantation System in Louisiana," *Journal of Southern History,* August 1937.

Sitterson, J. C., *Sugar Country—The Cane Sugar Industry in the South, 1753–1950* (Lexington, Kentucky, 1953).

Smith, M. G., *A Report on Labour Supply in Rural Jamaica* (Government Printer, Kingston, Jamaica, 1956).

———, *The Plural Society in the British West Indies* (Berkeley and Los Angeles, 1965).

Smith, R. T., *British Guiana* (London, 1962).

———, "Social Stratification, Cultural Pluralism and Integration in West Indian Societies," in S. Lewis and T. G. Mathews, eds., *Carribean Integration* (University of Puerto Rico, 1967).

Snodgrass, D. R., *Ceylon—An Export Economy in Transition* (Homewood, Illinois, 1966).

Stahl, Kathleen M., *The Metropolitan Organization of British Colonial Trade* (London, 1951).

Steward, Julian, *et al., The People of Puerto Rico* (Urbana, Illinois, 1956).

Tate & Lyle Limited, *Tate & Lyle Report and Accounts,* annual.

————, *Tate & Lyle Times International,* quarterly.

Taylor, K. S., "The Dynamics of Underdevelopment in a Plantation Economy: The Sugar Sector of Northeastern Brazil" (unpublished M.Sc. thesis, University of Florida, 1969).

Taylor, P. S., "Plantation Agriculture in the United States: Seventeenth to Twentieth Centuries," *Land Economics,* May 1954.

Taylor, W. C., *The Firestone Operations in Liberia* (Washington, D. C., 1956).

Thomas, C. Y., *Monetary and Financial Arrangements in a Dependent Monetary Economy* (Mona, Jamaica, 1965).

Thomas, Clive, "Diversification and the Burden of Sugar to Jamaica," *New World Quarterly,* Dead Season / Croptime 1969.

Thompson, E. T., "The Plantation" (a part of a dissertation submitted to the Faculty of the Division of the Social Sciences in candidacy for the degree of Doctor of Philosophy, Department of Sociology, University of Chicago, 1932).

————, "The Plantation: The Physical Basis of Traditional Race Relations," in E. T. Thompson, ed., *Race Relations and the Race Problem* (Durham, North Carolina, 1939).

————, "The Planter in the Pattern of Race Relations in the South," *Social Forces,* December 1940.

————, *The Plantation—A Bibliography* (Pan American Union, Washington, D. C., 1957).

————, "The Plantation Cycle and Problems of Typology," in Vera Rubin, ed., *Caribbean Studies—A Symposium* (University of the West Indies, 1957).

————, "The Plantation as a Social System," in Pan American Union, *Plantation Systems of the New World* (Washington, D. C., 1959).

United Fruit Company, *Annual Report,* annual issues.

————, *The United Fruit Company in Middle America* (Company leaflet, Boston, n.d.).

United Nations, *Demographic Yearbook, 1967* (New York, 1968).

United Nations, Economic Commission for Latin America, "The Cuban Economy," Chapter III, *Economic Bulletin for Latin America,* July 1964.

United Nations, Economic Commission for Asia and the Far East, "Economic Problems of Export Dependent Countries," in *Economic Survey of Asia and the Far East, 1968* (Bangkok, 1969).

Wagley, Charles, "Plantation America: A Culture Sphere," in Vera Rubin, ed., *Caribbean Studies—A Symposium* (University of the West Indies, 1957; reissued by the University of Washington Press, 1960).

Wagley, Charles, "Recent Studies of Caribbean Local Societies," in Curtis Wilgus, ed., *The Caribbean: Natural Resources* (Gainesville, Florida, 1961).

————, ed., *Race and Class in Rural Brazil* (UNESCO, New York, 1963).

———— and Marvin Harris, "A Typology of Latin American Subcultures," *American Anthropologist,* June 1955.

Ward, R. G., *Land Use and Population in Fiji* (HMSO, Department of Technical Cooperation, Overseas Research Publication No. 9, London, 1965).

Watkins, Melville, "A Staple Theory of Economic Growth," *Canadian Journal of Economics and Political Science,* May 1963.

Watters, R. F., "Sugar Production and Culture Change in Fiji—A Comparison Between Peasant and Plantation Agriculture," *Pacific Viewpoint,* March 1963.

Welch, Frank, *The Plantation Land Tenure System in Mississippi* (Mississippi State College Experiment Station Bulletin 385, 1943).

West, R. C., and J. P. Augelli, *Middle America—Its Lands and Peoples* (Englewood Cliffs, New Jersey, 1966).

Wilbur, Walter, "Special Problems of the South," *Annals of the American Academy of Political and Social Science,* November 1934.

Williams, Eric, *Capitalism and Slavery* (London, 1964).

Wilson, Charles, *The History of Unilever* (2 volumes, London, 1954).

————, *Unilever, 1945–1965* (London, 1968).

Wolf, E. R., and S. W. Mintz, "Haciendas and Plantations in Middle America and the Antilles," *Social and Economic Studies,* September 1957.

Wolf, Howard, and Ralph Wolf, *Rubber—A Story of Glory and Greed* (New York, 1936).

Woofter, T. J., *Landlord and Tenant on the Cotton Plantation* (U.S. Works Progress Administration Research Monograph V, Washington, D. C., 1936).

Work, M. N., "Racial Factors and Economic Forces in Land Tenure in the South," *Social Forces,* December 1936.

Index